Stepping Forward Together

Stepping Forward Together

Creating Trust and Commitment in the Workplace

By
Mac McIntire

Innovative Management Group
Las Vegas, Nevada - U.S.A.

ISBN-13: 978-0-9674237-4-6
ISBN-10: 0-9674237-4-0

Published in the United States of America by
    Innovative Management Group
    702-258-8334
    www.imglv.com

Cover Design by Denis D. Hogen

Editing and Production Coordination by Carol Pettitt Communications, Inc.

To my wife, Nadine.
She and I have been stepping forward together
for 33 years.

And to our son, Daniel,
who joined our family team 23 years ago.

CONTENTS

Preface

I know why I "exist." All my life I have tried to help people understand the reason for their own existence – whether it be as an employee, committee member, spouse, child, student or any other role in which people find themselves. I strive to help people succeed both professionally and personally. This is my purpose. It is why I do what I do. It is also why I have finally written this book.

This book is about moving people. It's about getting people to understand their roles and to make the commitment needed to fulfill those roles as expected. In this book you will learn about the process people go through before they will commit to a specific course of action. You will learn how to get people to willingly climb the Ladder of Commitment to the point where they always do the right things for the right reasons.

My wife, friends, colleagues and clients have been pestering me for years to put my ideas about how to gain the enthusiasm and commitment of employees into a book. Participants in my management seminars have begged me for additional reference materials to remind them of the key points I make in my presentations about the Ladder of Commitment.

Unfortunately, even though this book is about commitment, I've had a hard time making the commitment to write down my thoughts because I couldn't figure out how to *write* something I normally *tell*. I didn't know how to translate what I *say* into the *written* word so it would have the same powerful, life-changing impact it has when people see and hear my presentation in person. I tried to write about the principles of the Ladder of Commitment as a management book, a text book, and a scholarly piece. But none of those approaches seemed to work.

Then a friend said to me: "Mac, you're a consultant, so consult. Just explain it like you would in person. Make it easy. Make it real. Just tell people how to do it."

That sounded like a great idea, but I was then afraid, if I wrote it like I tell it, that people who had been through my seminars would be disappointed because the book would duplicate what they had already heard. Then I remembered something another client once told me: "Mac, you are like a good movie. I never tire of watching or listening to you. Every time I hear you talk about the Ladder of Commitment, I get more out of it and enjoy it more."

A short time later, another client echoed the same sentiment. He was attending one of my workshops for the seventh time as the leader of another cross-functional problem solving team at his company. I was embarrassed to have him in the session because I always tell the exact same stories and deliver the seminar the same way each time. What could he possibly be hearing or learning that would be new? That's when he said: "Every time I've attended this workshop I've learned something new because each team had a different problem, so I've heard things from a different perspective. Finally, after seven times, I think I've got it! I have *become* what you teach. I *am* this stuff."

With that encouragement, I embarked on this writing journey. I put behind me my fear of not being able to *write* what I *tell*, as well as my fear of being repetitive. I communicated my story as though I was speaking one-on-one with you. I've carefully included every point, and a lot of new ones, so you can use this book as a reference any time problems arise as you strive to develop a strong team. It is my hope, when you have worked your way through this book and climbed the Ladder of Commitment, that you, too, will *become* "this stuff."

Introduction

Now more than ever, organizations require collaboration in order to succeed. The complexities of technology, increased competition, and global interdependence have created a work environment that requires people to work well together to achieve common goals.

Unfortunately, the conditions that characterize today's work environment – faster, cheaper, geographic dispersion, competition for scarce resources, downsizing, mergers and acquisitions – also create conditions that contribute to mistrust and a feeling of betrayal. All of the downsizing and decreases in employee benefits have led people to feel they can no longer rely upon their organizations for support. Consequently, employees today are much more hesitant to make a commitment to work hard or to go the extra mile when there is no perceived reciprocal loyalty from their employers.

The consequences of current business decisions (no matter how necessary), make the reestablishment of trust and commitment in the workplace an imperative. Trust is an essential ingredient for improving productivity and maintaining stability during turbulent times. In high trust environments, people are more willing to keep agreements, share information, admit mistakes, learn from those mistakes, and take on greater responsibility. They are more committed to and aligned with the organization's business objectives and vision. By creating work environments where trust flourishes, leaders can dramatically improve morale, productivity and profitability.

This book tells how to establish that trust, plus commitment, in the workplace. It offers a step-by step guide for how to get people to

Stepping Forward Together

"step forward together" as a team by using a powerful tool, called the Ladder of Commitment®. The Ladder of Commitment explains the internal process people go through in order to commit to a specific course of action. It shows how to effectively move people out of their comfort zones (what I call a "closed" response), and get them to be "open" and receptive to new ideas or changes. It describes the "seven things that matter most" in a relationship – both professionally and personally – that must be addressed in order to develop mutual and reciprocal trust, respect, confidence and support. It describes how to create a work environment where management and employees believe one another to the point where they will fully commit to work together to achieve common goals. It describes how to get a group of people to go in the same direction at the same time and do the right things right for the right reasons.

Although this book is primarily geared toward work teams, the commitment model also can be used to get couples, families, church groups, clubs, organizations, neighborhoods and communities to step forward together as a team. The principles learned can be applied in any situation where two or more people need to work together to achieve the same goals.

The precepts outlined in this book are not based on scholarly research or analytical data. I've conducted no in-depth surveys or held numberless interviews with effective managers or productive work teams to discern why they are successful. Instead, the ideas in this book are based on years of personal observations, testing of my own theories, trial and error, and practical application in my own company and personal life. I've proven that these ideas work!

You may be surprised, or pleased, to discover you already know the basic truths I'm about to share with you. Consciously or subconsciously, you, too, have been collecting data on what you can do, or should not do, in order to build relationships of trust and commitment. This book provides you with a conscious means to apply your data. Step by step, it will show you how to accelerate the process of building committed partnerships early in any relationship. As a result of what you learn, you can become a much better manager, employee, husband, wife, partner, father, mother or whatever role you find yourself in.

Introduction

This is not a book to be read quickly and then put on the shelf. To build trusting relationships, you may need to change some of your behaviors. Therefore, I encourage you to stop frequently as you read to ponder the points presented. Reflect upon your own situations and assess how these precepts apply to you. Go inside yourself to gain introspective understanding of your strengths, as well as your opportunities for improvement. Identify what you can do differently to strengthen your interpersonal relationships. Also, note how you might be able to help others to better interact with you.

I promise that, as you climb the Ladder of Commitment in your professional and personal relationships, you will find yourself stepping forward together with the people who matter most in your life. More important, you will become more successful in all that you do.

ONE

A Common Complaint

It had been a great day – a wonderful ending to a great week. Like most of my business trips, this one, too, had ended on a successful note. I was exhausted and wanted nothing more than a few hours of solitude and sleep on my night flight home. The man sitting next to me, however, had other plans. He was full of questions: where was I from, where was I going, what did I do for a living....

"I'm a consultant," I answered, unenthusiastically.

It was my typical, brief answer. I thought that would end his questions, as it usually does. I didn't want to be rude, but I'd facilitated a grueling strategic planning session with a team of executives at a large, respected company, and I was physically drained. Normally, on the flight home from a week-long meeting, I'm too tired to even read. After days of exhausting, organizational analysis, I don't feel like talking to anyone. The five-hour flight from Philadelphia to Las Vegas was going to be debilitating enough; the last thing I wanted to do was talk to a stranger.

I could tell my fellow passenger was a businessman – probably an executive, a decision maker, a potential client. He appeared to be in his early forties. His thick crop of dark, slicked-back hair had slight tinges of gray, unlike my balding head and silver temples. Like me, he wore a dress shirt, tie, slacks and well-shined shoes. He, too, had loosened his tie but not taken it off. I'd watched earlier as he had neatly folded his sport coat and placed it in the overhead bin next to his briefcase and carry-on bag. Any good salesperson would consider this a golden opportunity to sell the services of his consulting firm and possibly generate a new client. But I'm not a good salesman. Never have been.

"What kind of a consultant are you?" he continued.

"A management consultant," I responded, hoping the brevity of my answers would signal my desire to avoid conversation.

"What kind of management consulting do you do?" he persisted.

Since the short answers weren't working, I thought I might be able to silence him with the long version:

"I help companies define their strategic focus and align everything within their company to achieve long-term profitability and growth," I declared. "I show businesses how to stay focused on the things that matter most. I provide systematic tools and processes that enhance employee performance. I create teams out of groups of individuals. I build mutual trust and respect between managers and employees and create supportive relationships at every level of an organization. I build high performance companies staffed with committed and enthusiastic workers all going in the same direction at the same time. I teach managers how to get their employees to do the right things for the right reasons at the right time, each and every day at work."

"Wow! How do you do that?" he eagerly asked, sitting up in his chair and leaning closer toward me.

I could tell by the tone of his voice and the attentive look on his face that my plan had backfired. His question was sincere; he wanted the real answer. He was almost pleading with me to continue. The intensity of his attentiveness jolted me awake. Nothing energizes me more than someone who is truly interested in learning the deep truths of organizational and personal effectiveness. I thoroughly enjoy discussing what makes human beings and businesses tick and will gladly forego sleep to help a troubled company, a struggling manager, an unchallenged employee, or despondent soul.

My need for sleep and to be left alone vanished. I was suddenly alert and revived as I switched into my training and consulting mode and introduced myself as we shook hands. My seatmate was Paul Spencer, the general manager of a tool manufacturing company in North Las Vegas that employs about 200, mostly blue-collar, workers. Paul had been the plant manager for

almost two years, having started his career with the same company as an engi-
neer in the design department at the corporate headquarters in Ohio. He spent
several years in sales and marketing and was eventually promoted to head of
the Midwest region. He was awarded his current general manager position as
a result of his thorough understanding of the business. Like me, he was returning home after a week-long business trip.

"Is that true what you said about getting people to work together, all
going in the same direction toward the same goal?" Paul asked. "Can you really get employees to be enthusiastic and committed?" He shook his head as if
he didn't believe it.

"Of course," I responded. "Why are you wondering?"

"I'm not so sure it's possible," he countered. "I'm having a heck of a
time getting people at my plant to be enthusiastic about our goals, and I don't
know why. I'm constantly reading articles and management books that talk
about building trust between managers and employees, but I can't seem to pull
it off with the type of people working in my plant. When I was the sales manager it was easy to motivate salespeople. But I really struggle with the line
staff on my shop floor.

"And, to tell you the truth," he continued, "my managers aren't much
better. They aren't team players, either. Communication is horrible, and cross-
functional cooperation seems like a foreign concept. It's hard to fathom how,
in such a small company, people can become so territorial. It's like there are
huge walls separating the departments. I'm about 'this close' to calling it quits
and going back into sales," he said, holding up his thumb and index finger
about a quarter inch apart.

"So, is there any hope for me?" he asked, shaking his head as if he
thought there wasn't. "Can you really get people to work as a team, even in
my type of business?"

"It sounds to me like you face the same challenges many managers
face, regardless of the type of business in which they operate," I suggested.
"Your situation is not unique. You hire what you hope are the best people, only
to discover they don't always work well together. You put together what you
think is a winning combination of individuals, and then find out they don't

Getting good people
and managing them well
isn't hard if you know how to do it.
The key is knowing *what it takes*
to be successful,
and then doing *it until you succeed.*

necessarily gel as a team. You probably feel the same way Casey Stengle did when he said, '*It's easy to get good players. Gettin' 'em to play together, that's the hard part.*'"

"He's right!"

"No," I countered, shaking my head. "He's not right. I think Casey Stengel was wrong."

"Yeah, you're right. It's not just getting them to play together that's hard: it's also hard to get *good players*," Paul sighed, disheartened.

"That's not what I meant. I firmly believe that it's hard to get people to play together, or even to get good players, only if you don't know how."

Paul looked at me as if I had just made a ridiculously obvious statement. So I reiterated. "Getting good people and managing them well isn't hard if you know how to do it. I firmly believe that succeeding in business or in your job – even succeeding in life – is easy if you know how. The key is *knowing* what it takes to be successful, and then *doing* it until you succeed.

I continued, "You and I have something in common, Paul. Both of us design, build, and sell tools. Your company's tools allow people to build things better, faster, and easier. I create tools that help people and organizations do the same thing. My tools make people more effective at work, both in their individual and collaborative team roles. My tools help companies, and the people within them, move in the right direction and do the right things at the right time for the right reasons. And you, of all people, should know that having the right tools makes all the difference in the world."

Paul nodded as he listened. He turned and faced me in his seat so he could hear better above the cabin noise.

"A competent manager – one who is a master of the craft, if you will – needs a toolbox full of techniques and methods for managing effectively. Just as a carpenter is only as good as the tools he uses, so, too, managers are no better than the tools they possess and their ability to use them. Having the right tools – and knowing when and how to use them – is absolutely critical to success."

Paul nodded his agreement with my analogy.

"I'm a tools guy," I explained. "I've spent most of my adult life developing techniques that make companies and people more productive. I've ana-

Real learning takes place internally.
Personal growth only comes
after serious introspection
where you 'go inside yourself'
to assess what is right or wrong,
helpful or not helpful,
effective or ineffective.

lyzed human interactions and reactions in nearly every professional situation you can imagine. I've scrutinized the workplace from every angle. At this point, I dare say I know how to get people to work better together. And it's not as hard as you think. That's why I say that, contrary to what Casey Stengle said and you might believe, it's easy to both get good players *and* get them to play well together – but only if you have the right tools."

"That makes sense," Paul agreed.

"If you're interested, I'll share one of those tools with you right now. I'll bet by the time we've landed in Las Vegas I will have given you something to help fix whatever problems you're facing at your tool manufacturing plant."

"I'm definitely interested!"

"Great," I smiled, "because I could talk about this stuff all night. And it sure will make the flight go a lot faster."

With that, I quickly did what I could to transform our row into a makeshift meeting room. I reached under the seat in front of me, pulled out my briefcase, and took out a yellow notepad and a mechanical pencil. I grabbed a couple of printed 3x5 cards and slipped them into my shirt pocket. I'd show Paul what was on the card later. I pulled down the tray tables in front of both of our seats so we would have plenty of room to work. Then I began.

"Paul, in a few minutes I'm going to teach you a powerful model that will show you how to build strong work teams. I'm going to teach you how to get your employees to be enthusiastic about and committed to their jobs. But I first need to tell you a little bit about myself and my core philosophies so you'll know where I'm coming from.

"One thing you need to know about me is that I try to reduce every-thing to its simplest, most basic form. I believe in making things as easy to understand as possible. That's why I develop systematic tools and models to help people grasp how things work – particularly how organizations and human beings work – at the most basic level. So you'll hear a lot of simple concepts and pithy statements from me – but that doesn't mean we aren't nav-igating complex territory. I've found the easier a complex concept is to grasp the more likely it is people will internalize what they learn and they'll use that knowledge to improve their performance.

Stepping Forward Together

"Real learning takes place internally," I said, motioning up and down my body with both hands. "Learning is an internal process, not something that happens externally. Deep, personal, profound learning comes only after serious introspection and contemplation. I believe most managers and employees have a wealth of experience and knowledge already stored within them. They've been collecting information consciously and subconsciously all of their lives. Consequently, sometimes the best place to look for answers to your problems is by searching within your own mind, heart or intuitive senses. Serious introspection can often disclose what is right or wrong or effective or ineffective.

"That's why, as we talk about your business tonight, I'm going to tell you over and over again to 'go inside yourself.' When I say that, it means I want you to process this information in the context of what you believe, how you think, and what you feel is appropriate or inappropriate. To manage others effectively you need to gain a firm understanding of your core philosophies, your values and your personal beliefs – because until you know and understand who *you* are, you can't know and understand others. You cannot manage others effectively until you can manage *yourself*."

Paul was listening intently.

"As we sit here and discuss these concepts, I want you to constantly go inside yourself to search your mind, your heart, and your intuition for the answers you seek. When these three processing centers are in harmony – your head, your heart, and your intuition – you'll know when you've come to the right conclusion. This is your innate system of internal checks and balances. If something seems right intellectually, but your heart tells you otherwise, you probably should listen to your heart. If your heart tells you to go in one direction and your head tells you to go in another, you should pay attention to your head. And, if something feels right or wrong in your stomach, your intuitive hunch may be correct. Therefore, the best way to know what is right or wrong is to confirm it in your head, your heart, and your intuitive senses."

I told Paul the process for moving others is the same as it is for moving oneself. "To get people to move in the direction you want and to do what you want them to do, you have to appeal to people's heads, hearts, and intuitive senses. When you align all three of these decision centers, the odds are higher people will commit to whatever you ask of them."

I needed Paul to fully grasp the significance of what I was saying. It was critical to his knowing whether the tool I wanted to share with him would work for him. While discussing the model, I wanted him to constantly evaluate the usefulness of what I was saying based upon the validation he received in his head, heart and intuitive senses.

"Paul, I'm telling you this very important point before I explain anything else to you for two reasons. I'm assuming you're sincerely interested in learning how to move your employees to do what you want them to do?"

"Yes, I'm interested," he confirmed.

"OK. But before I can help you move your employees, I have to first move *you*. I have to convince you that whatever I tell you is true so you'll commit to doing the things I tell you. And I won't get you to believe me unless I can convince you in *your* head, *your* heart, and *your* personal intuition.

"Then, once I've convinced you, I have to teach you how to convince your employees and managers so they'll also get it in *their* heads, *their* hearts and *their* intuitive senses. This is the key to moving people. If you want to get people to do what you want them to do the way you want them to do it, you have to convince them in all three locations. Again, when you tap all three decision making centers, the odds are higher your workers will commit to whatever you ask of them.

"What I'm about to explain to you is the internal process people go through before they will commit to a specific course of action," I continued. "Much of what I'll tell you, you probably already know. That's because your head, heart, and intuitive insights contain a wealth of knowledge and experiences you've been capturing throughout your life, both consciously and subconsciously. You may know a lot more about effective management than you think. The answers to a lot of the problems over which you've been struggling may already be inside of you. The problem is that much of what you know subconsciously you can't explain. My talent lies in developing tools and models that tap into your subconscious knowledge so it can be consciously evaluated, processed, altered and assimilated."

Management is a science, not an art form.
The skills, abilities and attributes
of the 'natural' manager
are subconscious processes that, as yet,
have not been exposed
to the conscious scrutiny of lesser skilled managers.
Once exposed to the consciousness of others,
the qualities of exceptional managers
can be understood, learned, and transferred
to lesser skilled managers.

A Common Complaint

I could see Paul was pondering what I was saying. I paused to give him time to process the information. When I sensed he had concluded his internal dialogue, I continued.

"You've probably heard people express the belief that good managers are born, not made, haven't you Paul?" I asked.

"Yes," he replied.

"I don't believe it," I submitted. "Clearly, some managers seem to have a greater innate ability than others; but the belief that managers are born, not developed, is a convenient excuse for those who cannot discern the 'science' behind good management. It's easier for less astute people to claim that management is an 'art form' that cannot be taught to less endowed supervisors. That way they don't have to take the time or invest the energy to try to figure out how they can be better managers themselves.

"In reality, there are no inherent secrets or mysteries to managing competently. The skills, abilities and attributes of the 'natural' manager are subconscious processes that, as yet, have not been exposed to the conscious scrutiny of lesser skilled managers. Once exposed to the consciousness of others, the qualities of exceptional managers can be understood, learned, and transferred to lesser skilled managers.

"There is a reason and a motivation behind every human action, no matter how subconscious it may be. Good managers understand these subconscious processes, both in themselves and in others. Armed with that information, they can rouse the enthusiasm and commitment of their employees and get them to perform as expected."

I hoped I wasn't going too deep too quickly. I normally don't start my conversations with such philosophical pronouncements, but he seemed to be following my points.

"Before you can get someone to change or improve his performance, you first have to get him to acknowledge there is a need to change," I suggested. "Would you agree that people can't or won't change their behavior until they are aware there is a need to change?"

"Of course," he said.

"Likewise, people cannot alter or improve a subconscious process – like how they manage – until they become conscious about that process. The key to self-improvement is becoming aware of what one does, how one does it, and why one does it. If people are unaware of what, how and why they do something, not only can they not learn from 'it' and improve 'it', but they also cannot transfer their knowledge, behaviors or actions to others so they, too, can benefit from 'it'.

"The ultimate goal in any organization is for everyone in the company to get 'it' – to understand what it takes to succeed at both the company and individual level. And that's what I do as a consultant: I build tools and models to help people get 'it' and anchor 'it' in themselves and others so they can succeed at work and in life."

I could tell Paul was tracking what I was saying. It was time for me to move from the philosophical to the practical.

"Now let me explain what 'it' is. Tell me, Paul, are there things at work that you get, but your employees don't seem to get at all? Are there things that are obviously important to you as the plant general manager, but they don't even show up on the radar screens of your employees? For example, are there things you notice all the time – such as a mess on the shop floor or a safety problem at your plant – that are blatantly apparent to you, but are oblivious to your employees?"

"Yes!" Paul reacted, surprising himself with how strongly his answer came out. "That really irritates me. It seems like I'm the only one who sees that stuff. Just last week I walked the assembly line and was disgusted at how filthy and cluttered some of the work stations were."

"There's a reason you seem to be the only one who sees it, Paul," I said, thrilled to have been handed such a perfect example. "You're *conscious* about cleanliness and safety. Your employees aren't."

"Why aren't they?" he demanded. "I harp about those things all the time!"

"Yes, I'm sure you do," I said with an amused smile. "And I'll bet there are other things that you, as a manager, are conscious about that your employees may not seem to care about at all – things like operating costs, waste, yield rates, productivity, quality control, customer satisfaction, and other critical elements of your business. No doubt you've harped about those things, too. I'm quite sure you've tried to get everyone in your organization to be just as conscious about those issues as you are. After all," I chided, "they are the things that matter most, aren't they?"

Paul wasn't smiling. He actually was gritting his teeth: his frustration about these issues was written all over his face.

"Why don't your employees get 'it'?" I queried.

"I don't know!" he said irritably. "I've talked about those things until I'm blue in the face. Sometimes it's as if I'm talking to a blank wall. I think I'm the only one who cares about those things."

"Oh, I think other people care about them, too," I explained. "You're just at a higher level of consciousness than they are because you're the general manager of the company. These things are constantly in your consciousness because of your position. They're important to you."

"But those things are important to everybody's position!" Paul lamented. "Or at least they ought to be!"

"Yes. You're absolutely right. They ought to be," I agreed. "Cost containment, yield management, increased productivity, quality control, and better customer service ought to be at the forefront of the minds of every employee in every organization. Unfortunately, too often they are not. But, I can tell you how to get it into your employees' minds so these things are just as important to them. And that's through a concept I call *conscious management.*"

"I like the sound of that."

"*Conscious management* is a process that ensures every employee is constantly focused on the things that matter most," I explained. "It is how you get every single manager and employee to be alert, attentive, and adamantly focused on doing the right things right for the right reasons. It's how you get everyone in an organization moving in the same direction at the same time.

"You see, Paul, the reason why you are conscious about specific things at your plant is because of what you know, what you think, what you see, what you hear, what you feel, and what you intuitively sense. You know what the company's goals are and why they are important. You think about what is best for the business. You see inefficiencies on the production line and want to fix them. You hear customers complain and you take quality failures personally

Conscious Management
is a systematic process
whereby you consciously transfer
what you know, think, see, hear, feel and intuit
into your employees and managers
so they can know, think, see,
hear, feel and intuit
everything the same way you do.

because of your concern about the business. You feel bad when the company is not as profitable as it could be. When you sense something is wrong, you dive right in and try to figure out what is going on."

"That's right, I do," he confirmed.

"So now, try to imagine what would happen if all of your employees responded the way you do to the situations in your company. Imagine how productive your plant would be if every manager and employee knew what you knew, thought what you thought, saw what you saw, heard what you heard, felt what you felt, and sensed what you intuitively sensed. Because that's the real issue, isn't it? If you could be assured that every single employee on the line and every manager in every department at your company were as conscious – or conscientious – about the same things you are, your life as the general manager would be a whole lot easier."

"You're right," Paul said, obviously pondering my premise. "That's an interesting thought!"

"That's what *conscious management* is," I declared. "*Conscious management* is a systematic process whereby you consciously transfer what you know, think, see, hear, feel and intuit into your employees and managers so they can know, think, see, hear, feel and intuit everything the same way you do. The only way your employees can do what *you* would do, the way *you* would do it, is if they process things the same way you do."

"That's a fascinating notion," Paul exclaimed.

"And that leads us to another critical management concept I'm constantly promoting in my seminars. I call it: *managerless management.*"

"That sounds even better than *conscious management.*"

"Yes, I'm sure you'll like this one too. The question I ask managers is this: Whom do you really want to manage your employees?" I asked, expecting Paul to answer.

Paul was stumped for a moment. He then rightly declared he wanted his employees to manage themselves.

"You're absolutely right, Paul. The best form of management is where employees manage themselves."

"That would be nice," Paul said facetiously. "But that will never happen."

Managerless Management
entails creating a work environment
and organizational structure
where employees have
all of the information, tools, resources
and incentive they need
to stay on task, meet performance standards,
and be productive
without the need for close supervision.

"It *has* to happen!" I declared.

"Why's that?"

"It HAS to happen," I said, emphasizing my words even more strongly, "because the only way you can truly be a successful manager today is if you can raise the commitment level of your employees to a point where they manage themselves.

"Most managers today don't have time to manage. Unlike 15 or 20 years ago when a manager spent a great deal of time in the office, most managers today are 'working managers.' They're out on the line. The majority of supervisors today perform the same front-line tasks as the employees they supervise. They work the front desk of the hotel while managing the front-desk staff. They supervise the production line while operating one of its stations. They cook with the cooks, design with the designers and write while managing the writers.

"The problem with this," I continued. "is that when you're a working manager, and push comes to shove and there's not enough time in the day, which of these two responsibilities falls by the wayside: working or managing?"

"Managing," Paul rightly surmised.

"Why?"

"Because the work has to get done," Paul suggested.

"Right. The work has to get done. So when do managers *manage*?"

"In their spare time. Whenever they can."

"Hence the problem," I said. "Managers are managing whenever: whenever there is a crisis, whenever a problem comes up, whenever they have a minute, whenever they get around to it, whenever a situation forces them to deal with their employees.

"The biggest problem with management today is that managing is a spare-time, whenever job – not the primary focus of the manager. It's no wonder there are so many management problems in so many businesses. Employees are being neglected because management is too busy *working*. Managers everywhere make sure the pressing production needs are met, but when the whistle blows at the end of the day they've neglected to manage their people. That's why they fail to generate the enthusiasm and commitment necessary to achieve high levels of performance and greater profitability. By being singularly focused on results, they actually produce fewer results than they could if they'd take a greater interest in their employees."

Paul was listening attentively. I could tell he was pondering what I was saying; no doubt mentally assessing how much time he and his managers spend managing their staffs.

"That's what makes *managerless management* such a valuable leadership tool," I continued. "If the reality of the workplace is that managers don't have time to manage, then we have to create a work environment and organizational structure where employees can stay on task, meet performance standards, and be productive without close supervision. *Managerless management* entails putting in place systems and processes that allow employees to manage themselves without having a manager lording over them. *Managerless management* practices provide your workforce with the knowledge and understanding – or *consciousness* – they need to perform to standard with far less management oversight. It raises your employees' consciousness level to your level of consciousness so they can do what you would do in the same situation.

"And guess what the best part is about getting employees to manage themselves? It frees *you* up to focus on other important issues – like strategically positioning your company for the future, monitoring the bottom-line, or interacting with the customers and employees. You know," I chided again, "the stuff you're supposed to be doing as the general manager of the company."

"Oh, is that what I'm supposed to be doing?" Paul said, smiling.

"That's the ultimate goal of both *conscious management* and *managerless management*: to get people to do what *you* would do the way *you* would do it without *you* having to be there. *Conscious management* is getting your employees to be so conscious about their work there is no need for you to be their consciousness for them. And the only way that can happen," I reemphasized, "is when your employees know what you know, think what you think, see what you see, hear what you hear, feel what you feel, and sense what you sense. That's what management is all about. Management is the transference of everything that is within your head, heart and gut so your employees become just as conscious as you are about the things that matter most at work. When that happens, everyone at your company will be going in the same direction at the same time."

"Wow!" Paul exclaimed, falling back into his seat. "If you can tell me how to do that, I'd love you forever!"

It was fun to see Paul's excitement. I couldn't wait to tell him how to do it. I knew we'd be talking for a long time; probably until our plane landed in Las Vegas. I was looking forward to a great discussion.

Two

The Definition of a Team

We had taken off and the plane was climbing toward our cruising altitude. The flight attendants were up from their jump seats preparing to serve the passengers the usual fare of drinks and pretzels. Paul and I were settling in for what I knew would be a very enlightening conversation.

"Paul, I know I've already given you a lot to think about and you're anxious for me to tell you how to get everyone in your company committed to going in the same direction at the same time," I continued, "but I need you to understand one more very important concept before I share a model with you.

"At the end of the day, what you're really talking about when you say you want to get everyone going in the same direction at the same time is that you want everyone in your company to perform as a cohesive team," I suggested. "Is that right?"

"That's true," Paul agreed.

"So I need to explain *my* definition of a team. My definition is so simple and descriptive you can tell immediately whether you have a team or not.

"Paul, I'm sure in all the reading you've done over the years about managing you've probably read several books about teams and teamwork."

Paul nodded.

"So you've probably come across several good definitions of what a team is. Some definitions you've read might be really great. They're philosophical, profound and make you think. But others are trite and silly; like the poster you see on the wall that says: 'There is no I in team.' Give me a break!

Stepping Forward Together

A team
steps forward together.

The Definition of a Team

"My definition of a team may seem equally simplistic, but I think it describes a team quite well. My definition of a team is simply this: *A team steps forward together*."

I paused momentarily to see Paul's reaction.

"That's it. A team steps forward together. No complex or convoluted descriptor. It's that basic. That's all you need in order to know whether or not you have a team." I repeated.

"If you want to know whether you have a team, all you have to do is ask yourself some basic questions: Are the people within your organization stepping forward together? Are your executives stepping forward together as they run your plant? Are the various departments within your company stepping forward together in a coordinated and collaborative effort to achieve your production goals? Are your union employees stepping forward together with management's support to produce high-quality products for your customers?"

"Those are easy questions to answer," Paul said, shaking his head. "They're not."

"Then you don't have a team," I declared. "Members of a real team, a cohesive team, step forward *together*. They move in the same direction at the same time. When the company says 'go right,' everyone moves to the right. When told to 'go left,' a real team shifts to the left – all in unison. All in agreement.

"When a real team has tasks to perform, everyone does his or her part without hesitation. No one says: 'It's not my job.' Producing quality products and providing great service is *everyone's* job. On a true team, there are no weak links; and there are no lone heroes. No one is left behind to take the blame; and no one steps forward alone to take the credit. A real team advances as a cohesive, singular entity. Members of a real team recognize themselves as part of a collective whole – not as individuals. And they act accordingly, by working in coordinated harmony.

"If *anyone* in any work group is not stepping forward with the rest of the group, then you don't have a team," I stressed.

Paul glanced out the airplane window, weighing his organization against my description of a true team. "That's pretty straightforward. By that definition, it's easy to spot teamwork – or the lack of it."

Stepping Forward Together

"That's what makes it a good definition," I replied, with the mischievous grin I'm known for flashing when I've successfully driven home a point.

"The sales team I managed just before moving to Las Vegas was a real team," Paul said, as if testing my theory against situations in his past. "They didn't just step forward together; they *ran*. They were the best sales team in the company, and their results proved it. They worked hard together. They even played hard together."

A smile spread across Paul's face as he remembered another defining characteristic of this star team. "The thing that really amazed me about that team is everyone made sure everyone else on the team reached his or her sales quota. That's almost unheard of in our industry. They really *did* function as one."

Yet Paul had also seen the opposite of an effective team.

"I've seen all the maneuvers, political and otherwise, in the corporate world: turf wars, empire building, people who take all the credit and others who place all the blame. I believe most people in most businesses aren't stepping forward together."

"And of the non-team behaviors you just listed, are you experiencing any of those at your manufacturing plant right now?" I asked.

"It's one thing when your front-line employees don't see eye to eye," Paul began, "but even the managers at my plant don't work as a team. Departments march off in different directions, pursuing individual tasks and neglecting the goals of the group. Managers bicker among themselves. Some even refuse to work with peers who don't share their opinions. Some of my managers are just as bad as some of the employees; maybe worse.

"But let's face it," Paul said, his skepticism bolstered by memories of his current work situation. "In every group there are always some employees who are strong and others who are weak. So I'm not sure it's even possible to get every single person in an organization to step forward together as a team. Remember, I have over 200 people at my plant."

"That's the problem, isn't it," I stated. "The more people you have in an organization the harder it is to get everyone to step forward together as a team. It's easy to step forward together by yourself. For example, when you're single you pretty much get to do whatever you want and go in any direction you want. But when you get married, life changes. Now two people have to work hard at becoming one. You have to coordinate your activities. You have to make sure you are not at odds with your spouse. Couples often struggle until they become unified in their views, goals, expectations, values, attitudes and beliefs. But then you have a child and the 'team' changes again. Driving three people toward a common goal is harder still. With each subsequent child added to the family come additional challenges to creating harmony in the home and unity in the family.

"Getting two, or 200, or 2,000 people to step forward together can be difficult," I agreed. "How would you like to be the President of the United States and try to get over three hundred million people to step forward together?"

"That's impossible!"

"Ah, nothing is impossible," I said, in my best Jedi Master voice. "Some things are just a little harder to do. You ought to consider yourself fortunate to be general manager over only 200 people."

"Go ahead and rub it in: I can't get a measly 200 people on the same page," Paul bemoaned. "It seems like the only time I see my workers stepping forward together is when they're stepping forward to pick up their paycheck. All they want to do is put in their eight hours and do the bare minimum to keep their jobs. They're not enthusiastic or committed. They're only interested in themselves."

"Are you sure about that?" I questioned.

"Well, that's the way it seems to me," he said solemnly.

"You may be right," I offered. "But my experience tells me your employees may be more capable and more motivated than you think. I've worked with hundreds of companies across the country and thousands of employees throughout the world; and I'd venture that you'd be surprised at the sleeping giants you have within your company."

"Yeah, so how do I wake them up?"

"Ah! That's the fun part. There's nothing more exhilarating than turning employees who appear to be unmotivated and non-caring into enthusiastic, highly committed, self-managed team players. Now we're getting to the good stuff. It's definitely possible, and I'll tell you exactly how to do it.

Stepping Forward Together

And the best part of all is that the process is exactly the same for getting commitment from employees, managers, your boss, your customers – and even from your spouse and children."

I looked down at Paul's ring finger and noticed a gold band.

"Are you married?" I asked.

"Yes."

"Do you have children?"

"Yes. I have a daughter who is 15, and an 11-year-old son."

"Would you like your spouse to be fully committed to you and to your marriage?"

"I hope she's committed to me by now," Paul said. "We've been married for 23 years."

"The length of a marriage doesn't necessarily indicate a committed relationship," I countered, "just as the length of service of an employee doesn't necessarily mean he or she is loyal to the company. Some people stay in marriages or employment relationships long after their commitment has waned."

"That's encouraging," Paul said, sarcastically.

"How about your kids?" I continued. "Would you like them to be committed?"

Paul roared with laughter at the alternate meaning of my question. "Yeah, sometimes I *would* like them to be committed: committed to an institution somewhere! At least until they get through their teenage years. Then I'll take them back," he joked.

"Paul, I promise that what I'm about to show you will benefit you both professionally and personally – at work and at home. I can guarantee if you *want* to be a better company general manager, you *can* be if you listen carefully to what I'm about to tell you and then apply it in your work life.

"But I'll go even further than that. I will promise you that if you want to become a better husband to your wife or a better father to your children, you can if you apply in your personal life the concepts I'll share with you tonight."

The Definition of a Team

I expressed to Paul a paradox that has puzzled and saddened me for a long time. I'm shocked at the number of managers who appear to be great managers at work, yet they're estranged from their spouse or children at home. They communicate brilliantly with their employees and colleagues; they have unlimited patience and potential at the office; they are highly respected and loved by their staff at work; yet at home they alienate their spouse, ignore their children, and interact poorly with the members of their family – the very people who should matter most to them.

On the other hand, I also know people who are wonderful husbands or wives, outstanding fathers or mothers, great leaders within the walls of their home; yet they are horrible bosses at work. They have the patience of Job with their children; they listen attentively; they're understanding and compassionate; they are considerate and kind; and they're wise and inspirational in their counsel. Some even coach their son's Little League team or daughter's gymnastics team. They seem to have an uncanny ability to motivate nine- to 12-year-olds to do anything; yet, at work, these same people can't motivate their employees to do the simplest tasks. At the office they are impatient, intolerant, unsympathetic, demanding and demoralizing. The same person who is loved and respected at home, is despised and barely tolerated at work.

"How is it that a person so good in one situation can be so bad in another?" I inquired. "It seems to me that someone capable of being a great manager at work or a wonderful spouse at home ought to be able to transfer those skills and characteristics to the other environment. The interpersonal skills required at work are the same as those needed at home; and the qualities that make someone a good partner or parent at home are the same characteristics needed at work. If a person is good in one location, he or she ought to be equally good in the other. Work and home situations are exactly the same."

Paul looked like he was trying to decide whether he agreed. So, I asked him if he thought there was much difference between employees and children. He huffed and said no.

"Have you ever seen employees who act like children?" I asked. "Do you have any employees who seem stuck in the 'terrible twos'? Do you have employees – or even managers – who fight amongst themselves like competing siblings? Have you ever experienced employees who run to 'momma' when they don't get what they want from 'dad,' or who manipulatively play mom against dad? Are there any employees at your plant who don't play well with others or who pout when they don't get their own way."

"Pfffft. No kidding," Paul said, shaking his head in disgust.

"That's why I say there's no difference between managing employees and managing one's family. The skills and techniques you use in one situation are the same skills and techniques you use in the other."

I went on to explain that the role of a manager and a parent is to increase the maturity level of a person to the point where they get 'it'. Managers and parents nurture individuals through coaching and counseling in order to teach them how to succeed in life. Those individuals who achieve the greatest success are the ones who get the 'its' of every situation early in their life – whether at school, at work, at church, in marriage, in society, or in life.

"Obviously maturity has nothing to do with age," I said. "Yet maturity is what managers need to instill in their employees if they want them to manage themselves. Maturity also is what parents try to teach to their children before they leave the home and go off on their own. Managers and parents hope their employees and children will become thoughtful, responsible, self-disciplined individuals. They want them to make wise decisions and mature choices. They hope they'll figure out the 'its' of life sooner, rather than later, in their life and career.

"The point of all this is simple," I said. "It doesn't matter to me where you learn what I'm about to teach you, as long as you learn it. If what I say makes more sense to you as it relates to work, then think about your business. But if it makes more sense to you from a personal perspective, then think about your marriage and your family. As long as you think about these concepts and ponder them in some meaningful context, you'll be able to understand them, learn them, and use them. I promise, if you practice at work the concepts I'm about to teach you, you will also benefit at home. Likewise, if you can get your family 'team' to step forward together, you can get your work team to do the same.

"All I ask is that while I explain this model to you, you go inside yourself and confirm what I'm saying by checking it against your head, your heart, and your intuition. That's how you will know what I am saying is true."

I paused briefly to allow Paul to internalize what I'd said.

"OK. Are you ready to learn how to create a highly effective, enthusiastic and committed team?"

"I'm ready," Paul eagerly responded.

THREE

Beginning the Climb to Commitment

Paul and I had been talking for almost 20 minutes and we were just now getting to what I wanted to share with him. It had taken us some time to get to this point but I felt it was important he understand the key concepts we'd just discussed before I showed him my model for getting people to step forward together as a team.

I picked up my mechanical pencil and drew two parallel vertical lines on my yellow notepad. I then connected the vertical lines with four equally spaced horizontal lines (as shown in the diagram on page 46). I wrote the word COMMITMENT above the top rung of the ladder.

I pointed to my diagram and said, "OK. What I'm going to show you is a model I developed many years ago I call the Ladder of Commitment®. Sometimes, however, when I'm really humble, I refer to it as the 'Holy Grail'," I said, only half facetiously.

Paul smiled.

"I really do believe this model *is* the Holy Grail because this simple visual powerfully explains a complex process – the subconscious evolution people go through before they commit to a specific course of action. The Ladder shows what happens inside a person's head, heart and intuitive senses before they will accept and enthusiastically embrace something," I explained.

"Once you understand the Ladder of Commitment, you can use it to accelerate the process of gaining the commitment of your employees. By knowing this you can propel people to the top of the Ladder quickly. You

Stepping Forward Together

COMMITMENT

can get your employees to perform at a higher production level earlier in their employment. Most important, you can get people to do what you want them to do, the way you want them to do it, when you want it done.

"You can also use this model in your personal life. Husbands and wives who understand the Ladder of Commitment can use it to build a stronger relationship early in their marriage. They can create an enduring partnership that truly does last forever. Parents who consciously climb the Ladder in their relationships with their children can form strong family bonds of love and support and get everyone in the family to step forward together."

I went on to explain to Paul that before he could get a company of people to step forward together as a team, each employee must first step forward as a committed *individual*. Likewise, each partner in a marriage must be committed to the relationship *individually* before a collective bond of unity can be formed in the marriage. The process of obtaining one's commitment begins as a solo climb up the Ladder. And it is, indeed, a *climb* up, because most people don't start out in their relationships – work or personal – at the top of the Ladder.

I took my wedding ring off of my finger and held it in the air, showing it to Paul.

"When a bride and groom stand at the altar, place wedding bands on each other's fingers, and say the words 'I do', where do you think they think they are on the Ladder at that moment in time?" I asked, pointing to my drawing.

"At COMMITMENT," he rightly concluded, pointing to the top of the Ladder diagram.

"That's exactly right. They think they are making a commitment. In fact, they usually make vows to that effect, saying such things as: 'until death do us part', 'in sickness and in health', 'in good times and in bad'. Yet 52 percent of all marriages in the United States end in divorce. That's a pretty horrific statistic. That means every other person sitting here on this plane – if they are or have been married – are divorced, in the process of getting a divorce, or will be divorced in the future."

"Well, that's encouraging," Paul said, sarcastically.

Stepping Forward Together

"Even if you've been married 23 years, like you have, does that mean your marriage is secure?" I asked.

"I guess not."

"That's because commitment has a short shelf life. It's something that has to be continually reinforced and strengthened day after day," I offered. "The commitment process starts on day one of a relationship and continues as long as the relationship lasts. Of course, you could change your partner and start all over again, but the odds get worse in second marriages. Seventy-five percent of second marriages end in divorce. Since the odds are against you with each subsequent marriage – or each subsequent new hire – it's much better to get it right the first time.

"So, if over 50 percent of marriages end in divorce, what does this wedding ring really mean?" I asked, again showing my wedding ring to him.

"Apparently it doesn't mean anything," Paul replied.

"That's right. Placing a wedding ring on someone's finger and making a vow of commitment apparently *doesn't* mean the person is committed. Saying words of commitment doesn't mean a person actually is committed. So I guess the wedding vows recited by one out of two marriages in this country actually mean: 'I do for *now*', 'I do until something else comes up', or 'I do until someone better than you comes along'."

Paul chuckled.

"Obviously there must be more to the commitment process in marriage than just proclaiming one's commitment," I suggested. "The same is true at work. Unfortunately, employers make the mistake of assuming employees are making a vow of commitment when they accept a job offer. That would be wonderful if it were true. But people don't automatically commit to something – to a task, to an organization, to a team, to a manager, or anything else – even if it that thing is something they themselves chose."

"I accept that a lot of marriages end in divorce," Paul countered. "But I'm not ready to buy the premise that newlyweds aren't committed to each other on their wedding day. It seems more likely that they lose that commitment over the course of their relationship. I'd argue the same is true for employees. Why would anyone apply for a job and then not want to do it?" Paul asked.

Beginning the Climb to Commitment

As he verbalized the question I could tell the gears were turning in his head. His push back was a way of confirming or denying my premise in his own mind, thereby firmly grounding his understanding. I did not respond.

"I think that, at my plant, almost all my employees showed at least some initial enthusiasm," Paul suggested. "But I'm shocked at how quickly that wanes. I just hired a supervisor who looked, sounded, and acted great during the interview. He seemed motivated and genuinely interested in the position. But once we hired him, that motivation just evaporated. I guess you just need to weed them out early."

"No!" I countered. "Don't start weeding, start nurturing. You need to start building real commitment early in the relationship."

I explained that when couples make vows at the marriage altar or a job candidate accepts an employment offer, they're not at the *top* of the Ladder at COMMITMENT. They're at the bottom! They're in the unstable, scary, I-hope-everything-works-out-OK stage. They *hope* it will be a good marriage or a good job. They hope everything will work out – 'Please let her be a good wife', 'Please let this job be a good one', 'Please don't let my boss (or husband) turn out to be a jerk'.

In the early stages of a relationship what people actually experience is *hope*; not commitment. It would be great if people started out on the first day of a marriage or new job at COMMITMENT. But most people don't. When two people look into each other's eyes across the marriage altar or the interview desk and say yes, it is only the beginning of the commitment process. It's not real commitment or total commitment. Not yet.

Prudent managers seize the opportunity at the early stages of a person's job to consciously secure lasting commitment from an employee. Wise newlyweds turn their initial hope into long-lasting reality by moving up the Ladder as fast as they can. Sensible parents anchor the commitment of their children to family values and parental teaching while their children are young, knowing they have to start early if they want their influence to last.

Paul nodded as he thought about this. "So how do you get people to the top of the Ladder?"

"When I'm done explaining the entire model you'll see how everything fits together," I replied. "But, first, let me tell you how I would conduct an interview if I was hiring a person for a job. I want to test the job applicant's commitment early on, during the interview. I want to know exactly where he stands. I don't want someone taking a job and then finding out later he didn't want to do the work. I also don't want someone to take a job he doesn't want, just to get his foot in the door. When I interview someone for a job I want him to be committed to *that* job. So this is how I would conduct the interview. . ."

I turned in my seat and faced Paul so I could model my mock job interview. I looked directly into his eyes, acting as if he were the job candidate. I then began my interview role play.

"If I owned a restaurant and was interviewing you for a pot washer position, this is what I would say: *'I noticed you applied for the pot washer position, Paul. Are you interested in a job washing pots?'*"

Paul played along, nodding his head and saying yes.

"*'Just to be sure that you understand the job, let me explain what a pot washer does. A pot washer washes dirty pots. These pots are huge, heavy metal pots that usually are very greasy and sticky. Sometimes the pots have burnt stuff stuck to the bottom that is extremely hard to scrape off. Your job, as a pot washer, would be to scrub those pots clean, no matter how dirty they get and no matter how yucky they become, and return the pots completely clean to the cook. Then, after you've worked hard scrubbing those pots, guess what the cook is going to do with them? He's going to get them dirty again. You might get those same pots back three or four times during your shift. It's your job to clean those pots again and again no matter how many times they come back to you, no matter how dirty they get, and to wash them cheerfully without complaint. Does that sound like something you want to do? Is this the job you're interested in?'*"

Paul smiled. He knew during an interview people will say and commit to almost anything in order to get the job. He said yes.

"*'That's good,'*" I said, continuing my example. "*'So you're saying you'll commit to wash the pots as I've explained. That's your commitment. And in return the company will make a commitment to pay you for washing those pots. That's our commitment. See the connection? You wash pots . . . and we pay you. Your pay is directly connected to your washing pots. As long as you keep your commitment to wash pots we'll keep our commitment to pay*" *you for working. How does that sound? Does that seem fair to you?'"*

Paul and I agreed an honest day's pay for an honest day's work is a fair trade. We both knew, however, it doesn't take long to discover some new employees have no intention of keeping the commitment they made during the job interview.

"So how soon do you find out they aren't keeping their commitment?" I asked.

"Not long," Paul replied with a laugh. "Sometimes you can tell within days. Sometimes you don't find out until after the 90-day probationary period when the employee starts to slack off. It's like they think they can't be fired after that."

I smiled and asked, "Yet even though the employee is no longer keeping his commitment, what does he still expect the company to do?"

"To pay him!" Paul exclaimed.

"I don't get that part, do you? Why should the company have to keep its commitment to pay the employee when the employee is no longer keeping his commitment to work? Personally, I think a manager should be able to go up to an employee during the workday and say: 'I've been observing your performance today and noticed you've rendered six hours of behaviors we pay for and two hours of behaviors we don't pay for. Consequently, you can expect your paycheck to reflect your effort accordingly. We'll only pay you for the six hours you actually worked.'"

"That would be great!" Paul chuckled.

"I agree. But I know a lot of employment lawyers who won't let you do it. They'd sue you if you tried. That's because the employment laws say you have to pay people for their *time* at work, not for *working* at work. And, unfortunately, it doesn't take long for some employees to realize all they have to do at work is put in their *time*, rather than work, to earn their paycheck."

Paul nodded his head in disgust, knowingly.

"So, let's talk for a minute about what you would like your managers and employees to be committed to at your plant in Las Vegas," I said. "What commitments do you expect from them?"

"I expect them to do their jobs," he said firmly. Then he added, "I also hope they'll be committed to the goals of the company. I want them to do a

Company Goals
Quality
Customer Service
Team
Me
Change

COMMITMENT

quality job and to provide good customer service. And I expect them to work as a team."

I wrote down on my notepad the words *company goals, quality, customer service,* and *team* on my Ladder diagram just to the left of the COMMITMENT level.

"Do you also expect your managers and employees to be committed to *you* as the general manager of the company?" I suggested. "Would you like them to be committed to following your leadership, accepting your direction, and doing what you ask?"

"I was going to say no, not as long as they're committed to the company. But, you're right. I *do* expect them to be committed to me as the general manager."

I added the word *me* to the list I was making.

"And when there are changes made at your company, do you expect your employees to commit to those changes?"

"Of course," Paul confirmed.

I added the word *change* to the list.

"OK. So let's talk about the process people go through in order to commit to your list," I said, pointing to the bottom of the Ladder. "Typically, how do your employees respond when you roll out the production goals for the year? When you introduce quality or service improvement programs, do your employees rally in support of those programs?"

Paul listened to my questions without responding.

"Whenever you announce a new policy or major change in your organization, do your employees get all excited, pump their fists in the air, and shout: 'Yes! This change is going to be great!'" I asked in my most enthusiastic and patronizing tone.

Paul rolled his eyes and looked at me with a funny smirk on his face.

"No?" I questioned. "You mean when you implement new procedures, change the processes, or alter the work on the shop floor, your employees don't get jazzed about it? Are you saying your employees don't commit right away when you implement a change at your company?"

"No! They hate change!"

"Yes, most people resist change," I concurred. "Resistance is a

Company Goals
Quality
Customer Service
Team
Me
Change

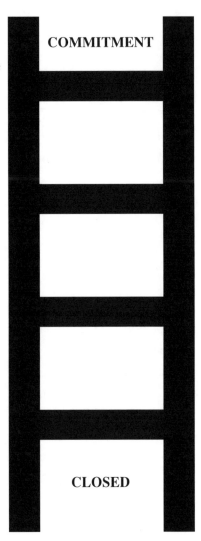

COMMITMENT

CLOSED

natural and normal first response to change. In other words, most people respond CLOSED to the introduction of any new idea, process or program," I said, writing the word CLOSED at the bottom of the Ladder.

"As I said earlier, Paul, it would be wonderful if people started out at COMMITMENT when the company goals are announced, quality or service programs are rolled out, or a new manager is hired; but they don't. I'm going to explain why people respond CLOSED to new ideas or concepts by using how they respond to *change* as the example. All of the things you've listed here where you expect commitment from your employees – company goals, quality, customer service, etc.," I said, pointing to his list. "Each requires accepting some degree of change before a person can commit to them.

"When you declare the company goals for the upcoming year, those goals are almost always higher than the previous year's goals. That means the employees have to do something different than they did the year before in order to perform at a higher level to accomplish the new goals.

"If the level of quality and customer service is not where you want it to be in your company, the employees must modify their performance according to the new standards you wish them to achieve.

"And anytime you add new members to a team, there is a period of adjustment while the new and long-term members become accustomed to each other."

Paul nodded his assent to these points.

"Practically every commitment you desire from your employees, and even from your family members, requires some sort of change," I emphasized. "So knowing how people react to change will help you understand how to get people up the Ladder to the COMMITMENT level. The problem is, as you so rightly said, most people don't like change. They are CLOSED to it.

"Therefore, you ought to thank your lucky stars whenever people are responding CLOSED because it means they are at the threshold of commitment. They're at the bottom of the Ladder just waiting for someone or something to convince them to climb up to COMMITMENT," I declared. "Since being CLOSED is the first step in the commitment process, you shouldn't feel discouraged or frustrated when you sense resistance in your organization. You just need to give people a reason to climb up the Ladder."

FOUR

Why People Resist Change

I could tell Paul was amused at my suggestion that the first step toward COMMITMENT is being CLOSED to it. It didn't seem to him that being closed would be an indicator people were at the threshold of commitment.

"Why do you think people respond CLOSED to change?" I asked.

"People don't like change," Paul replied.

"Yes. But why don't they like change?"

"People are afraid of change. They're afraid of the unknown."

I tore off a blank sheet of my notepad and wrote down our thoughts as we discussed the reasons why people resist change.

"What is it about the unknown that they're afraid of?" I pressed.

"It's scary. They don't know what's going to happen. They're afraid of failure."

"I'm sure that's true. But are they afraid the change will fail, or are they afraid *they* will fail?"

"Probably both," Paul suggested.

"I'll talk about fear of personal failure in a moment. But let's first address the suggestion that people are afraid the change will fail."

Paul and I agreed many people hesitate to commit to a change because they're not sure the change will succeed. No one wants to put a lot of energy into something that doesn't work. Rather than commit early in the process and be disappointed should the change fail, some people wait to see how successful the change will be before expending energy and effort supporting it.

Stepping Forward Together

Some people don't support a change because they think it is the wrong course of action and it's destined to fail. Since they believe it's a bad idea that probably won't work, they don't commit to it.

"Don't you think it's interesting that some people's response to a proposed change is to assume it will fail?" I asked. "It's as if they feel upper management cloistered themselves in a room, brainstormed a list of the worst ideas they could think of, prioritized the list, and then picked the dumbest of the ideas to spring on the employees."

Paul roared with laughter. He said he was sure he had employees at his plant who thought that way.

"Sorry, I just had to get that off my chest. It's just amazing to me that some employees seem to think all managers are idiots. I doubt anyone implements what he feels is a bad change."

I continued: "OK, what are some other reasons why people respond CLOSED to change?"

"People fear they may lose something in the change. They may lose their job, lose status, or lose power," Paul surmised.

"Certainly that's a legitimate fear," I agreed.

Organizational improvements often result in job elimination. Employees tend to resist any change that suggests people might lose their jobs. Managers who spend years building their fiefdom may have a hard time supporting any effort to reduce or alter the boundaries of their kingdom. The loss of job security or positional status is a major reason why people resist change.

I went on to explain that one of the primary reasons why people resist change is because the change takes people out of their comfort zones by altering their routines. Most people prefer to "routinize" their work and personal lives. Routine tasks are easier to perform because they can be done with minimal thinking. We program our minds and bodies to perform routine tasks without conscious thought. When we are in a comfortable routine, our minds are at ease. We work without mental effort. It's comforting and less stressful to be able to perform competently without thinking.

When their routines are disrupted, employees have to consciously think about the new processes. They have to stay mentally focused until they become comfortable with the new way of doing things. Where previously the employee could work without thinking, a change requires conscious thought until the task becomes routine once again.

"Nothing irritates employees more than having to think at work," I joked. "People don't like to be conscious at work; it taxes their brains when they have to consciously think about what they're doing. Employees prefer to work on auto pilot so they can think about other things while they're toiling. That's why people develop routines for almost everything they do. It's also why they resist any change to their routines."

I went on to explain that, when people like what they are doing and are comfortable with it, they usually fight to keep their routines in place. They've already gone through the commitment process to get to where they are, and they're not eager to change their routines and commit to new procedures. This is particularly true of people who had a personal hand in creating the processes they use. People are naturally loyal to objects of their own design. They have a hard time relinquishing their commitment and shifting their loyalty to someone else's change.

"When you create something new, more often than not, you have to destroy something old, but human beings will not easily destroy that which they have created. Once people have created their personal routines, it will be harder for them to accept imposed change. That's why it's important to get employees involved prior to implementing a change. People are more inclined to accept changes they helped design."

Paul suggested people also will resist any change that implies the current way of doing things is wrong or inadequate. People are proud of their effort and they often take it as a personal affront when someone suggests they need to change.

"If a person develops his routine and someone wants to change it, that's like saying what he's been doing is wrong or stupid," Paul said. "It just dawned on me how arrogant it must appear when management, particularly new management, comes in and starts changing work processes. It's like saying: 'You've been doing it all wrong in the past, and aren't you glad I'm finally here with all my brilliance to keep you from being stupid?'"

"That's why it's so important to get conscious about what happens to human beings internally during the commitment process," I said, attempting

People resist change for two primary reasons:
All changes, whether large or small,
make people feel uncomfortable and incompetent.

to anchor an earlier point I'd made. "The Ladder of Commitment consciously shows the internal, subconscious issues people tussle with at the CLOSED stage before they can climb higher up the Ladder to COMMITMENT."

I reemphasized to Paul that one of the major reasons people resist change is because it makes them feel uncomfortable. But I wanted him to understand another, even more powerful, subconscious concern that keeps people from willingly accepting change.

"In addition to the discomfort entailed in every change, there is another super-subtle impact hidden within every change," I declared. "Every change to the routine automatically makes a person feel *incompetent*, even if just for a small moment, until she learns the new routine. Whereas, before the change, the employee could perform the task competently without thinking, a change requires her to learn the new routine. It demands conscious thought and creates a sudden awareness that the person can no longer do a task that she once could do so easily."

I wanted to give Paul an example to help him understand how a change makes a person incompetent.

"Paul, in your job as the general manager of your company, do you have certain forms that you have to fill out regularly, perhaps daily?"

"Yes. A few."

"When you fill out those forms, do you have to read them before you fill them out? Each time you use the forms, do you have to read where it says 'name' before filling in the name, read the word 'address' before writing down the address, and so forth?" I asked.

"Of course not. I just start filling them out."

"That's because you already know what the form says and you're competent at filling it out," I declared. "It's unconscious competence. You don't even think about what you're doing. You just start doing it. In fact, filling out that form is so routine, I'll bet you can reach for the form and start filling it out without even thinking about it."

"Yes, that's true," Paul confirmed.

"But what happens if someone changes the form?"

"I have to read it," Paul said.

Stepping Forward Together

"Yes. For just a brief moment you can't do something you used to do without thinking. You're incompetent. And that's irritating, isn't it? It's particularly irritating to be incompetent on something as trivial as filling out a form. Even minor changes, such as changing a form, can cause irritation at work because it makes people incompetent and forces them to think, even if it's just for a few seconds."

"That's interesting," Paul said, apparently going inside himself and reflecting back to changes made at his company. "I've been shocked that minor changes on the assembly line cause a major ruckus from the workers. To me they are no big deal, but they always seem to be a major irritant to the employees. I guess that's why."

"Let's explore that even further," I continued. "What happens if they not only change the form, but they also move it to a new location? Now you have to both learn how to fill out the new form and remember where it is located. You have to retrain your mind and your body to retrieve the form from the new location and fill it out the new way.

"Like I said before, even if the new task takes only a few short minutes to learn, people hate being incompetent for even a few seconds as they struggle to learn the new way. They don't like having to think about something they previously could do without thinking. Minor adjustments can be major irritations to some people."

I told Paul, if he really wanted to see how people react to a simple change, he should go home and move the silverware drawer in the kitchen and see what happens.

"No thanks!" Paul shot back with a look of horror on his face. "I already know what will happen." He didn't want to incur the wrath of his family.

"And you know what's really funny?" I added. "Moving the silverware drawer would irritate you, too, even though you're the one who moved it, because you know you're going to keep going back to the old location!"

I pointed out that if short-term incompetence is so abhorrent, longer-term incompetence is almost intolerable, particularly to adults. This is why adults are often hesitant to learn new things. An adult, for example, may wish to learn how to play the piano, yet shy away from attempting to do so out of fear of appearing incompetent while learning the new skill. Subconsciously, adults dread going through the beginner-level piano books. Adults want to be fully competent instantaneously, expecting to play Tchaikovsky's Piano Concerto #1 immediately or within an unreasonably short period of time. Many of the people who say: "I've always wanted to . . . .," never do, because they cannot bear being incompetent at the beginning of the journey as they learn the new skill.

"Paul, if small changes, like moving the location of an object or changing a form are so irritating, think of the emotional impact of large scale organizational change," I stressed. "Sometimes I think managers have no inkling of just how intrinsically difficult it is for people to alter their present course or perspective. Failure on management's part to understand the commitment process on major organizational changes is bad enough, but managers need to realize employees will become annoyed at even minor changes. That's why you need to fully grasp what happens to people internally before they will climb the Ladder of Commitment."

I switched to a personal example to better anchor my point. I told him the transition from single-life to married-life is an example of how difficult it can be to adjust to change. Marriage requires a major modification to one's routine. Two single people bring to the marriage their set ways of doing things and then have to meld their individual routines into one. Each has to consciously adjust to the other person's habits, customs and personal schedule. They have to give and take, compromise and collaborate, until they develop new routines that are comfortable and acceptable to both parties. The high divorce rate may merely be a result of couples who could not adjust to the cumulative changes the marriage brought into their lives.

As stated earlier, the married couple's routine changes again with the addition of their first child. Children dramatically disrupt the routine the couple worked so hard to establish in the formative years of their marriage. Now they must consciously create new routines that are effective in the new situation. For some, the stress of adjusting to the multitude of changes wrought by the addition of a child can be overwhelming. Some couples postpone this disruption for as long as they can, consciously or subconsciously anticipating the impact a child will have on their routine. A few couples decide not to have children at all. Some explain their decision by saying, "We don't want to bring children into this horrible world," when what they may actually mean is they don't want to bring children into *their* world – their world of a well-established routine that would be disrupted by having children.

"Employees are no different," I suggested. "They offer a similar rationalization for why their routine should not be altered when they say such things as: 'It will never work here,' 'That's been tried before and it didn't work,' or 'It won't make any difference, so we might as well leave it the way it is.'"

I told Paul there are countless reasons why people are CLOSED to change, and almost all of them are directly tied to feelings of discomfort and incompetence. I wanted to demonstrate what happens to people during a change so Paul could understand how he should respond in the future when he sensed resistance to his organizational changes.

I asked him to fold his arms. It was a silly exercise, one that is used frequently in training courses, but this simple example demonstrates some very profound points regarding the commitment process that every manager should understand.

I told Paul to get conscious about how he folds his arms. Notice which arm folds over the other arm and tucks under, and which arm folds under his arm and lies on top. Once Paul was sure how he normally folds his arms, I then asked him to reverse his fold.

I watched as he tried to figure out how to reverse the folding of his arms. It took a moment, but he finally got it. He smiled and shook his head in frustration at having to struggle with such a simple task as folding his arms.

"How does it feel?" I asked.

"Weird. Uncomfortable."

"You've just experienced a change. And, as with almost all changes, it feels weird and uncomfortable."

I told Paul that from now on whenever he folded his arms in the future he had to fold his arms this new way. "This is the right way to fold your arms." I firmly declared. "Anytime you fold your arms from this moment forward, you must do it the right way – this new way. This is my policy for folding arms.

Why People Resist Change

"I want to make sure I'm clear," I stressed. "From now on you will fold your arms this new way, not the way you used to do it. Are you clear on the new policy? Do you know what I expect from you regarding folding your arms in the future?"

Paul looked at me as if I were crazy.

"So, what question is going through your head right now?" I asked.

"Why?"

"Remember that," I counseled. "You've just learned something very important about change. People always want to know *why* the change is necessary before they will commit to it. I will explain more about the importance of the *why* questions later, but for now, my answer to your question about why you need to fold your arms the new way is: *'Because that's my policy.'*"

"But why?" Paul asked again.

I smiled at Paul's response. "You're just like those whiney employees: always asking why. Like I said, I'll come back to that in a minute."

I then told Paul he could unfold his arms, waited a couple of seconds and then quickly told him to fold his arms again, the new way, clapping my hands to speed him up. I watched as he again struggled to fold his arms the *right* way. He was a model of incompetence. He obviously had to think about it before he could get it right. He first folded his arms the old way, the way he used to do it. Then, after reminding himself of how he used to do it, he switched and did it the new way.

"What's wrong, Paul? Why did it take you so long to get it right?" I queried.

"I guess I'm stupid," Paul responded.

"No, you're *incompetent*. But don't take it personally. What you're really doing is modeling someone who is in the process of learning to change. There are some key things you just modeled that will help you understand how people react to change.

"The first thing managers need to realize whenever a change is implemented is most people will not be able to competently perform the task in the early stage of the change," I explained. "It may take a while for some people to figure out how to 'fold their arms' properly. When employees are learning new tasks, you need to give them time to work through their incompetence.

Never use yelling, threats, sarcasm,
belittling comments or punishment
as a training tool. It does not work!
You cannot achieve a positive outcome
by negative means. When people are learning,
you need to be quick to reinforce
and slow to point out mistakes.

Why People Resist Change

You can't expect people to adapt and commit to a change immediately. It seldom happens that way."

I stressed that when people are learning a new task or process, they need an encouragement and reinforcement while they struggle to become competent in the new endeavor. Managers should never yell, threaten, discipline, or criticize people when they're learning. They should never talk down, belittle, or be sarcastic with those who are struggling to learn. When people are dealing with their own incompetence it can often look like resistance; but they're not resisting the change, they're fighting their incompetence. They just need time to work through it. What may look and sound like resistance may actually be fear of personal failure.

Some people may need more time than others. Needing more time doesn't mean people are slow or bad. It means they are learning. People adjust to change at different speeds. Good managers know they need to be patient when implementing change, particularly large scale change that requires a great deal of adjustment. Managers can greatly accelerate the commitment process by being supportive, rather than critical, of those who seem reluctant to change. Sadly, far too many managers wrongly use discipline or threats when their employees are struggling to learn a new skill, hoping it will motivate them to improve.

"Never use yelling, threats, sarcasm, belittling comments or punishment as a training tool. It's not helpful and it doesn't work!" I counseled. "You cannot achieve a positive outcome by negative means. You cannot get people to commit to the action you want by yelling, threatening, belittling or punishing them. Those things don't cause people to move toward what you want them to do; it only makes them move away from you."

I really wanted Paul to understand and accept this point.

"When people are learning, you need to be quick to reinforce and slow to point out mistakes. Help people get it right by encouraging them and reinforcing their progress as they learn to 'fold their arms' the new way."

I could tell Paul was thinking about his own behaviors and how he interacted with others both at work and at home. He had written himself some notes while I was speaking.

Stepping Forward Together

"One last thing to think about: How long are your children in the learning stage while they're in your home?" I asked.

"They're always learning," Paul rightly answered. "Even when they're adults, there are still things they can learn from their parents."

"So, do you ever yell at your children? Do you ever threaten them or punish them? Do you ever talk down to your kids or criticize or belittle them?" I pressed, wanting him to internalize my point. He didn't respond, but I could tell he understood.

"You may want to remember that," I stressed. "If it's true that children are always learning, then it might be helpful to realize that employees are always learning, too. The business environment is constantly changing. There are always new policies, procedures, processes or systems to learn. So purge yelling, criticism, condescending comments, threats and punishment from your repertoire of communication methods – both at home and at work."

There were several other important lessons about change I wanted Paul to learn from the arm-folding exercise, so I continued talking about the demonstration.

"Did you notice you went back to the old way of folding your arms when I told you to fold your arms the second time? Why was that?" I asked.

"I didn't even think about it. I did it out of habit."

I explained some people naturally go back to the old way after a change is implemented, without even noticing they did it. This isn't out of resistance or malice. It's natural for people to fall back into old patterns and habits. It takes a long time to engrain into one's consciousness the fact that the silverware drawer has been moved. They may keep going back to the old way out of habit long after the change has been implemented.

Another reason why people go back to the old way is to help them remember the new way. Sometimes people have to momentarily revert to the old way in order to recall the new way they are supposed to perform. Some people cannot access the new instructions in their brain and do what they know they are supposed to do until they refer back to the old map and recall where they have been. Then, getting their bearings from old landmarks, they can then proceed in the new direction.

Why People Resist Change

"Come on," Paul interrupted. "Don't you think some people resist change just because they don't want to do it?"

"Sure," I agreed. "I think there are a small number of individuals who may fold their arms the old way out of obstinacy. I've seen employees who figuratively stand on the sidelines stubbornly folding their arms and planting their feet in defiance. But I think the number of truly defiant employees is few. I think most 'rebellious' people have reasons for their defiance. When managers uncover what those reasons are, and address them in a positive way, they usually can get most resisters to climb up the Ladder to COMMITMENT."

I explained that sometimes people look and sound like they are resisting change when, in fact, they are just waiting for someone to convince them of the value of the new way. Some people resolutely fold their arms the old way until given a good reason to fold their arms the new way. If the change doesn't make sense to employees – if they don't know why it's necessary or important – they may keep doing things the old way until someone gives a reasonable explanation for why they need to do things differently.

"What really irritates people is when someone changes things for no apparent reason," I suggested. "Employees get really frustrated when someone changes a form they've been using, then discover the new form asks for the same information, only in a different format. Employees tend to get irritated and remain on the CLOSED rung on the Ladder over changes that have no apparent purpose. If the change doesn't make sense, is not logical, or has no perceived value, you can be sure people will be CLOSED to the idea."

As an example, I suggested a lot of new managers come in and implement changes to current formats or long established processes because they prefer the format or process they used at their previous employer. A manager who changes things just because the manager wants to maintain a routine he or she is comfortable with will infuriate the employees. Why should the employees have to change to the new manager's processes when the manager could just as easily, or perhaps even easier, adjust to the way things have always been done at the present company?

"People *do* resist change," I agreed, "but there is usually a logical reason for it. For example, I once had a guy in a management training session I was conducting tell me, after I did the folding arms exercise, that when I instructed the group to reverse the fold, he didn't do it. When I asked why, he said, 'I knew with 25 people in the room you wouldn't notice how I folded my arms the first time, so I never changed.'"

"What a jerk!" Paul declared.

"No, he's not a jerk," I countered. "He's just acting normally. Some people may appear to be resisting change when, in fact, they actually are acting rationally and reasonably, according to their own sense of what is rational or reasonable."

"That guy's response isn't rational. It's defiance!" Paul insisted.

"I disagree. I think he's just being a normal, rational human being," I offered. "Employees sometimes don't go along with a change because they think no one will notice whether they changed or not. Employees on the graveyard shift, for example, often get away with doing things their own way because they seldom see the boss late at night. People in remote offices may believe they can ignore corporate dictates because of the distance between them and their corporate overseers. A lot of managers are notorious for attending management training sessions with little intention of making any alteration to their managerial style. They know their bosses will not follow-up to see if what was learned was actually implemented.

"Lack of follow-through or management involvement, not resistance, is a major contributor to the lack of employee commitment to many change initiatives. People respond CLOSED to any change where they feel their own manager is not committed to the change, as evidenced by the manager's own inaction. The major question I get from employees as a consultant when I'm involved in an organizational improvement initiative is: 'Does my manager agree with the change and is she committed to it?'"

There were a few more points I wanted to make about why people resist change, so I returned to the arm-folding example.

"So, do you think folding your arms the new way will ever become comfortable to you?" I asked.

"Probably. After I've done it for awhile."

"That's right. That's another important point about commitment. Whenever a change is implemented it needs to be left in place long enough for people to get comfortable with it and competent at doing it. Companies that implement frequent changes make it difficult for employees to reach the COMMITMENT level. Just when they're getting comfortable again, and have become competent in the new routine, another change comes along and throws them out of whack again. Where there is constant change, people tend to stay CLOSED.

"Paul, I realize your tool company, like most companies, has to be adaptive and fluid in order to compete in today's tough markets. But changing procedures or processes too frequently can greatly diminish employee commitment to the change."

I told Paul I frequently hear complaints from employees about executives who seem to chase every new management fad. Whenever their CEO reads another management book, the company charges off in a new direction based on what the CEO is reading at the time. Then, when the CEO reads another book with a different approach, she gets excited about these additional concepts and she takes the company in a whole new direction. Repeatedly the company swings from one management principle to another as the CEO tries to implement each management technique she reads about in a book. No wonder employees respond unenthusiastically to new fads. They don't get excited about the latest trend because they know it won't be long before they will be asked to head off in a new direction.

I could see the wheels turning in Paul's head.

"You can always tell when you've chased too many new programs," I said, offering him a way to discern whether he may be trying to change too frequently. "Next time you roll out a new program, listen in the wings to what the employees say about it. If you hear comments such as, 'Here we go again,' it might be time to ease up on implementing new programs."

"That's me," he admitted. "I keep reading books and implementing new things, trying to find something that will get my people to be more focused and more productive."

"And does it work?" I asked.

"No."

"Then why don't you stop doing it?" I advised.

I told Paul, when I find an executive who seems to be influenced by

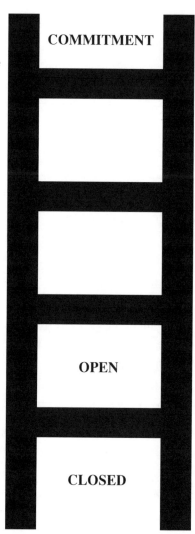

Company Goals
Quality
Customer Service
Team
Me
Change

COMMITMENT

OPEN

CLOSED

every new management philosophy or organizational whim, I tell him to stop reading management books for a while. It's best to find one good management approach, figure out how to make it work, and then leave it in place long enough for people to become proficient at it.

Paul sat reflectively for a moment. "You're hitting the nail on the head with this one. I know I'm guilty of this. I want to be a good manager. That's why I read so many management books. I get excited about the things I'm reading and want the other managers at my company to be excited about them, too. I buy copies of the books and pass them out to the managers in my staff meetings. But I doubt they read them. Maybe I'm giving them so many different things to read they don't know what is important and what isn't."

"And they're probably thinking, 'here we go again,'" I said softly, reinforcing the point.

"No wonder nothing ever changes. I keep giving managers these books and I expect them to change their management style based on what the books say. I assume they'll figure out what I want just by reading the book. But I never tell them I want them to change. I never tell them *why* I gave them the book in the first place or say what parts of the book I think we need to implement. I just assume they'll figure out what they need to do differently."

Paul had a look on his face that I'd seen many times before. It was the look of someone who knows he has made a mistake but he's afraid it may be too late to fix it.

He continued, "It just dawned on me that every time I give these mangers a new book, they probably think I think they're incompetent. Every new book I give them sends the message: 'You're inadequate. You're not managing right.' That's not why I'm giving them the books. I'm just trying to . . ."

"You're just trying to be helpful," I said, finishing his sentence. "Don't feel bad. You're doing the right thing for the right reason. You just need to be OPEN about why you're giving your managers the books," I said, pointing to the next rung on the Ladder.

I wrote the word OPEN on the second rung.

Stepping Forward Together

"I'll tell you about the OPEN rung on the Ladder in a minute," I said. "But first I want to connect what you just learned about giving out too many books to a point we discussed earlier about implementing too many changes.

"Just as your managers respond negatively to the numerous books you give them, so, too, do employees respond poorly with a lot of changes. Some companies re-engineer their structure and processes so frequently there's no way for the employees to commit to the change. They get shell-shocked from the bombardment of changes. Consequently, they just sit back and wait for the next realignment. Why get excited about something if you know it will eventually change again? Too much change too frequently kills commitment.

"The same goes for frequent changes in management personnel. I once did some consulting work with a company that had six presidents in four years. Each time a new president joined the firm the president had absolutely no credibility with the employees. The new presidents might as well have been talking to the wall when he shared his vision of where he wanted to take the company. Based on the history of turnover in the top spot, the employees just looked at their watches and wondered how long it would be before another new president arrived with yet another new vision."

I wanted Paul to understand that many attempts at organizational change fail because management doesn't leave the change in place long enough to make it work. A change must be kept in place long enough for people to get comfortable and competent with the change. Companies that implement program after program to improve quality, customer service, teamwork, production, or other deficiencies, seldom achieve a level of true employee commitment because the change never becomes firmly rooted. When employees make comments such as "been there, done that" or "here we go again," it is an indication they are responding CLOSED to the too-frequent changes in the organization. One of the key components of gaining employee commitment to change is this: Find the right change, plan it well, implement it well, and leave it in place long enough to work.

"That makes a lot of sense," Paul agreed. "I certainly can see mistakes I've made in my own organization."

Why People Resist Change

"Then you'll probably really enjoy my favorite point about why people resist change. I've saved it for last on purpose," I said, smiling.

I told Paul a great deal can be learned from the laws of physics about motivating people. Newton apparently knew the difficulties of managing people because his *First Law of Motion* describes quite well why some employees respond CLOSED to change.

Newton's First Law of Motion has three primary premises. I've changed the words slightly so they apply to the change process:

Premise number one: An employee at rest tends to stay at rest.

Premise two: An employee in motion tends to follow his natural trajectory at the same speed and in the same direction until he is stopped or influenced by an outside force.

Premise three: An employee in a state of motion tends to resist acceleration.

"This describes the CLOSED area on the Ladder in a nutshell," I declared. "Premise number one: Non-committed employees tend to stay not committed. Premise number two: Employees going down a certain path tend to stay on that path at the same speed and in the same direction until the manager does something about it. And finally, premise number three: Employees tend to resist management attempts to accelerate them down a different path."

"You're talking about my employees!" Paul exclaimed. "They want to stay at rest and they definitely resist acceleration."

"That's why management has to provide the accelerant," I suggested. "The way to light a fire within employees, propelling them toward COMMITMENT, is to get them to step up to the next rung on the Ladder. To do that, managers need to OPEN up to their employees and get their employees to OPEN up to them."

FIVE

Getting People to be OPEN

Our conversation was briefly interrupted when the flight attendant brought our drinks – white wine for Paul and water, no ice, for me. She generously gave each of us two small packages of pretzels. It was the usual gourmet cuisine provided on airplanes these days. For a few hundred dollars more I could have flown first class and received complimentary bags of *mixed* nuts instead. Tempting, but then I wouldn't have met Paul and had such a stimulating discussion. I was enjoying our conversation and was glad he had awakened me from my usual flight-home stupor.

"OK," I continued when the flight attendant moved her cart to the next row. "Before I tell you about the OPEN area on the Ladder of Commitment, you need to understand the factors that determine whether people will open up to one another. I'll use the two of us as the example.

"We just met for the first time when we sat down on this plane tonight. We could have sat silently in our respective seats and never said a word to each other. Yet you opened up to me. What caused you to be open?"

"I don't know. I pretty much will talk to anyone," Paul offered. "It's part of my personality. Maybe it's the salesman in me. I'm an extrovert."

"Yes, extroverts tend to be more open than introverts," I agreed, "but there's a difference between talking to someone and being OPEN with someone. Being open, really open, means you're willing to share what you generally might hold close to your vest. Being open means you readily express your innermost thoughts, motivations, and feelings. You freely share your ideas and opinions. True openness is a process of give and take involving both personal disclosure – the sharing of your thoughts and ideas – and the solicitation of feedback from others regarding those thoughts and ideas.

"So, Paul, based on that limited description of OPEN, do you feel like you are an open person?" I inquired.

"I'm not *that* open," he conceded. "I certainly don't go around sharing my innermost thoughts with just anyone. In fact, based on your description of OPEN, I really haven't been open with you yet. We've just been talking."

"That's right. Talking is a first step toward OPEN, but it's only a step," I explained. "There's a big difference between mere talking versus a truly OPEN and frank discussion.

"So what would it take for you to feel you could be totally candid and OPEN with me? What would determine whether you would OPEN up to me?"

"I'd have to trust you," Paul surmised.

"Trust is a good word," I agreed. "A lot of people say they need to trust someone before they open up to them. So that could be what it will take. But what else might determine whether you would be open with me?"

"If I was comfortable around you. Or if you were open with me . . ." He thought for a few more seconds and then added, ". . . or if I respected you. I don't know. I'd really have to think about it for awhile."

"All of those are good answers. Certainly the things you mention might impact your openness toward me," I nodded. "But I think the determining factor of one's openness is much simpler than that. Every reason you gave, and any others you could give for whether you might open up to someone, can be summarized in one word. I'll tell you what that word is in a minute after I've demonstrated it to you in a role play."

I paused as I pondered how to proceed. In my training seminars it's easy to demonstrate what I was about to explain. But that role play gets very loud and animated. Since Paul and I were seated on an airplane, I was afraid my normal demonstration would cause quite a stir among our fellow passengers. I told Paul he would have to imagine the intensity of some of the things I was about to demonstrate.

Before I started my role play I suggested the majority of employees inside a company typically are hesitant to open up at work. Workers seldom share their most significant thoughts or ideas with their bosses. Most employees sit in silence during meetings rather than openly divulge any questions or concerns they may have about an issue. Even when there are serious matters needing to be addressed, employees often keep quiet.

"You can always tell when people are afraid to open up because they seek out the extroverts to carry their torch," I chided, giving Paul a little nudge, since he had declared he is an extrovert. "Inside every company you'll see people going around prior to a meeting trying to enlist the one person they feel will have the courage to be a spokesman. They draft the extroverted individual by saying: *'Somebody ought to bring this up in the meeting,' 'Somebody should say something about that,' 'Why don't you bring that up in the meeting?',* or *'I think you should raise that issue next time we meet.'"*

Paul smiled and said he'd seen this hallway ballet many times before.

"Why are they asking someone else to bring it up in the meeting?" I asked. "Why don't *they* bring it up themselves?"

"Because they don't want to stick their own necks out," Paul replied.

"That's right," I said. "They want to see what happens to the sacrificial extrovert who brings up the issue before they chime in."

Paul roared with laughter. I could tell he was quickly reassessing the value of his extroversion. Obviously he had been the sacrificial spokesman before.

I raised my index finger and said, "Now, let me demonstrate the one factor that determines whether a person will open up. Again, I'm going to model this a lot quieter than normal, but I'm sure you'll get my point."

I first set up the role play by reminding him I earlier had mentioned a client company of mine that had had six presidents in less than four years. The company had gone through a major downsizing, eliminating 25 percent of its workforce. To further cut costs, the company also reduced the salaries of all of its mid-level mangers by 15 percent. The company's board kept changing the president every few months in a fruitless effort to find a leader who could restore the company to profitability. Each new president came to the company determined to make a difference. Each had his own vision about where he wanted to take the company. Each tried to get the employees of the company committed to his vision and focused on the future. And each had failed.

Stepping Forward Together

"How do you think the employees responded to each new president's vision when he or she came in? Do you think they got excited about the new vision?"

Paul shook his head and said no.

"What about the executive staff? Do you think they got behind the new president's vision?"

"I doubt it."

"That's right. The employees actually started an office pool on how long the new president was going to last."

I then started role playing by telling Paul to imagine I had been hired as the seventh new president of the company. I told him I've called a meeting of my key managers so I can share my vision for turning the company around. I begin the hypothetical meeting by telling my managers we need to step forward together as a team if we want to be successful in the future. I state my desire for people to be OPEN and honest. I believe the only way we can make the company successful is if everyone opens up and talks freely about the business.

I ask them to openly share their ideas of what we need to do to improve the company. I tell them every problem or issue is fair game to address in the meeting. We can talk openly. I again encourage the managers to be open and honest, and then turn the time over to the participants in my make-believe meeting to ask any questions they wish.

"What do you think it would sound like in that meeting when I open it up for questions?" I asked. "Do you think the managers would open up to me?"

"Probably not," Paul replied. "I'm sure they'd sit there in total silence."

I agreed that first-time meetings with a new boss usually are very quiet. Most introductory encounters are one-way communication meetings where the manager talks and the staff members listen quietly, not knowing if it is safe to express their opinions or share their ideas.

"Fortunately, there's always someone in the group – that one brave soul, the lone extrovert – who is willing to test the situation," I said, nodding toward Paul to signal his role in the demonstration. (In reality his role was to just sit there, since I was acting out both his part and mine in the role play. I just wanted him to imagine he was the target of my response to his openness.)

"Paul, you get to play the role of the typical lone extrovert who opens up during a meeting."

"That sounds like me. I'm always the sucker," Paul sighed.

I told him that, as the seventh president in the role play, when I open the meeting for comments from the group, he will be reluctant at first to ask his question. But I will encourage him by restating my expectation that people need to be open and honest. I reiterate that all comments will be acceptable, so, with renewed courage, he finally blurts out his question.

"'*OK*,'" he says. "'*I have a question. Since we've been going through downsizing and major cost cutting, even to the point of cutting 25 percent of our staff and reducing managers' salaries by 15 percent, I'm curious,* (he pauses) *how much money are they paying you as the new president of this company? Did you take a cut in your salary like we did in ours?*'"

Paul laughed at the absurdity of the question. He said he'd heard some whopper questions like that from employees in his career.

I continued the role play by getting a stern look on my face and in as loud a voice as I dared use on the airplane, I said firmly: "*Look, we are not here to talk about executive compensation in a forum such as this! We are here to talk about what YOU need to do to serve our customers better, what WE need to do to turn this company around. WE'RE NOT GOING TO TALK ABOUT COMPENSATION OR PERSONNEL ISSUES. THIS IS NOT THE PLACE OR TIME FOR THAT! DO YOU UNDERSTAND ME!!!!?*"

Paul smiled and feigned cowering in fear. I quickly returned to the role play and, pretending to regain my composure, turned to the rest of the managers in the make-believe meeting room, and calmly said: "*Now, are there any other questions I can answer for anyone?*"

Paul grinned from ear to ear. He knew after an outburst like that no one else in the meeting would say a word.

I gestured toward my drawing of the Ladder of Commitment and asked: "If someone actually did respond to you like that in a meeting, where would you go on the Ladder, Paul?"

Stepping Forward Together

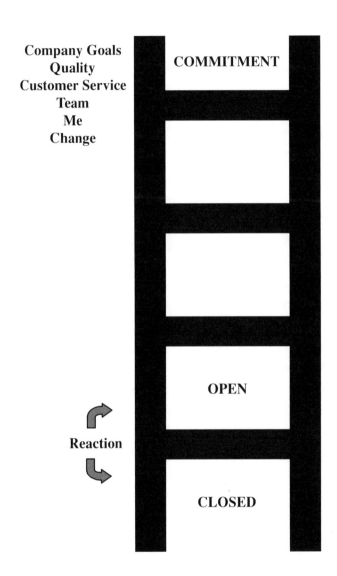

Company Goals
Quality
Customer Service
Team
Me
Change

COMMITMENT

OPEN

Reaction

CLOSED

"I'd go to CLOSED," he stated strongly.

"That's right. But would you just go slightly closed like this?" I said, indicating a minor backslide from the bottom of OPEN to the top of CLOSED.

"No way! I'd go all the way to the bottom of CLOSED."

I drew a thick, dark arrow from the OPEN area of the Ladder to the bottom of the CLOSED area showing where Paul said he would retreat after a stern reprimand like I just demonstrated. I then looked Paul directly in the eye to make sure I had his full attention before I made my next point.

"The key factor that determines whether a person will open up is the reaction he gets when he does so," I stressed. "The amount of openness a person exhibits is inversely proportionate to the amount of perceived punishment he might receive for doing so."

I wrote the word *reaction* down the side of the arrow I had drawn between the OPEN and CLOSED rungs of the Ladder.

"The reactions people get when they open up determines whether they move up the Ladder. If people get a good reaction to their openness, they generally open more. But if they get a negative reaction, people tend to close down. The more negative the reaction, the deeper the closure. If someone over-reacts, like I did in my example, people usually close down big time."

I could sense the wheels turning in Paul's head as he pondered this point. I paused to allow him to think about personal examples of where he, or others, may have reacted poorly and caused people to go to CLOSED. Then I continued.

"By the way, Paul, going back to the role play, do you think you would be the only one in that meeting to close down?"

"No. Everyone in the room would close down."

"That's right. Have you ever been in a meeting where someone got shot down?" I asked.

"You bet."

"How did the other people react to that reaction?"

"Everyone in the room shut down. No one said a word," Paul confirmed. "I've been in meetings where someone over-reacted and everyone in the room went to CLOSED." He was starting to pick up on the language of the Ladder. I was encouraged to see him internalizing the concepts.

"Actually," Paul continued, "once someone reacts poorly in a meeting; you might as well end the meeting. No one is going to open up after that."

"That's right. Sadly, negative reactions in one meeting can close people down for many subsequent meetings. I've been in some companies where managers in weekly department-head meetings remain CLOSED because of something that happened a long time ago. In some companies every meeting is a CLOSED meeting."

I went back to the role play to share some additional points about how reactions close people down.

"Are the people who witnessed my bad reaction in the meeting the only ones who close down?" I asked.

"No. When those people go back to their departments, the other employees will probably be able to tell it was a bad meeting by how they are acting," he suggested. "Those in attendance may even say something about what happened in the meeting. Everyone who hears about the bad reaction will close down."

"You're right," I agreed. "You know the minute the meeting is over someone is going to go right out and tell others what happened. They'll say something like: *'Man, you should have seen what happened to Paul. The new president came in and said he wanted everyone to be open and honest, and Paul believed him. He asked one question and bam! – off with his head.'*

"What do you think it will sound like in the next meeting the new president schedules with his employees?" I asked.

"Total silence."

"A bad reaction closes people down," I stressed, "but, as my role play demonstrates, a bad reaction doesn't just close down the one to whom the reaction was directed. Bad reactions can negatively impact everyone who hears about it. So let's review what we just discovered about bad reactions," I said, turning my notepad to a fresh page and writing down my points as we discussed them.

"First, **the bad reaction did not have to happen to *you* to close *you* down.** Seeing someone else get shot down can send you into a nose dive to CLOSED.

"Second, **you did not have to witness the bad reaction to be negatively affected by it.** Just hearing that someone has reacted poorly to a situation can cause people to avoid the situation themselves. Bad news travels fast. Even though people were not there when it happened, once they hear about it, they tend to close down. People don't want to take the chance they might evoke the same reaction.

"The third point is related to this: Did a negative reaction have to happen at your manufacturing plant in order to close your employees down?"

Paul thought about the question for a second before responding.

"I guess not. Something could have happened to an employee at a previous employer that might have closed him down."

"Exactly. If you listen carefully to your employees they'll often send signals that something in their past is keeping them from opening up. For example, they may say, *'At the company I came from, employees never talked to management'* ; or, *'I'd never do that; I know what happened at my last company when someone did that'* ; or, *'I learned a long time ago to just keep quiet'* ; or, *'Never volunteer for anything; that's what I learned in the Army.'*

"You see, Paul, **the bad reaction did not have to happen at your company to close you down.** Negative experiences in the past can cause people to be less open now. Someone who has experienced a bad marriage or an adverse dating relationship may be very hesitant to open themselves up to another relationship. Likewise, someone who has been stymied at a previous place of employment may be less inclined to share their ideas at a new job.

"Unfortunately, one of the challenges of getting people out of CLOSED and into the OPEN is convincing them to leave at the door the baggage they bring with them from their past. Negative experiences in the past often keep people from moving forward in the present."

Paul slowly shook his head from side to side. "This is interesting. I have a guy in my company I've tried to get to open up, but it's like pulling teeth with him. No matter what I do I can't seem to convince him that I'm really interested in what he has to say. Maybe something happened to him in the past that caused him to close down."

"Remember the attitude of 'been there, done that' that I mentioned earlier?" I reminded. "Human beings have a tendency to believe that one bad

*'Killer phrases' are statements people make
that close others down without any attempt
to verify the integrity of the statement.
The dismissive statement
is accepted as true without question,
closing down any action
the individual may have proposed.*

reaction to a situation foretells all future reactions to similar situations. People paint the reactions from their past onto the canvas of the present. It's hard for some people to get over the horrible reactions they've experienced. They close down to current opportunities because of past obstructions.

"I heard a line in a movie that sums up pretty well how a lot of people tend to view things when they go to a new company. It said, 'Just because everything is different, doesn't mean anything has changed.' I think a lot of people think, *'Just because this is a new company doesn't mean anything is different here than at my old company. I'm sure they won't listen to me here either, so I'll just keep my mouth shut.'*"

"So what do you do about it? How do you overcome that attitude?" Paul asked.

"I was just about to tell you that," I said. "But then I thought of a couple more important points about reactions that might be helpful to understand before I move on.

"Now I want you to ponder my next question carefully," I said, pausing for effect.

"Did a bad reaction actually have to happen in order to close people down?"

Paul thought for a moment. "I'm not sure I know what you mean."

"*'You'll get fired for that,'*" I said, giving him the answer to the question in my statements. "*'THEY'LL never allow that.' 'MANAGEMENT won't support it.' 'The BOSS doesn't like it.' 'It will never get approved.' 'That's not what THEY want.' 'We tried that once.' 'Don't let THEM catch you doing that.' 'You'll get in trouble if you do that.' 'Trust me, THEY'LL never follow-through.' 'Don't let me ever catch you doing that again.' 'Just do what THEY want!'*"

"I see what you mean," Paul said, reflectively.

"I call these comments 'killer phrases'. Killer phrases are statements people make that close others down without any attempt to verify the integrity of the statement. The dismissive statement is accepted as true without question, closing down any action the individual may have proposed. Even though it can't be verified that anyone has, indeed, 'been fired' for an action, the mere

---

Bad reactions close people down

1 – The bad reaction did not have to happen to you to close you down.

2 – You did not have to witness the bad reaction to be negatively affected by it.

3 – The bad reaction did not have to happen at your company to close you down.

4 – The bad reaction did not have to actually happen to close you down.

5 – The bad reaction did not have to be all that bad to close you down.

---

mention that someone *might* be fired can cause a person to forsake their desire to act."

Paul huffed and shook his head again. "I can almost hear some of the killer phrases that are used at my plant. It seems like every time we try to do something new, someone makes a comment that kills any initial enthusiasm there might have been for the project."

He grew silent and glanced out the window of the plane. He let out a huge sigh as he turned back toward me.

"Just a few weeks ago I was conducting a meeting where I introduced a new production process to our assembly line supervisors. I thought everyone would like the idea. A few of the younger supervisors seemed enthusiastic about it until one of the more seasoned managers spoke at length about why it wouldn't work. After that, everyone was suspicious of the new process. People make a lot of 'closing' statements in organizations, don't they?" he lamented.

"Yes. Unfortunately, the first reaction of a lot of people to any new idea is a negative reaction. Their first comment when a new idea is presented is often critical and pessimistic. Good ideas get killed because people respond negatively to them."

Paul agreed. "I wish I could control my own killer statements."

"Yes, I wish I could control mine too," I bemoaned. "You would think I would know better, but I find myself making killer statements far too often. My wife swears negativity is in my blood because my blood type is B-negative."

Paul burst out laughing.

"That's why it's so important for each of us to become conscious about what we say and do. Instead of *reacting* we need to *respond* to the situation. Reactions just pop out, and often they pop out poorly. That's why we need to take a moment and think of our *response* before we react inappropriately."

I wrote down the fourth key point about reactions.

"So, in some instances **the bad reaction did not have to happen at all to close you down.** Just the mere hint that a bad reaction might happen can cause people to close. Rumors, gossip or killer statements can close people down faster than reality.

Stepping Forward Together

"I once had a manager tell me that after he opened up in a meeting and shared his thoughts with the president of the company, a colleague passed him a folded note warning that he may not want to be so open. The note said: 'Beware: Dead Manager Walking'."

"I've felt that way sometimes after I've opened up," Paul confessed.

"Finally, one last point," I added. "Did my reaction to you in this little role play have to be as dramatic as I demonstrated in order to cause you to close down?"

"No."

"I didn't have to yell at you, did I? My reaction could have been as simple as a stern look, an uncomfortable pause, a sarcastic tone, or a sharp retort. My facial expression, body posture, tone, volume, intensity, word choice – anything you perceive to be negative has the potential of closing you down. Consequently, **the bad reaction did not have to be dramatic to close you down.** Sadly, the bad reaction may not be all that bad, yet still closes someone down."

"That's true."

"That's why it's so difficult to get people to open up," I hammered. "Sometimes a boss' mere expression of a divergent opinion can close people down who are in the clutches of risk avoidance. Even the slightest hint of a negative reaction can cause people to clam up. And CLOSED people are a long way from COMMITMENT."

SIX

Managing Reactions

I had just finished explaining the one thing that determines whether people will be OPEN is the *reaction* they receive when they share their thoughts and ideas. I needed Paul to fully grasp my next point, so I turned in my seat and faced him to better emphasize what I wanted to say.

"Paul, if you learn nothing else tonight from what we talk about on this flight home, I want you to get this next point. It is a major, major point. It is the key to everything we've talked about so far and is critical to everything I will explain hereafter."

I spoke slowly and distinctly to emphasize my point. "Paul, when it comes to interpersonal relations in the workplace, *MOST OF WHAT A MAN-AGER DOES IS MANAGE REACTIONS.*"

I repeated my statement, wanting it to sink in. "Most of what a manager does in a typical workday is manage reactions. And whose reactions do you have to manage first?" I asked.

"My own," he responded without hesitation.

"Controlling one's reactions is one of the toughest things for people to do," I said. "It's hard to keep yourself from reacting poorly, particularly when the numbers are off, production is down, or operational goals are missed. It's also hard to control your response when people sometimes say and do some pretty dumb things. Have you ever had an employee ask you a stupid question or suggest an obviously silly idea?"

He smiled. "Yes, I have."

Most of what a manager does
in a typical work day
is manage reactions.
The first reactions you have to manage
are your own.

"How do you normally react to an employee's stupid suggestion or silly question?" I probed.

"I'm not sure," Paul said without going inside himself to find out.

"Come on, Paul. You know the answer to the question. What is your typical reaction – either verbally on non-verbally – to things you think are obviously ridiculous? Get conscious and tell me what you do."

"I probably roll my eyes," he offered.

"That's exactly what you do!"

"What?"

"Yes, you *do* roll your eyes. And you also look away and change the tone of your voice. And you get this little smirk on your face," I told him.

"How do you know?"

"Because you've done it with me a couple of times when I've said something that you probably thought was a little strange."

"I'm sorry," he apologized. "I didn't know I was doing it."

"That's why *conscious management* is so important. Every manager needs to get conscious about how he or she reacts. Most of what a manager does is manage reactions, and the first reactions we have to control are our own. And there is a very important reason why we should: If you react poorly to the stupid questions and the silly ideas, will you get the good ones later on?"

"Probably not."

This is a very important point to remember at work and at home. Too often managers and parents react harshly to simple questions or what we perceive to be asinine ideas, when a much gentler response would be more appropriate. The harshness of the reaction causes the other person to close down and makes them hesitant to share their ideas again. Parents can stunt the growth of their children and managers can thwart the development of their employees by reacting negatively to the innocent questions one asks and the naive ideas one offers when one is learning.

"Have you ever reacted poorly to a silly question from one of your kids?" I asked, switching to a personal example to again emphasize the point.

"I'm sure I have."

Stepping Forward Together

"You need to be very careful," I warned. "If you react negatively to their silly questions when they are young, you may not get their serious questions when it really matters, during the teenage years. There will come a day when you will want them to be OPEN and talk to you frankly. But if you CLOSE them down now, they may not open up to you at the time when you need them to be open the most."

"That's a good point," Paul said thoughtfully.

"I don't know about you, but I've found it's hard *not* to react negatively to a silly comment," I offered. "Almost everyone has an uncontrollable reaction to an inane comment. We roll our eyes, change our tone, contort our face or exhibit some other subconscious response without even knowing we do it. But if you want people to open up and climb the Ladder of Commitment, you have to learn to control the reactions of every part of your body. Every little thing you do has the potential of turning a person off and closing him down. You must control your reactions if you want to keep people in the OPEN."

Paul told me about a few situations where he did not handle his reactions well. Although he never thought about it in terms of the Ladder of Commitment, he instinctively knew his outbursts had caused people to close down.

"That's so weird," he said softly, shaking his head as if he'd just come to realize something important.

"What's weird?" I asked.

"I was just thinking of things I've said to people in the past. I can be pretty sarcastic sometimes. I also have a tendency to yell when things aren't going well. When we're on a tight production schedule I start barking out orders, hoping to motivate people to work harder or to think before they act. But, after listening to you, I realize my yelling doesn't move people the way I want."

"So what's weird about that?" I asked.

"What's weird is what I think I'm doing by reacting the way I do and what I'm actually doing is just the opposite from what I want. I think by

yelling at people it will cause them to do what I want – to COMMIT to do the right thing," he said, pointing to the top of the Ladder. "But what it's really doing is causing people to CLOSE down. That's so weird. I think I'm moving them up the Ladder, but I'm really causing them to go down the Ladder. Why do managers – why do I – yell or get angry at people and think it will have a positive effect?"

"Like I said earlier, you cannot achieve a positive outcome through negative means. So why do you do it?"

He just shook his head.

"Don't beat yourself up for what you've done in the past; just learn from it. Anger and yelling are natural human reactions when we're frustrated. It takes a very mature, stable, introspective and conscious person to be able to control one's reactions."

"Oh! So now you're saying I'm unstable and immature," Paul jokingly challenged.

"Well, aren't you? Don't you think a manager who yells at his or her employees is unstable and immature?" I retorted. "I'm not saying there aren't times when a manager needs to be firm with his employees in order to keep them focused on the right things. But firmness and yelling are two different things. You can be firm without losing control of your emotions – without reacting in an irrational manner.

"Firmness seldom closes people down, but lashing out in anger or yelling at people almost always does. Negativity never causes people to move toward a positive outcome; it only causes people to move away from the negative. That's why no one wants to be around you after you've blown up at someone. Remember, the negative reaction didn't have to happen to you to close you down. When you fly off the handle at one person, everyone around the situation is affected by it."

Because this point was so important, I switched to an example at home to firmly anchor the concept within Paul's mind.

"I don't mean to pry, but have you ever had an argument with your wife or children?" I asked.

"Of course."

"Have you ever had a bad one – one where you, your spouse, or your child was louder than you needed to be or said things you really shouldn't have said?"

"Yes."

"Did the yelling and hurtful comments help the situation?" I pressed.

"No. Of course not. It never does," he said dejectedly, possibly thinking of a past conflict that didn't go well.

"We all make mistakes. We're all human," I said, trying to relieve his distress. "The key is to get conscious about how we react and then to control it.

"Normally I wouldn't share with anyone what I'm about to tell you," I said softly, "but everything we've talked about so far is so essential, I think this story might help drive home the importance of this point. Hopefully you can learn from my sad experience.

"My son had a very severe anger problem during his teen years. It was so severe he actually broke furniture and punched holes in the walls of our home. There were times when he was completely out of control. But what's even worse is when he was so angry and out of control, guess how I reacted to my son's anger?"

"By getting angry," Paul rightly surmised.

"And do you think it ever worked? Do you think my getting angry when my son was angry actually fixed the problem?"

"Probably not."

"It *never* fixed the problem! It never helped; not even once. So why did I do it? Why did I continually scream at him when it was so obvious it only exacerbated the problem?" I lamented.

"Because you're human," Paul said.

"Yeah, I hate that part. I hate reacting according to my human weaknesses rather than using the wisdom that is in my subconscious mind. I knew better, but it wasn't until I became conscious of my bad reactions that I stopped getting angry at my son's anger. And when I started controlling my anger, his anger diminished."

I could tell by the look in Paul's watery eyes that he had gone inside himself and was accessing a personal experience. When that happens I know to sit back and wait for the internal process to conclude. I wanted to ask what was going on inside him, but didn't want to violate his privacy. I knew he would be more OPEN later as we climbed the Ladder of Commitment together.

"Just remember, the most important reactions you need to control are your own," I reminded. "But that's just the beginning. Who else's reactions do you have to control as a manager?"

"I have to control the reactions of my employees."

"That's right. Do employees ever react poorly toward each other?"

Paul just shook his head affirmatively.

"Nothing disrupts the unity of a team more than disharmony among its members. That's why a major part of a manager's job is to help employees control their reactions to each other so everyone on the team can step forward together." I explained. I then asked: "In addition to your reactions and those of your employees, who else's reactions do you have to control as a manager?"

"I have to control the reactions of other managers," he declared.

"Really? Are you saying there are other managers out there who may not react well in certain situations? You mean you're not the only manager who freaks out sometimes?"

Paul smiled, chuckling quietly.

"You are right. Sometimes cross-functional cooperation and collaboration are adversely affected by the negative reactions of the department managers. Very good! Who else's reactions do you have to control as a manager?"

"I guess a manager is responsible for controlling the reactions of the customers," Paul surmised.

"You mean customers can freak out, get upset and yell and scream too? There's nothing worse than freaking customers is there?" I joked.

"Yes there is," he shot back. "A freaking boss is much worse!"

We both laughed at his comment. Although most managers may never have thought about it, the reality is that most of what a manager does all day is control reactions. Managers control the reactions of employees to employees, managers to managers, managers to employees, employees to customers, customers to employees, customers to customers, employees to suppliers, suppliers to employees – pretty much any interaction between two human beings in the workplace.

"No wonder it's so hard to get people to OPEN up in the workplace," Paul lamented. "When you put a lot of people together in an enclosed work environment the chances are high someone is going to react poorly. How is anyone supposed to manage all this?"

"Obviously by starting with you first," I answered. "Get your own reactions under control. That will go a long way to moving people up the Ladder. Then, do everything within your power to help other people control their reactions. Your job is to promote a calm, rational, self-controlled work environment."

"What if people are already CLOSED because of the way I've reacted in the past? Can I undo the damage?" Paul wondered.

"Of course you can. You just need to confess your sins, repent of your evil ways, and never do it again," I joked.

Paul wasn't laughing.

"Don't be so hard on yourself. Being aware of your reactions is the first step to controlling them. And if you've reacted poorly in the past, all you have to do to get people to react differently to your past reactions is to untrain the elephant."

"What?"

"Untrain the elephant," I repeated. "Whenever we react poorly, we train people over time to react to our reactions. Therefore, if you want people to learn how to react differently to you in the future, you need to untrain them first. The process for getting people to overcome past negative experiences is the same process used for untraining an elephant."

"OK?" Paul said suspiciously. He didn't have a clue about what I was talking about.

"Before you can untrain an elephant you first have to know how to train one," I suggested. "You do know how to train an elephant, don't you Paul?"

"I can't say that I do."

I explained the process for training an elephant is relatively simple. It often takes only a few weeks to tame a wild elephant. The training starts when a trainer locks a huge iron ring around one leg of the elephant. The trainer drives a long metal stake into the ground and secures the elephant to the stake by a chain that runs from the stake to the ring on the elephant's leg. The chain is about ten feet long. Once the wild elephant is chained to the stake it is left alone.

For days the captured animal pulls against the chain, struggling to get free. It tramples and trumpets endlessly, pulling at the chain, trying to break its shackle. But the stake and chain are firmly grounded. After a horrendous fight to get free, the elephant eventually tires of the fruitless pulling at the chain. It learns struggling against the chain is hopeless. Resolved that it cannot break free, the elephant begins to settle down.

At this point the elephant trainer replaces the sturdy chain with a flaxen rope. The elephant could easily break the rope and run free, but when it feels the tug of the rope on the metal ring, it assumes the rope is still the unbreakable chain. It believes it is still bound by an unbreakable bond. Thinking the rope is the chain, the elephant never pulls hard enough on the rope to break it.

Once the elephant stops pulling on the rope, the trainer removes the rope from the ring, discards the stake, and allows the elephant to roam freely within a few feet of the trainer. In the hand of the trainer is a long stick. The elephant feels the ring on its leg, sees the "stake" in the hand of the trainer, and assumes it is still chained to a short tether. It doesn't run off because it "knows" it cannot go past the distance of the original chain and stake.

Eventually even the ring can be removed from the elephant. The experience of the earlier, pointless struggle to get free remains locked in its memory. This is what's called "learned apathy." From its experience it has learned that fighting against the "system" is fruitless. The elephant goes to CLOSED and never again tests its freedom to roam, just like employees who learn over time to never again open their mouths or share their ideas because of past struggles against the organizational system.

"And that's all there is to training an elephant," I said.

"So how do you untrain an elephant?" Paul asked.

I told him untraining an elephant is also an easy process. All you have to do is allow the elephant to go outside the preconceived bounds of its chain. Take the elephant past all previous points of restriction. Let the elephant see there is no chain, no stake, and no tamer to restrict him.

At first the elephant will be hesitant and confused. It won't know whether to proceed. It will take one step, pause, look around suspiciously, hesitate, and then take another. Then it will step out again, testing the boundaries, trying to acquire the confidence to press forward. Finally, the elephant will sense freedom. When that happens, look out. The elephant will take off running.

"Employees are like elephants," I proclaimed. "They grow weary of endless changes. They get tired of being shut out by managers who won't listen to them. They grow frustrated from butting their heads against a wall of opposition. Eventually they stop trying to make a difference in their organization. They stop sharing their ideas. They exhibit learned apathy, just like the elephant."

"Again, what can you do about it?" Paul pressed. "I know I have apathetic employees in my company. I accept that I may have caused it. What do I do when I have apathetic people?"

"Take them beyond their previous bounds," I answered. "Remove the shackles. Take them past the point where they previously got squelched. Walk them to the edge of the mental boundaries etched from their past experience. Give them a taste of freedom.

"This is why it is so important for the manager to take the first step. The manager has to OPEN up first or the employees will not believe it. The manager has to control his or her reactions and allow for open communication. Managers have to start the process by removing the chains and stakes that, in the past, CLOSED people down.

"At first the employees will not believe they are free to open up, free to share their opinions, free to express their views without getting shut down. They'll hesitate. They won't say much. They won't believe the freedom is real. They'll expect their chain to be yanked at any moment. But when it isn't, the apathetic anchors will slowly start to dissolve. If management reacts well to the openness and doesn't freak out, the unrestricted trickle of employee input will eventually become a flood of comments and ideas."

"I don't know whether that's good or bad," Paul said.

I jumped on Paul's comment.

Managing Reactions

"See! You just reacted negatively! And the reason you reacted negatively is because you are afraid of the *reaction* you'll get if you open up. You're afraid of how the employees will react if given freedom of speech.

"So many managers are afraid to open up to their employees – or allow their employees to open up to them – because they aren't sure how they or their employees will react. Reaction, or assumption of reaction, is what keeps people from moving forward. A bad reaction didn't have to happen to them, it didn't have to happen at your company, and it didn't have to happen at all, to close people down. We've learned over time to remain CLOSED because we fear the reaction that *might* happen. We think being closed is the safest place. We think if we give employees the freedom to speak openly, they will ask tough questions or somehow react poorly. We don't have faith that people will do what is right when the situation is right. A few bad experiences in our past cause us to be hesitant and not open up today."

Paul had just expressed the first hurdle managers must tackle before they can climb the Ladder of Commitment. They must answer the question of whether they actually *want* to climb the Ladder with their employees. Some managers don't *want* an OPEN work environment. They prefer the "I'm the boss, you're the employee," "my way or the highway"-type of work environment. For some obtuse reason they don't want input from employees. They just want to give orders and have people obey their commands without question. They don't care about COMMITMENT; they only want compliance.

I could tell Paul was mulling over my comments. He seemed to want to challenge what I just said, but he didn't. I was going to draw out this perceived hesitation, but decided instead to see if it would come out later when he felt more comfortable with me.

"Managers need to go inside themselves," I continued. "They need to discover how they really feel about openness and honesty. They need to assess whether they can treat people like adults, and allow the normal give and take of adult interaction, or whether they prefer the demeaning parent-child relationship that is exhibited in far too many organizations.

"So much of a manager's actions and reactions are based upon who they are and what they believe internally. Great managers have the gift of introspection. They know who they are. They know what they believe. They know intuitively that their behaviors and actions are tied to their innate management philosophies and values. The more managers are conscious of their internal processes, the better they will be at controlling and using those processes to achieve a successful outcome as managers."

I pointed to Paul's head, then to his heart, and then to his stomach.

"I told you earlier to go inside your head, heart and intuitive senses to find out what you really want. You need to ask yourself if you really want to climb the Ladder of Commitment with your managers and employees. Do you really want to go into the OPEN with the people at your plant? Or do you feel it's better – safer – to operate in a CLOSED work environment? Because, believe me, it's possible to still reach your company's production and financial goals in a CLOSED shop. It happens all the time. There are thousands of companies in this world operating as CLOSED companies that still achieve significant performance results. It's possible to achieve the outcomes you want in a CLOSED company. It just takes longer, it's not as enjoyable, and you don't reach the heights of success you could reach when everyone within your organization is committed to stepping forward together toward the same goals.

"It's the same in a marriage, you know," I said, again wishing to reinforce my point with a personal example. "Is it possible to have a marriage where the husband and wife don't talk to each other openly? Can a CLOSED marriage survive? Sure, it happens all the time. People stay married even though they are closed. But it's not a lot of fun and it's not a nice way to live. Their marriage certainly would be a lot happier if they opened up and climbed the Ladder together. Unfortunately, for some sad reason a lot of managers and married couples seem to prefer to live in a closed environment rather than go into the OPEN and climb up the Ladder."

"I'm not sure they *prefer* it," he corrected.

"Then why do they do it?" I countered. "Why remain in a closed relationship when it's not helpful and could be a lot better if they'd just open up?"

"Maybe it's because of apathy," Paul wisely proposed. "Maybe they've just given up over time because they're tired of the fights they've had in the past. It's that elephant thing."

Managing Reactions

"You're good, Paul!" I praised. "That's introspection. Go inside yourself – go inside other people – because that's where the answers are. That's where truth is. To move up the Ladder of Commitment you have to know what's happening inside yourself and others. When you discover *who* you are and who *they* are, you'll be able to move up this Ladder a lot faster. Go to a quiet place and ponder what is inside you and others. When you know yourself and you know others, you'll be surprised at how quickly you can move up this Ladder.

"One of my favorite quotes comes from the Chinese philosopher Lao Tzu. He said: *'He who knows others is learned; he who knows himself is wise.'* Only after you truly know yourself can you be wise in knowing how to handle others. The more time you spend getting to know yourself and then getting to know others, the better off you will be as a manager, as a spouse, as a parent, and as a human being."

SEVEN

Communicating
the Business Imperative

Most of the people on the flight were either reading or trying to sleep. Some, like us, were engrossed in conversation. Although Paul and I had been talking for quite some time, his interest was not waning. We both were becoming more energized as our discussion went on.

"All right," I continued, "You've just learned the most important thing to understand about how to get people out of CLOSED and up the Ladder into the OPEN is to control your own reactions. If you react well, people will move up the Ladder; if you react poorly, they will remain closed. Closed people are never committed. Therefore, to get people to the COMMITMENT rung, you have to move them into the OPEN so they will be receptive to whatever you want them to commit to.

"Now I want to tell you about the seven things you need to address with your employees in the OPEN area if you want them to move up to the next rung on the Ladder. These seven things entail the essential information employees need before they will become committed at work. They are so important to the COMMITMENT process I call them: *the things that matter most.* When you know these seven things and proactively communicate them to your employees, you can greatly accelerate the speed at which they climb the Ladder to COMMITMENT."

I pointed to the right side of the Ladder and told Paul I was going to list the seven elements in their logical order. I stressed it was essential that

Stepping Forward Together

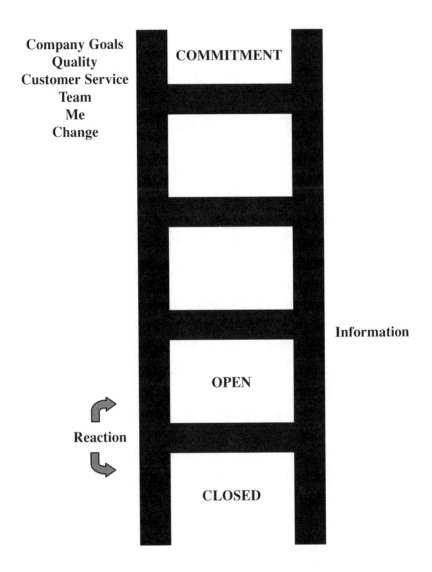

Company Goals
Quality
Customer Service
Team
Me
Change

COMMITMENT

Information

OPEN

Reaction

CLOSED

each element be addressed in sequential order to effectively move people up the Ladder.

"The first thing employees need before they can commit to something is INFORMATION. Lots of it," I said, writing the word "information" on the right side of the Ladder next to the OPEN area.

"Paul, it is impossible for people to commit to something if they don't know what it is," I suggested. "That may sound obvious, yet so many companies keep their employees in the dark regarding the most important aspects of the business. They expect their employees to be excited about things that seldom get shared outside of the board room or executive office – things like where the company is headed, how well the company is doing financially, what new products the company may be rolling out, or organizational changes that are coming down the pike. Employees often learn from the newspaper what they should have heard from their managers. Nothing makes employees feel less valued than being kept out of the loop on important work-related matters.

I stressed very heavily that many organizations have been destroyed through lack of communication. An employee's judgment and decision making is only as good as the information upon which they are based. Employees need an enormous amount of information to perform well, yet so many companies grossly neglect to share vital information with their front-line employees. They hold close to the vest the very information workers need to perform at optimum levels.

"Managers need to realize sharing information is critical to gaining employee commitment," I said. "But on a more practical note, it's also the best way to share the workload. I often hear managers complain they are overworked. Yet many of these managers overwork themselves because they don't delegate tasks that could easily be delegated. They refuse to entrust work to others out of fear the tasks will not be performed to their satisfaction. Consequently, managers do the tasks themselves to make sure the tasks are done right.

"What these managers fail to realize is their employees *could* perform the tasks satisfactorily if they were given all of the information necessary to perform well. Overworked managers can lessen their burden by remembering

Stepping Forward Together

*People cannot do what you would do
until they know what you know.
When they know what you know,
the odds are higher
they will do what you would do.*

this important maxim: *People cannot do what you would do until they know what you know. When they know what you know, the odds are higher they will do what you would do.*"

Paul was listening intently. He hadn't said much, but I knew he was tracking everything I was saying.

"The reason why you can do a task well, Paul, is because of what you know," I explained. "There is a reason why you are excited, optimistic or committed to a task. When you share what you know, think, see, hear, feel or sense, other people can get excited about it, too. One of the keys to getting your employees committed to do what you want is to share with them the information that motivates you to do what you do. This is how you get your employees to think with *your* head, see with *your* eyes, hear with *your* ears, feel with *your* heart, and perceive with *your* intuition. When your employees know what you know you can delegate with confidence, knowing they will do what you would do."

I went on to suggest employees literally beg for more information in the work place. Statements such as: 'nobody tells us anything,' 'we're always the last to know,' or 'nobody knows what's going on around here,' are strong signals employees covet the essential information needed to gain their commitment. Managers should communicate to their employees that which they would want communicated to them if their positions were reversed.

Employees need a lot of background information about a task, a strategy, a company, or a proposed action before they will commit to it. The background information helps people decide whether something is worth committing to. It motivates the employees by providing the reason why a proposed action is necessary.

"The most important background information employees need as they climb toward COMMITMENT is the *business imperative*," I said. "Most people will not move unless there is an imperative for them to so. The imperative provides the impetus that causes people to act. People must believe an action is inherently worthwhile before they will commit to doing it.

"Let me give you an example," I said. "Have you ever moved out of a home you loved?"

"Yes. We left our dream home in Ohio when we moved to Las Vegas," he said, still sounding somewhat disappointed.

"Why would you leave your dream home?" I asked, challenging his decision.

"We had to. The new job required it."

"Why? Was the commute too far from Ohio to Nevada?" I said, glibly. "You mean you'd leave your dream house just to save a few hours in commuting time?"

"Apparently."

"That's right," I reinforced. "Having a valid imperative, such as a long commute, made it much easier to accept the fact you had to leave your dream home, change your routine, and start a new life in Las Vegas. The valid imperative made the tough decision much easier."

I gave him another personal example to anchor the point.

"Newlyweds may be perfectly happy living in a small apartment. But when they have children they're compelled to move to a larger home or apartment. The fact that they can't afford the larger home then compels them to find a higher paying job or take on a second job so they can pay the higher mortgage. The compelling reason provides the motivation to take an action that one normally might not take without the imperative to do so."

I could tell Paul was already pondering the business imperatives at his manufacturing plant even though I was using personal examples.

"Paul, you left your dream home in Ohio because it was imperative for you to do so. A person with a bigger mortgage switches to a higher paying job or gets a second job because it is imperative to pay the mortgage payment. If you want to move your employees, you need to find an imperative that will cause them to do what you want them to do. You have to give them a compelling reason why they should move, particularly if that course of action requires a change to their routine. If there isn't a business imperative for them to complete a specified task, perform at a certain level, or make a necessary change, they either will stay where they are or revert back to the comfortable routine they're used to performing."

I wanted to give him a couple of examples of business imperatives, so I told him about two companies I worked with as a consultant that had to make dramatic changes in their strategic direction in order to survive. Both required the commitment of long-term, deeply entrenched employees if they were to successfully transition to the required future state.

The first company was a Las Vegas Strip casino that was a dwarf among giants. It had only 700 hotel rooms, while its mega-resort competitors had 3,000 rooms or more. It relied on revenue from 300 slot machines, when casinos just across the street generated income from thousands of machines. It only had three restaurants to its competitors' multiple food venues. There was no way it could compete unless it could find a unique niche in the market.

The casino decided to promote itself as a boutique property that offered five-star service, something unheard of in Las Vegas at the time. The problem was its employees were barely performing at a three-star level. The average longevity of the staff was 26 years. The average age of the valet parkers was 56. There were three 75-year-old cocktail waitresses and an 82-year-old security officer. Some of the employees had worked at the casino for over 40 years. They were set in their ways. No one had raised the bar on them for many years.

"When the casino called me to help obtain the five-star rating, I didn't think there was any way we could get their long-term employees to make the commitment necessary to improve their service levels," I confessed. "I was sure when we rolled out the five-star initiative we would have to terminate a lot of people who I knew would resist the change. I told the company president to get ready for a lot of age discrimination law suits and union grievances."

"So what happened?" Paul asked.

"Boy, was I ever surprised! When we shared with the employees the future vision for the property, we were very upfront and open. We told everyone exactly where the company stood in relation to its competitors. We told them of the changing conditions in the market and explained how the small casino could not compete against the mega-properties without making revolutionary changes to the way it did business. We explained the boutique hotel/casino concept and the business proposition behind it. We stressed the necessity of providing five-star service and going after the five-star rating so we could raise our room rates to a profitable level. We opened the books, shared the numbers, compared and contrasted various options, and enlisted their support. And it worked! Those employees amazed me. They were energized. They were focused. They had a business imperative and they were determined to make it work. Every single employee, manager and executive at the property stepped forward together.

"The three 75-year-old cocktail waitresses became my benchmark. I watched in awe as they performed at the five-star level. The 'old' valet parkers started to run again – something they hadn't done in years. Out of the 750 employees, only 10 left the company because of the change, and they left on their own. Everyone exuded tremendous pride when we were awarded the five-star designation."

The second company I described was a large New York City-based financial institution. The company was considering moving one of its divisions from Manhattan to Salt Lake City. I'd been asked to facilitate the team that analyzed the feasibility and logistics of the move. When our study was complete, we presented our conclusions to the executive team of the division for approval. Those who needed to approve the decision would also be personally affected by it. They would have to move to Salt Lake City.

"During the meeting the business imperative for the move was so strong it was impossible to deny that it had to be done. A vote against the move could only be based on personal bias or one's own agenda. Yet it was a tough choice for many. The senior marketing executive was a single parent who had never lived outside of Manhattan. She actually lived in the same apartment building where she was raised by her parents, who just happened to live across the hallway from her and her daughter.

"Another executive had children who were in their senior and junior years of high school. Almost every executive had a personal reason for voting against the change. But the validity of the business imperative solidified everyone's commitment, even at tremendous personal cost. The marketing executive cried as she said she would make the commitment to move to Utah. Two years later she told me it was the best decision she'd ever made. Both she and her daughter felt living in Salt Lake City was a wonderful growth experience they would never have had had they remained in their comfort zone."

Communicating the Business Imperative

I told Paul, if he wants to move the employees at his plant, the business imperative must be something that is compelling to the workers, not just the company. The business imperative also has to make sense to *everyone* involved, as my five-star example showed. Managers have the unique challenge of identifying a business imperative that appeals to shareholders and employees alike. The best imperatives are those that link the business imperative with an equally valid personal imperative. The business and personal imperatives provide the "why" explanation as well as the incentive people need before they will commit to a specific course of action.

"Do you remember in the arm folding demonstration what your first question was when I told you to reverse the way you fold your arms?" I asked.

"Yes. I wanted to know why I needed to do it."

"That is the first question whenever a change is proposed," I explained. "If you change a policy, people want to know why. If you change a procedure, people want to know why. If you move something from one place to another, people want to know why. The first question people wonder whenever you make any change is why the change is being made. What they are really asking, however, is: What is the business imperative behind the change? They also are wondering what the personal imperative is that would cause them to commit to the change.

"Since you know the *why* question is in everyone's head whenever a change is proposed, you can greatly accelerate your employees' commitment to the change by explaining the *why* before they ask," I counseled. "Consequently, here is an important rule of thumb to always remember whenever you propose a change: *Always state the 'why' first, then the 'what.'* Always in that order!"

I could tell Paul was wondering why the order matters.

"If instead you first tell *what* changes are being asked of your employees, your workers will be wondering *why* the entire time you're telling them the *what*. They won't be listening to the *what* because they're waiting to hear the *why*. Sometimes the *what* is such a shock to the employees they're too stunned to hear the *why* once the *what* has been dropped on them.

---

*Always state the 'why' first,
then the 'what.'*

Communicating the Business Imperative

"On the other hand, if you tell them the *why* first, they will be more inclined to listen to the *what*. Your employees may not necessarily accept the *what*, but at least they will understand *why* the change is needed."

I switched to a home example to better explain my point.

"Parents make a big mistake when they tell their kids the *what* before the *why*. For example, they declare to their teenage daughter: 'You can't go to the party'. That's the what. Having been denied what she wants, the daughter probably will become defensive and argue her case without ever hearing her parents' reasons for saying no.

"Her parents should have stated the *why* first. They should have explained their reasons for their refusal first by saying something like: 'Since it's a school night, and because there may be drinking at the party and no adult chaperones, I'm going to have to say no to this one. Hopefully there will be another party you can go to in the future.' Although the daughter may not like or accept the answer, at least she will understand the reasons why her parents made the decision."

"I need to remember that," Paul said. "That's something that may help me when I talk to my daughter. It's also something I can use in a meeting I have next week at work. There's a corporate initiative I'm being asked to implement at my plant, so I'll test and see if stating the *why* first will lessen people's resistance to it."

"I'm pretty sure it will," I said confidently. "Now let me ask you another question to further emphasize the importance of communicating the *why*," I continued. "I want you to 'go inside yourself' before you respond to this next question. Here is the question: Can you get committed to something if you don't know the *why* behind it?"

Paul pondered the question for a few seconds then shook his head, saying, "No, not really."

"But even though you don't know why; can you still do it?"

"Yes," Paul said hesitantly.

"That's not commitment; that's compliance," I warned. "Anyone can do what you want them to do out of compliance. But compliance isn't commitment."

I started to continue, but then Paul interrupted.

Stepping Forward Together

"What difference does it make? I'll tell you what: I'd be happy if my employees would just comply," he bemoaned. "I can't get simple compliance from some of them. So that would be wonderful if they'd just comply. Besides, why do I care whether an employee performs out of commitment or out of compliance? As long as they do what I want, I don't care whether it's out of commitment or compliance. Isn't compliance all I expect anyway? I just want people to obey the company rules and do what they are told."

"Is that truly how you feel, Paul, or are you just curious about the difference between compliance and commitment?"

Paul didn't say anything. I could tell by his silence he wasn't quite sure how he felt or what he believed.

"I don't know," he said. "I honestly believe I'd be happy to settle for compliance."

"I understand your frustration. But do you just want employees who work because they are told to, or do you want workers who perform the right way because they *want* to? Do you want employees who need a manager to tell them what to do, or do you want employees who manage themselves through *managerless management*?"

"But aren't there some situations where you don't want employees to ask why; you just want them to do it without question?" he countered.

"Sure . . . in the military. When you tell soldiers to take the hill in a war situation, you don't want the soldiers to stand around asking why. Likewise, when there's an emergency, such as a fire, you can't take the time to get everyone's buy-in before you evacuate the building. There are times at work when it's necessary to shout orders and have everyone jump to immediate action. There are situations that call for an autocratic, authoritative, direct approach to accomplish an immediate result. But a dictatorial posture is a poor long-term management style. An imperious style will hurt you and your company in the long run."

"Yes," Paul protested, "but in the situation you just mentioned about the parents telling their daughter she couldn't go to the party, shouldn't the daughter just do what her parents ask out of respect for them? And shouldn't an employee obey the boss out of respect for the boss? Show a little respect and do what you're told!"

Communicating the Business Imperative

"Sure. That would be wonderful," I answered. "But, 'respect' for one's superiors is on the next rung of the Ladder. Without giving you too much information in advance about the next rung, let me just say that once a person has reached the respect level in a relationship it is much easier to do something without knowing all of the reasons why. But, to get to that level, they first have to be OPEN and receptive to that person's direction. And, as you probably have already discovered, people who are CLOSED to a parent or boss always need justification before taking action. So I submit a child or employee will not do anything without knowing the *why* unless they have already surpassed the OPEN rung on the Ladder and climbed to a higher level."

"That makes sense . . . ," Paul responded hesitatingly.

"But . . .," I said, sensing he was still puzzling over this concept. "I don't think you're convinced yet, are you Paul?"

"I'm not sure. Right now I still think I'd be happy with compliance."

I assumed this was the hesitation I'd sensed in Paul earlier when I stressed the importance of having committed workers instead of compliant employees. He was struggling with the primary premise and core value of the management philosophies I espouse. If I couldn't convince him of the need for commitment over compliance there was no need for me to continue explaining the Ladder of Commitment.

"All right Paul, let me present what I think are logical arguments for why you should want committed employees instead of compliant workers."

I flipped to a new page on my notepad and wrote down my points as I articulated them one by one.

"Point One: **If your employees perform out of compliance rather than commitment, they do it only because you told them to, not because they *want* to.**

"Compliant employees typically do only what they are told. Workers who do only what they are told are mere order-takers and order-fillers. Order-taking workers are like animatronic robots that simply go through pre-programmed motions. They are not sentient beings who think and act for themselves. In today's fast-paced competitive economy you don't need order takers; you need decision makers. You want employees who can think and act for themselves, doing what is best for the company when there are no rote guidelines or policies to follow.

"Compliant workers seldom, if ever, take initiative. They are seldom creative and almost never think outside the box. Compliant workers dutifully do what they are told to do; nothing more, nothing less.

"Committed employees, on the other hand, see what needs to be done and they do it no matter what it takes. They are conscientious about their work and come up with new ways to achieve results better, cheaper and faster. Only sentient workers can react favorably to the ever-changing requirements of the business.

"There is an old African proverb that says: 'one volunteer is worth ten forced men'. Committed employees step forward on their own; compliant workers have to be pushed to perform. Compliant workers only do what they are told when they are told. More important, compliant workers go out of compliance when the boss is not around.

"Point Two: **If non-thinking employees need you to think for them, which is the case if orders have to be given, then your employees can only act when you are there to think for them.**

"If external pressure, rather than internal commitment, is the driving force behind your employees' behavior, then you have to be present to keep the pressure on the employees to maintain their compliance.

"Conversely, committed employees keep the pressure on themselves even when you're not around because they are internally motivated to do so. Committed employees don't wait for orders. They see what needs to be done and they take the initiative out of an intrinsic need to do so.

"There is a saying that 'two heads are better than one.' If that's the case, then the 200 heads at your plant in Las Vegas must be better than your one head, Paul. If your employees are merely complying with your orders then *your* head is the only head doing the thinking and decision making in the business. That means your single head has to be smarter than all of the other heads in the company combined.

"The whole purpose of *managerless management* is to wean employees from their reliance upon management. Again, you want your workers to think and act for themselves. That's what *managerless management* is all about. You want the motivation of your workers to come from within. You want them to be driven internally, not externally. You want your employees to perform for the right reasons, not just because you told them to."

"Point Three: **If you only want compliance from your employees, there is no need for you to create a productive work environment or a quality work life.**

"If employee compliance is all you want from your workers, then all you have to do to ensure their compliance is either reward them well or punish them well. Reward and punishment are the only managerial practices that will have any effect on employee compliance. Compliant workers require either a carrot or a stick to keep them moving. Committed employees require neither of these external stimuli to keep them focused.

"Rewarding and punishing employees is a very small part of what a manager does. The primary role of a manager is to provide a supportive work environment where employees could excel if they wanted to. Getting productive ideas from employees is not so much a matter of having creative employees as it is one of having supportive management. The more supportive you are of your employees, the more productive they will be. When you fail to provide a supportive work environment you limit the output of your employees through your negligence."

"What do you mean by supportive?" Paul asked. "Isn't offering employees a monetary reward for their performance being supportive?"

"People want more than a paycheck at work," I answered. "They want more than just a bigger piece of the pie. Clearly they need a fair wage to keep them moving and remain satisfied, but once their basic financial needs are met, non-monetary support is far more valuable in motivating your employees than money.

"Employees want managers who communicate openly. They want to be kept informed. They want to know what is expected of them and what it takes to win at work. They want managers who are fair and consistent in their management practices and leaders who treat them with respect. And most important of all, employees want managers who stand behind them and support them in their efforts as they strive to achieve the company goals."

I continued.

"Point Four: **Employees who are not committed to something, who toil merely out of compliance, have to fake the behaviors they exhibit at work.**

"If you force your employees to comply with your customer service standards of friendliness or courtesy, you'll soon find out that customers are seldom fooled by pseudo-customer service. Customers know when your workers are merely complying with a customer service directive rather than being fully committed to it. Those who serve out of compliance do so unwillingly, and begrudged behavior is easily detected.

"Point Five: **It is difficult to be positive and enthusiastic about something you do not feel or believe in.**

"Employees who are not committed to customer service, who only comply because they have to, will find it extremely difficult to fake being positive or enthusiastic toward the customers.

"Committed employees are genuine. They do what they do because it is who they are. They serve because they are service oriented. They work hard because they are hard workers. They do what is right because it feels right. They genuinely exude what they sincerely feel inside themselves.

"Compliant employees can't fake it forever. If it isn't in them, it isn't in them. Eventually they will tire of the act and end it. Compliant workers can never stick with bogus behaviors for the long haul. Only committed workers – those who have it within them – can maintain the proper attitude and behaviors over time. Eventually the compliant workers will tire of the façade and cease performing at the expected level. Eventually the phoniness will shine through."

I reminded Paul that earlier he agreed he wants employees who "get it" in their head and their heart.

"You want workers who understand and agree with the business imperative, not just those who placate or acquiesce to it. When people get 'it', right actions invariably and naturally follow. They do the right things because it is natural for them. But when employees are not committed to something – such as quality work or customer service – they have to *act* committed instead of *being* committed.

"Point Six: **When your employees are committed to something in their heads and hearts, certain behaviors and actions naturally follow. But when they are merely complying, they focus on 'acting' properly rather than working effectively.**

"When your workers' actions come from unnatural compliance, they have to constantly think about their actions and consciously remember how to act. Workers who have to work hard just to remember how to act spend less time actually working.

"Committed workers do that which comes easy and natural. Their performance is real, not an act. By not having to act, they can focus on their work rather than their actions.

"Point Seven: **People cannot motivate others if they are not motivated themselves.**

"Employees cannot convert others if they are not converted themselves. Compliant employees cannot have a positive influence performance-wise on other employees in any sincere or significant way. In fact, employees who are simply compliant usually try to bring committed employees down. Bad workers tell the good workers to stop working so hard. Compliant workers seldom are cheerleaders for the company. They don't try to raise themselves or others up; they try to bring everyone else down to their minimal level of compliance.

"Committed employees, on the other hand, invariably try to convert others to their positive way of thinking. Committed employees seek to better themselves and those around them. They raise their productive output because they *want* to perform well. And they usually try to get others to perform equally well, too, because they want everyone to be equally committed.

"Remember *managerless management?* I DON'T WANT TO MANAGE MY EMPLOYEES; I WANT THEM TO MANAGE THEM-SELVES," I said, enunciating my words firmly to emphasize my point. "I want my employees to be self-motivated and self-directed. I want every member of my team to be energized, and I want them to energize every other member of my team. Compliant workers never do that. Compliant workers just drag everyone else down."

"Point Eight: **It is difficult to trust or respect someone who only complies out of a requirement to do so.**

"Since compliance is an act, it is an act of hypocrisy. Compliant workers are not honest. They are not true to their own feelings and beliefs. They are acting out of compliance, not out of their own intrinsic principles or values.

"Since compliant workers are not true to themselves, they cannot be trusted or respected. And since they cannot be trusted or respected, they cannot be fully supported.

"It's hard to support someone whose motivations are suspect," I suggested. "You never know with compliant workers whether they are performing because they want to or only because they are told to.

"How can you trust an employee who is merely complying? How do you know the act will continue? The problem with an act is that the act eventually ends, whereas commitment never does."

"Finally, Point Nine: **If you are interested only in the compliance of your employees rather than their commitment, then you obviously don't fully understand your role as a manager.**

"Your role as a manager is to increase the efficiency and effectiveness of your employees so they can produce more. Your job is to raise the productive output of your employees by increasing the value and worth of their accomplishments. True value and true worth are achieved when employees reach their fullest potential. Yet an employee's potential is often far beyond the maximum level of full compliance with a manager's dictated job requirements. Compliant workers rarely go beyond the performance expectations set by the manager, while committed employees often astonish management by their ability to far exceed what is expected of them.

"Managers who harvest the full commitment of their employees get far greater output from their workers because the employees do the right things for the right reasons. Committed employees do it because they want to, not because they have to. Employees who are committed to something far outperform workers who only comply out of fear of punishment or promise of reward.

Communicating the Business Imperative

"So there you have it, Paul: My nine reasons why you should want committed employees rather than compliant ones. I think you want a company full of workers who are passionate about your business, not employees who merely go through the motions in a job to which they have no real commitment. You want workers who respect your leadership, heed your counsel, and follow your direction. You want your staff to maintain the company values even when you're not around. You want your workers to do what *you* would do in every situation. You want them to follow your example because you always do the right things for the right reasons."

"Well, I don't think I'm always right," Paul countered.

"But that's the point, isn't it? Because you're committed to your values, committed to a specific course of action, and committed to your company, you *try* to do what is right. You *try* to make it better. You do everything within your power to stay the course. You set the example for others by being committed yourself.

"But what do compliant workers do? Do they stay the course and always try to do what is right? Do they do everything within their power to make the business better?" I prodded.

"No. They only do what they are told," he stated flatly.

"Exactly! So, are you convinced yet?"

"I think I was convinced before," he conceded. "I just needed to hear it."

"OK, then hear this: The only way you can create employees who are as passionate about your business as you are is to give them the information you have that makes you so passionate. Tell them everything you know that makes you feel the way you do about the business. Sharing *information* is the first of seven critical elements on the OPEN rung that will get people to climb up the Ladder to COMMITMENT," I said, pointing to where I had written the word "information" next to the Ladder.

"It all makes sense," Paul concurred.

EIGHT

Answering the Why *Questions*

A few minutes ago I told Paul how important it is to explain the *why* behind every proposed action. I said it was the first question people have whenever a change is announced. I also suggested managers can build rapport and gain the commitment of their employees faster by answering the *why* questions before they are asked. Now I wanted to share a couple of additional critical points about the power of explaining *why* to employees.

I wrote the word *why* next to the word *information* on the Ladder.

"Paul, there are two additional things you need to understand about the psychological importance of answering *why* questions. Let me demonstrate the first one by asking you a question," I offered. "If you had a great idea you wanted to implement at your tool manufacturing company – an idea you thought would be perfect for the business, something you felt was a sure-fire winner, but you needed my approval before you could implement it – to what extent would you explain your idea to me to gain my approval?"

"To whatever extent necessary, I guess," Paul declared.

"And what if, after you explained your idea, I still didn't 'get it'? Then what would you do?"

"I'd explain it again. Maybe explain it better."

"And if I'm still not with you, then what would you do."

Paul looked perplexed. "I don't know. I'd probably give up."

"You're probably right! You might give up," I declared. "That's the problem! A lot of people have great ideas but they give up too easily when other people fail to immediately latch on to their thoughts. As soon as they get

Stepping Forward Together

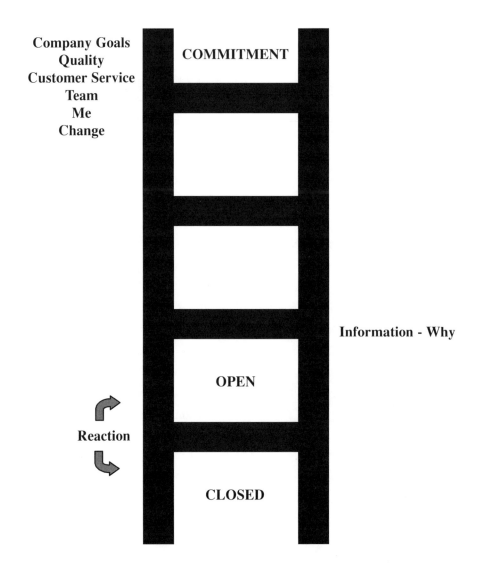

Company Goals
Quality
Customer Service
Team
Me
Change

COMMITMENT

Information - Why

OPEN

Reaction

CLOSED

a little pushback or sense confusion from others about their ideas, most people withdraw rather than press their point. Instead of finding a different way to communicate to gain the other person's COMMITMENT, they clam up and go to CLOSED. And that's the worst thing they can do. So many great ideas have been abandoned because of a few bad reactions. People need to learn to stand firm on their ideas and find a different way to communicate until they get the buy-in they need."

Paul leaned against the window as he thought about my last statement.

"Think it through, Paul. If you really did have a fantastic idea you felt was important to the business, but you needed my approval, what else might you do to get my buy-in?"

"I could ask you what you don't understand," Paul continued.

"Yes. What else?" I encouraged.

After a few seconds another idea came to him. "I could break my idea down into a simpler explanation."

"That's right. You may need to get the crayons out and draw a picture for me because I'm a little slow. What else could you do?" I pressed.

He paused to think for a moment, and then the flood gate of alternatives opened. He rattled off several more ways to express his idea.

"I could explain the benefits of my idea. . . . I could state what's in it for you if you support my idea. . . . I could engage the support of other people who might influence your decision. . . . I could find someone else who knows how to communicate with you more effectively than I can. . . . I could sell my idea to someone else who could then sell it to you. . . . I could . . ."

Paul was thinking outside the box. I hated to interrupt his stream of thoughts, but I knew he got the point.

"There are literally dozens of ways you could explain your idea. You just need to find the one that finally gets through to me," I explained. "So why are you spending so much time explaining your idea to me?"

"Because I believe in it. I believe my idea is good for the company."

"Because you're *committed* to your idea," I repeated. "When people are committed to their idea they tend to stick with it and find alternative ways to communicate. But why are you spending so much time with *me*?"

*The meaning of your communication
is the* response *you get.
If you get the wrong response,
change the way* you *communicate.*

- Virginia Satir

*How well we communicate is determined
not by how well we say things,
but by how well we are understood.*

- Andy Grove

"Because I need your approval."

"That's exactly right. Because you NEED me," I emphasized. "If you want to implement your idea you need my commitment, my buy-in. I'm important. You see, before you can get my buy-in you first have to get ME. You need to get through to me and get me to understand your idea or position. The method you use to get my buy-in could be as simple as drawing me a picture or as complex as having to explain it to me several different ways before I get it. But no matter what, you should never give up until you've gained my support. There's always a way to get through to every single person. You just need to find the right key to unlock their commitment."

I shared with him a quote by Virginia Satir, the renowned psychotherapist and author of several excellent books on effective communication, which echoes my comments. She explained the importance of altering the way we communicate this way: "The meaning of your communication is the response you get. If you get the wrong response, change the way you communicate." Andy Grove, the former CEO of Intel said it this way: "How well we communicate is determined not by how well we say things, but by how well we are understood."

"It's not what you say that matters, Paul, it's how people *respond* to what you say," I said. "The key is not to become irritated or frustrated when people don't respond the way you would like. You just need to find a different way to communicate until they do."

Paul had just demonstrated the first psychological thing managers need to understand about answering *why* questions. The reason why he had taken the time and energy to communicate his idea to me is because he needed me. I was *important* to him and his idea.

"The first thing you have to remember about a *why* question is this: **For people who are important, we take whatever time is needed to explain ourselves until they 'get it'.** We change the way we communicate until we get the other person's buy-in and commitment. By continuing to communicate until we gain their support, we send a very powerful, subtle message that the other person is important to us. And that's how we gain their commitment. When people feel they are important to us they feel more inclined to go along with our ideas. The time we take to truly communicate, versus ramrodding our ideas, lets the person know we value them. And that's a very strong message to send to people when you want their commitment."

As usual, I switched to a home example to better anchor this point.

"When our kids ask why, what's the answer?" I asked.

"Because I said so," Paul answered quickly, apparently having used this answer in his relationship with his children.

"And when you answer like that, does it work with your kids? When you say 'because I said so' do your daughter or son respond saying: 'Great answer, Dad. I'm with you now. That's all I needed to hear. Now I'm committed'?"

"No."

"So what do your kids say to your 'because I said so' answer?"

"They ask why again."

"And I'll bet your next answer is something like, 'because I'm your father, that's why,' or 'because I told you to,'" I mocked. "And does that work? Does that get them to do what you want?"

"No, it doesn't."

"Isn't it amazing that throughout the eons of time parents have answered their children's *why* questions with the same answer – even though it never works," I offered. "Although 'because I said so' may get the child to comply, it seldom gets their commitment. Only by taking the time to communicate fully will parents gain the legitimate commitment of their children."

I suggested to Paul that when parents don't invest the time to communicate with their child they send a very strong, super-subtle message that the child is not important. The failure to explain why sends a strong message that the inferior child is not important enough for the superior parent to explain his thoughts and reasons. Subtly, very subconsciously, the failure to explain why gets translated in the child's mind to something like this: "Who in the heck do you think you are? I don't have to explain myself to you. I'm your father. You are a seven-year-old. You are not important enough for me to take the time to explain myself to you. You just do what you are told because I said so."

Paul grimaced and looked away.

"Just out of curiosity, Paul, are your kids important?"

"Yes," he said emphatically, looking back at me with watery eyes.

"And are your employees important?"

"Of course they are. We can't do anything without them," he stated.

"Then take the time to communicate with them until they get it. Tell them why. Tell them the business imperative. Explain the reasons behind your actions. Communicate with them until you get the response you want."

Paul shook his head slowly from side to side.

"I'm sitting here thinking of a bunch of situations where I've failed to provide an adequate answer to my children's *why* questions. I never thought I was sending them a message that they're not important," he groaned.

I wanted Paul to feel even more emphatically what his children felt.

"So, Paul, have you ever felt not important at work? I asked.

"Yes," he said sadly.

"When?"

"Just a couple of weeks ago I was talking to my boss back at our corporate headquarters in Ohio. The company was implementing a change in the bonus structure. I didn't understand what precipitated the change. All I wanted to know was why . . ."

Paul stopped mid sentence, exhaling loudly. "All I wanted to know was *why* the change was made."

"And when you asked why, what happened?" I asked.

"I don't know. I guess my boss thought I was challenging the change. He became defensive. He didn't answer my question. He made a couple of comments about how I needed to get on board. And then he ended the discussion abruptly by saying, 'Well, that's what we're doing. It goes into effect next quarter.'"

I paused for a moment, and then said, "And how did that make you feel?"

I could tell just by looking at him that he was still hurting from the experience.

"It made me feel like crap," he said, angrily.

"Isn't that interesting? By not answering your *why* question it made you feel bad; yet your boss wanted you to 'get on board' – he wanted your COMMITMENT," I said, pointing to the top of the Ladder. "But where did his reaction send you on the Ladder?"

"To CLOSED!" Paul stated with finality.

"Just the opposite of what the boss wanted," I emphasized. "And this brings us to the second very important psychological aspect of *why* questions. Why did you ask your boss why in the first place?"

"Because I wanted to know the reason for the change. I just wanted to understand it."

"That's right. You wanted to understand," I repeated. "You wanted to understand the reason behind the change so you could 'get on board', didn't you? But you couldn't get committed until you understood the *why* behind the decision to change the bonus structure. The extent of your commitment was directly connected to the extent you understood the reasons behind the decision. And the extent of your understanding was predicated upon the depth your boss was willing to go to explain the *why* behind the decision."

I re-emphasized that people cannot get committed to something they do not understand, and people cannot understand something fully until they know the *why* behind it. Knowing the *why* is often more important than knowing the *what*. People who know why can commit to almost any *what*.

"And that's the second important element you need to understand about how people react psychologically to *why* questions. When *you* ask why it is an honest inquiry for information. But what does it sound like when *I* ask why?"

I proceeded to drill him for the answers to my *why* questions. *Why weren't you in your office? Why didn't you get back to me? Why didn't you do what I told you? Why did you do it like that? Why do I have to do it your way?*

"What does it sound like when I ask why, Paul?"

"It sounds accusatory."

"And if I'm an employee and I ask *why* questions of you like these: *Why do I have to do it like that? Why can't I do it my own way? Why do I have to use that form? Why can't I use the old form? Why do we have to change?* What do those questions sound like?"

"They sound like whining and complaining?"

"Does it sound like I'm committed to whatever it is I'm inquiring about? Does it sound like I even *want* to commit?"

"No. It sounds like you're being critical. It sounds like you're resistant to it."

"And when you hear people who sound accusatory or who whine, complain, or seem resistant to what you want, where do you go on the Ladder?" I asked.

"I go to CLOSED," Paul said, pointing to the bottom of my Ladder drawing.

"Isn't that interesting? When *you* ask why, it's an honest inquiry for information. But when other people ask why of you, it sounds like a complaint or criticism. For some reason I don't fully understand, *why* questions tend to rouse negative reactions from people. Being asked why makes people feel like they are being challenged. *Why* questions don't feel like honest inquiries for information, they feel like criticisms, complaints or resistance." I explained.

"If you want to test this one, Paul, here's something you can try at home. The next time your wife cooks you a meal, calmly ask her why the food is so salty. See if she interprets your *why* question as an honest inquiry for information."

Paul wasn't interested in testing it. He already knew how she would respond.

"So, the second psychological thing you need to understand about *why* questions is: **Most *why* questions are an honest inquiry for information**. *Why* questions are an honest inquiry to get the information necessary in order to move up the Ladder to COMMITMENT," I stressed. "Unfortunately, *why* questions don't come across that way. They almost always sound negative or critical, which causes the other person to become defensive and close down. But the key thing you need to understand is this: if a *why* question is an honest inquiry for information, then what kind of response does it require?"

"An honest answer," Paul said firmly.

"That's right. Honest questions deserve honest answers. They deserve an OPEN response," I affirmed. "Do you remember the little role play I did with you earlier where I pretended to be the seventh president of the company that had had six presidents in four years? What was the question the employee in the role play asked the new president?"

Paul smiled as he recalled the situation. "He asked how much money the president made."

"Even though it was not stated as a *why* question, do you think that question was an honest inquiry for information?"

"No way! The employee was just making a smart aleck comment," Paul declared.

"And according to my reaction as the president in the role play, the president heard that question as a criticism, didn't he? That's why he reacted so strongly. He thought he was being challenged. But what if it was an honest inquiry for information? What if it was an important question where the answer would gain the commitment of that employee? Don't you think there's a possibility the employee really was looking for an honest answer to his question?"

"I don't see how a question like that can be an honest inquiry for information. It's none of his business how much the president makes," Paul maintained.

"Actually, when a company has gone through downsizing and cut the salaries of its management staff, don't you think the employees might wonder if the new president has made a similar sacrifice for the good of the company? Don't you think the employees might wonder if he, too, is going to step forward with the rest of the team and also make a sacrifice for the good of the company?" I proposed.

Paul conceded there was some logic behind the question.

"So if the question is an honest inquiry for information, what kind of a response does it deserve?"

"An honest answer," Paul said, shaking his head in disgust that he hadn't thought about these points during the role play.

"That's the trouble with *why* questions," I said, trying to reinforce what Paul was now figuring out. "Too often, *why* questions are perceived as challenges, criticism, or resistance, when they actually are honest inquiries for information. When people feel they are being attacked, they react negatively rather than respond openly and calmly. They attack when no offense was ever intended. And that causes both parties to go to CLOSED."

Answering the WHY *Questions*

I reminded Paul in the role play the president said he believed in being open and honest. He told his employees to feel free to ask any questions or make any comments. This meeting was a perfect opportunity for the new president to model the OPEN environment he espoused. But by not controlling his reaction to what appeared to be a stupid question, the president killed all hope of creating the type of company he knew was necessary to turn the business around.

"You're right," Paul exclaimed. "It's amazing how many times people do things that are just the opposite of what they want."

I wanted to give Paul another example of where managers go in the opposite direction from that which is right. I told him a lot of communication problems in organizations can be resolved by proximity. Management merely needs to be more visible and spend time with the employees. Yet, one of the toughest challenges I have as a management consultant is convincing executives to get out on the shop floor to mingle with the workers. *Management by Wandering Around* is one of the most powerful and productive management techniques available, yet too few managers ever do it. They barricade themselves in their offices and complain they don't have time to get out on the floor. But time is not the issue. If managers wanted to get out on the shop floor they could make the time. Something else keeps them in their offices.

I believe one of the reasons why they don't make the time to get out among the employees is because, subconsciously, they know what will happen when they do. Somehow, deep within the recesses of their subconscious mind, they know they will be peppered with *why* questions from the employees. And, also subconsciously, they know when they are asked those *why* questions they will feel criticized and challenged. And their subconscious mind warns them that when they are criticized they will react negatively to the challenge.

So, subconsciously, their body refuses to allow them to get into a situation where they might react poorly and damage relationships. Rather than react poorly and look bad in front of the employees, they stay in their office where they will not be faced with a plethora of *why* questions. Seclusion is a subconscious (or sometimes conscious) way to avoid an experience that one intuitively senses might be difficult to handle.

Stepping Forward Together

The most important lesson managers need to realize is that, by getting out on the shop floor and answering the *why* questions, they send a strong message to their employees about how important they are to the company. Being out among the employees also gives managers an opportunity to answer the honest inquiries regarding the information employees need to commit to the tasks and responsibilities required of them.

"Managers can do more to build rapport and get their employees to the top of the Ladder of Commitment by openly and honestly answering their workers' *why* questions than by any other means," I reminded. "And since the first question people have whenever a change is proposed is, 'Why is the change is necessary?', you can solidify your rapport with employees even more by answering the *why* questions *before* they are asked. Clearly, managers need to get much better at answering *why* questions without defensiveness or excuse."

NINE

Communicating the Things
that Matter Most - I

Paul and I had been talking for quite some time. I knew he had been listening attentively and participating in the discussion, but I wanted to make sure he had internalized all of the key points I'd made.

"OK, let's review what you've learned so far about the OPEN area on the Ladder of Commitment," I continued.

"The key to getting people to OPEN up is to control your *reactions* when they do. Once people open up they need a lot of *information* to keep them climbing up the Ladder. The most important information they need is the business imperative or compelling reason for taking whatever action you wish them to take. People will not commit to something unless they know the reasons *why* they should. When people ask *why* questions, it is an honest inquiry for information and should be answered honestly, without defensiveness. And finally, for people who are important we explain the reasons why until they get it. Taking the time to explain things to people sends a powerful and subtle message that they are important."

"I've got it," Paul said.

"Great! Now let me tell you about the second requirement in the OPEN area of the Ladder if you want to gain the commitment of your employees," I said pointing to the right side of the OPEN area on my Ladder diagram.

"Remember, I call the seven things I am listing down this side the *things that matter most* in the workplace. They are the seven elements

Stepping Forward Together

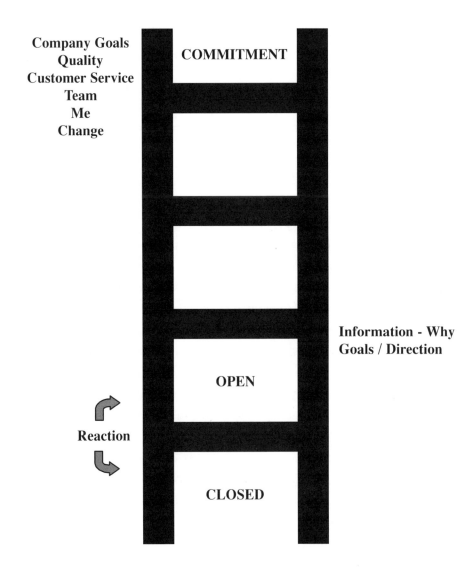

that determine whether employees will commit to do what you want. They provide your employees with the information that allows them to know what you know, think what you think, see what you see, hear what you hear, feel what you feel, and intuit what you intuit," I explained, reiterating the major premise behind the *conscious management* and *managerless management* concepts.

"After you've shared the background INFORMATION and explained the WHY behind a proposed change or action, your employees will be in a better position to understand the goals and direction of the company," I declared.

I wrote the words *goals* and *direction* under *information* to the right of the OPEN area on my Ladder diagram.

I reminded Paul that the order of the seven things I was listing is important. The goals and direction of the organization can only be fully understood in the context of the background information that precedes it. Managers sometimes have the tendency to announce organizational goals without providing an overview of how those goals were determined. The background information provides the foundation upon which to build the commitment of the employees to achieve the goals.

I gave Paul an example to show him why the background information must be established before the goals are announced.

"Since my consulting company is based in Las Vegas, I have a lot of casino clients. The majority of these casinos announce their strategic goals in annual all-employee meetings that typically involve a lot of fanfare and hoopla. The president or general manager of the property usually gets up and enthusiastically announces, '*The EBITDA goal for the company for the upcoming year is 22 percent.*' In most cases this pronouncement is met with a spattering of applause. But most of the employees just sit there with a blank look on their faces. Why aren't the employees excited about the EBITDA goal?" I asked.

"They probably don't know what EBITDA means," Paul surmised correctly.

Stepping Forward Together

Pretending to be the CEO of the casino and correcting my oversight, I said: *"Our Earnings **B**efore **I**nterest, **T**axes, **D**epreciation and **A**mortization goal for next year is 22 percent."*

"Now they should be excited about the goal, don't you think, Paul?"

"I doubt it."

"Why not?" I asked.

"That may be what EBITDA means, but just because you define something doesn't mean people understand it."

"You're absolutely right. As I said before, sometimes you have to explain things several different ways before people finally get it."

I was going to move on but Paul interrupted me. "So how do you explain EBITDA to employees?" Paul asked. "EBITDA is important in my business, too, but I'm sure I even have some *managers* who don't understand it."

"It's actually pretty easy. Forget the complicated words. Simply stated, EBITDA means 'operating cash flow.' This is how I would explain it to employees," I said, switching to role-play mode.

"As everyone very well knows from handling your personal finances at home, you have money that flows into your pocket and, unfortunately, you have money that flows out. That's called 'cash flow.' Invariably, what you hope at the end of the month is more money flowed into your pocket than flowed out. You want some cash left over in your pocket at the end of the month.

"It's the same in business. Money, called 'revenue,' flows in and money, called 'expenses,' flows out. As a business, what we hope at the end of the year is more money flowed in than flowed out. When we say we have an EBITDA goal of 22 percent, all we are saying is, at the end of the year, out of the money that flowed in and the money that flowed out, we'd like to have 22 percent of that money left over in our company pocket once our expenses are paid."

"It's that simple," Paul confirmed.

"So our EBITDA goal for this year is 22 percent!" I said enthusiastically, pumping both hands into the air to generate an enthusiastic response

from the imaginary employees. "Now the employees should be thrilled about the company goal, don't you think?" I asked.

He paused, and then shook his head no.

"What? Why not?"

"Twenty-two percent relative to what?" he asked. "The employees need more information. They need to know what the goal is this year relative to what it was last year. They also need to know whether last year's goal was achieved; and, if not, why not. And if this year's goal is higher than last year's goal, why does management think a higher goal is achievable? Is the goal realistic based on this year's economic and business conditions? And even if it is realistic, they'll probably want to hear what the company's plan is for achieving the EBITDA goal."

"Did you hear yourself, Paul? You just stated a lot of truths in your answer. You just confirmed employees need a lot of INFORMATION before they can understand the goal. You said workers need the background information about the goal relative to previous goals. You said they need to know WHY management feels confident the goal can be achieved. And most important, you said, to get excited about the goal, the employees need to hear the plan for achieving it.

"It would be much more helpful as the president of the company if, before announcing the EBITDA goal, I gave the employees some background information about the company's EBITDA position in the past. They also might want to know where we are in relation to our competitors regarding their EBITDA number. They also will need to know what is happening in our industry that might impact the company's EBITDA goal. Only after the employees have this information, and possibly a whole lot more, will the goal be meaningful enough to the employees for them to make sense of it."

"Why does this all sound so obvious and simple when you say it, yet so many managers like me don't take the time to explain things like this to our employees?" Paul asked.

"It's because we make a lot of assumptions about what the employees know and don't know," I suggested. "We assume they know a lot more than they usually do. It's pretty unrealistic to expect employees to be enthusiastic about things that seldom get shared outside of the executive office. And even

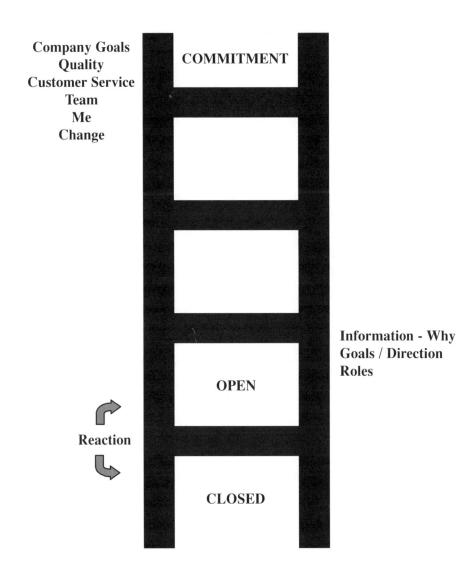

when information is shared, it's often stated in executive jargon that the employees can't understand. The front-line may not be able to decipher the often cryptic language of the financial world. That's why we have to communicate in such a way that they get it. And if they don't understand what we are saying, we have to change the way we communicate until they do."

"Good point!" Paul pushed. "What's the next item on the list?"

"Once your employees fully comprehend the goals and direction of the organization, they next need to be told their roles in achieving those goals," I explained.

I wrote the word *roles* below *goals* and *direction* and *information* on the right side of the Ladder.

"Paul, does anyone besides you at your manufacturing plant have a role in achieving the profitability goals of the company?"

"Yes. Almost everyone."

"Does the Sales Department have a role?"

"Of course."

"How big of a role do they have?"

"Obviously they have the biggest role. They're the ones who make the sales that generate the revenue to achieve the goals," Paul declared.

"Does the Design Department have a role in achieving your profitability goals?"

"Well, actually, all tool design is done out of our Ohio office," Paul said. Then, as an afterthought, he corrected himself. "But they definitely contribute to the achievement of our production goals in Las Vegas, even though we don't control that department. They provide us with quality designs so we can produce quality tools. So I guess they do have a role in our financial performance."

"How about your employees on the production line? Do they have a role in achieving the revenue goals of the company?"

"Of course they do," Paul said. "They're the ones who produce our products. If they don't make a quality product our sales force will have nothing to sell. If they produce defective products our scrap rates will increase and our customer return expenses will go up. Our front-line workers impact our financial goals probably more than anyone else."

Stepping Forward Together

"OK. One more question What about your custodial staff? What about the workers who clean up your shop floor and offices. Do they have a role in achieving your financial goals?"

"Yes. They clean up spills and other hazards that could cause injuries and result in costly litigation. So they help keep our costs down. And, just like everyone else, they need to do a quality job."

"You're absolutely right. Every single employee at your plant – from the president to the file clerk – has a role in achieving the profitability goals of the company," I stressed. "But is it possible that some of your employees don't understand their role in achieving your EBITDA goal?"

"Probably."

"So whose job is it to help them get it?"

"That's my job and their manager's job," Paul rightly responded.

Paul and I agreed that one of the key responsibilities of every manager is to ensure every employee knows his or her role and how they fit into the overall picture of the organization. Managers need to help employees understand why their position exists and what they must do in their position to achieve the company's performance goals. Employees perform better and are more committed when they see a direct link between what they do and how it impacts the company's overall success.

"Lack of role clarification is the number one reason why employees fail to perform in the workplace," I stated. "Unfortunately, some managers seem to think a person's role doesn't need to be clarified beyond telling the worker that he or she is a Pot Washer or Food Server. It's as if they think a person's job title *is* their role clarification."

"But isn't it obvious that a Pot Washer washes pots and a Food Server serves food?" Paul challenged.

"If you believe an employee's job title equates to role clarification, then I guess it's safe to assume that a Waiter is someone who makes the customers wait until the Waiter is good and ready to serve them," I retorted.

"I think I've eaten in those restaurants," Paul chuckled.

"As a manager I don't want to assume an employee's job title clarifies his role. I want to make sure he gets it. That's why, if I was interviewing a person who was applying for a Food Runner position at a restaurant, this is how I would do it," I said, again switching to a role play.

"*'I noticed that you applied for the Food RUNNER position,'*" I said, emphasizing the word runner.

"*'I don't know if you know exactly what a Food RUNNER does, but a Food RUNNER is the person who moves the food from the preparation area in the kitchen out to the buffet line out front. Your job is to make sure the buffet line is constantly full of food. Whenever the food is low, you need to go to the kitchen and get fresh pans of food to add to the line. And, since we call it the Food RUNNER position and not the food stand-around-and-talk-to-your-friends-all-day position, how do you think we want you to move the food from the kitchen to the buffet line?'*"

"By running?" Paul answered.

"Good guess. You see, I don't want there to be any confusion about what I expect from an employee. That's why in reality, if I were interviewing a candidate for a Food Runner position, the first thing I want to do in the interview is see how he *walks.*"

Paul smiled.

"I'm serious. Have you ever had an applicant come into a job interview loping along at a slow gait? Do you think he'll get faster after he gets the job? Believe me, if an employee walks slowly *before* he gets to work, he won't go any faster *after* he gets to work."

"That's so true."

"Job titles don't mean anything when it comes to role clarification. I've seen Food Runners who didn't run, Repairmen who didn't repair, Cleaners who didn't clean, and Salespeople who couldn't close a sale. So much for job title equating to role clarification."

"So how clear do you have to be?" Paul asked, even though I knew he already knew the answer.

"Crystal clear. I like to clarify roles in pithy statements that I can pound into an employee's conscious mind so I don't have to ever tell them again."

"Give me an example of a pithy role clarification statement," Paul asked.

*Lack of role clarification leads to role
    ambiguity.
Role ambiguity leads to role conflict.
Role conflict eventually leads to role
    failure.*

"Like telling a Casino Host (the person who brings the high-rollers into a casino) that she exists *to part people from their money and do it in such a way they want to do it again and again.*"

Paul shook his head at the simplicity, yet clarity, of the statement.

"Some casino hosts seem to think their job is to schmooze with the high roller," I explained. "They think they are there to take the high roller out to dinner, get them into a show, or ply them with all sorts of incentives."

"But isn't that what they do?" Paul said, somewhat puzzled.

"Yes, that is what they *do*, but it's not why they *exist*. If all they do is schmooze the high rollers without parting them from their money, believe me, that casino host will not be a casino host for long. The casino host was not hired to schmooze people; she was hired to part people from their money," I declared.

"Well, that's true. They have to get the high roller to gamble," Paul agreed.

"So, would you like to hear my pithy statement for why *you* exist as the general manager of your company?" I grinned. "You exist for one reason and one reason only: *EBITDA or die!* If you don't make your numbers, believe me, you won't be the general manager for long."

"You got that right. And I know it," Paul chuckled.

"Let me tell you why your tool company exists. You see, if your workers on the production line think all they do is manufacture tools, they are wrong and you are in jeopardy of going out of business. Your company exists to *produce power tools that are safe, durable, reliable, efficient and easy to use that perform the functions they are designed to perform at the level promised.* Do that and you will win every time."

I further explained that managers need to tell their employees exactly what to do and why. They can't assume their employees will understand their roles without clarification. Managers need to state why the job is important and how it helps achieve the company's short- and long-term goals. They should define the tasks, set the standards, explain the policies, go through the procedures, and do everything necessary to help their employees know exactly why their position exists and what it takes to win in their positions.

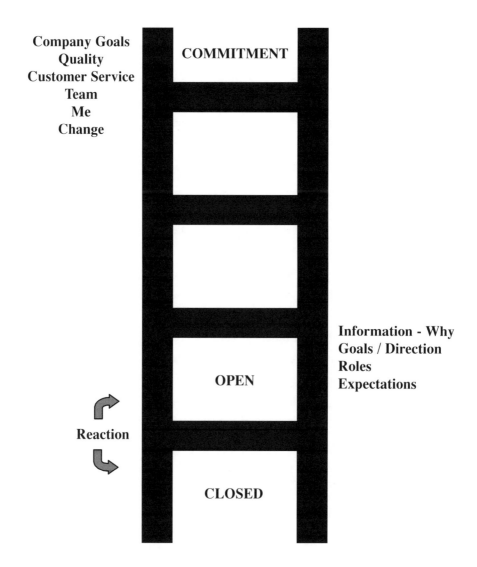

"Paul, when you don't clarify roles for your employees, it creates all sorts of problems," I explained, drawing another model on my note pad. "Lack of *role clarification* leads to role *ambiguity*. When your employees' roles are vague or hazy, they can easily do things that are wrong, unnecessary, unproductive, and sometimes even duplicitous. Any time two or more people are doing the same things or stepping into areas deemed to be outside of their role, this can lead to serious *role conflict*. Eventually, role conflict turns into *role failure* as the two competing employees either stop doing what they assume the other is doing, or they refuse to do the task because each feels the other employee is infringing on his or her area."

I told Paul managers can keep employees from failing or having conflict by clarifying roles so there is no ambiguity. The tools managers use to clarify roles include job descriptions, position statements, employee handbooks, policy manuals, performance standards, task sheets, departmental training, and other means that lay out the duties and responsibilities of a worker's job.

I asked Paul if he had any more questions about clarifying roles. He had none, so I continued.

"Once your employees know their *roles* and how they fit into the overall strategies of the company, the next step is to explain what is expected of them as they fulfill their roles. Clearly articulated attitudinal, behavioral and performance *expectations* tell employees how they should act and what they should do as they carry out their roles. Your employees cannot do what you want them to do the way you want them to do it unless you tell them exactly what you expect."

"Paul, what process do you use to inform your managers about your expectations?"

Paul stammered, trying to think of how he does it.

"When I interview a person for a management position I tell them what I'm looking for," he said. "Then, after the person is hired I meet with them on the first day and really stress what I expect."

"Do you have a list?" I probed.

"Of what?"

"Of your expectations. Are your expectations written down so you're sure you go over each and every expectation with each and every new manager?"

"No."

"Then how do you know you go over *all* of your expectations with *each* new manager when you hire them? Isn't it possible that you might forget some of your expectations during your discussion and not let the person know exactly what you want?"

"That's possible. I probably do forget some," Paul confessed.

"Yet, even though you might forget to tell the manager what you expect, I'll bet you still expect it from her, even if she's never been told."

"I'm sure that's true," Paul conceded, "but I've never thought about that before."

"That's why I'm raising this to your consciousness. That's what *conscious management* is all about. *conscious management* is where you consciously think about the *things that matter most* in the business and consciously address those things with your managers and employees in an organized and systematic way. And, speaking of your employees, what process do you use for sharing your expectations with your front-line workers?"

"Well, I don't interview the front line employees or meet with them when they are hired, so I don't have a process for sharing my expectations with them," Paul said reluctantly. Then, realizing he actually did do some things to share his expectations and wanting to redeem himself, he added: "Well, I do get out on the shop floor a lot. I spend time talking to the employees, so they should know what I expect from those conversations.

"I also hold an annual all-employee meeting where we talk about the company goals. And I write a general manager's column in our quarterly newsletter. So I'm doing some things to clarify my expectations!"

"Yes, it sounds like you are. And those things are good," I confirmed. "But are they enough to make sure every employee at every level of your company knows what you want?"

"Isn't that the job of the employee's manager?" he retorted. "They need to pass on my expectations and make sure everyone is on the same page. I think that's a manager's role."

"Yes it is. But you admitted that you may sometimes forget to share your expectations with your managers, so how can they pass on something they themselves have not heard?" I challenged. "Are you doing enough to make sure everyone in your company knows exactly what you expect and what it takes to win in their jobs?"

"Apparently not."

"This is why I'm spending so much time discussing the OPEN rung on the Ladder. Spending time talking to your employees about the *things that matter most* is the most effective way to motivate them to do what you want. It shouldn't be too surprising to learn that the number one motivator of employees is *quality* time spent with their managers."

"Are you sure about that? Don't you think employees are more motivated by money?" Paul questioned.

"That's what a lot of managers think. But survey after survey has shown employees rank pay way down on the list of motivators," I said.

I explained that according to the research the majority of employees rank meaningful work over pay as a motivator. They want to make a difference. They want to know their work matters and is important. When managers take the time to communicate with their employees – explaining the business imperative, telling them why it's important, sharing the goals and direction of the company, clarifying roles, and letting them know what is expected – they propel the employees up the Ladder of Commitment and motivate them to work at higher levels of performance.

"People crave meaningful interaction," I added. "Employees want the time and attention of their boss. They want to feel important – so important their boss would take the time to communicate with them. And that gets confirmed in exit interviews when employees leave a company. Do you know what employees say is the number one reason why they left a company?"

"I know this one," Paul interjected quickly, sitting up in his chair. "I just read this somewhere in an article. Most employees leave because of the way they were treated by their immediate supervisor."

"And you thought it was money," I chided.

"I just forgot."

"No, you didn't forget. You never learned it!" I hammered. "You read that article and you let an important piece of information slip quickly through your subconscious mind. You didn't internalize it. You didn't commit it to your conscious memory. If you had, you wouldn't have answered my question the way you did. You answered by reverting back to a well-held belief or bias that was already in your brain. That bias was so ingrained within you the statistical facts presented in the article you just read, and which have been upheld by countless surveys, didn't override what you already believed. Rather than absorbing the statistical facts and changing the way you thought, you let the truth bounce off your head and never enter into your conscious mind.

"That's why you have to get conscious, Paul. That's why you have to go inside yourself and learn what I'm telling you tonight about the Ladder of Commitment. Every single point I've made and will make is important. Every single point is true when it comes to gaining the enthusiasm and commitment of your employees. You need to check your head, your heart, and your intuitive senses if you want to be a far better general manager of your company when we land in Las Vegas."

TEN

Defining the Major Premise

I knew I was pushing Paul hard. I probably wouldn't have done it, but I sensed he wanted to be pushed. He wanted his thinking to be challenged. I knew he honestly wanted to learn, grow, and improve. So, as I always do, I switched to a personal example to better anchor my point.

"So, Paul, what is the number one thing your children want from you?"

"I'll bet the answer isn't money," Paul joked, referring back to his earlier comment. "Actually, I do know what it is. They want quality time with me and my wife."

"You're absolutely right," I agreed, "and any parent who doesn't get that, doesn't understand his or her role as a parent. You see, Paul, parents exist to help their children learn the *personal* imperative. Just as in business there is a business imperative, in life there is a personal imperative. The job of every parent is to help their children learn the things that are *imperative* they know in order to succeed in life. Parents need to explain *why* things are the way they are. They need to help their children establish meaningful *goals* and find purpose and *direction* in their lives. Most important, parents nurture their children best by helping them learn what is and will be *expected* of them at home, at school, at work, and in society so they can have a happy and successful future."

I had been pointing to each of the words listed down the right side of the OPEN area on the Ladder so Paul could see how the Ladder can also be used at home.

Stepping Forward Together

"The more I learn about the Ladder of Commitment the more useful it becomes," Paul exclaimed. "I wish I'd known this a long time ago. It would have helped me communicate better both at work and at home."

"Then maybe a tool I use in my own home on this very issue may be of value to you, too," I offered. "Your daughter is fifteen and your son is eleven, is that correct?"

"Yes."

"I hope you have a wonderful relationship with your kids. But the teenage years can be very difficult and stressful for both children and parents. It's typically a time of great conflict in the home as teenagers struggle to discover their identity and assert their freedom to choose who and what they will be. It is a time when roles become less clear and somewhat ambiguous. It is a time when children act like children, yet long to be treated as adults. It's a time when adults, angered by the teenager's behavior, lose their maturity and react like children when conflicts arise. It is a time when parents and children sometimes respond CLOSED to each other's wishes when openness is needed most.

"I don't know what it is about the teenage years, but for some reason that seems to be the time when people don't have a brain. When my son was a teenager he thought I was an idiot; and I felt the same about him sometimes. The fact is we were both idiots. For some reason we couldn't communicate. We weren't on the same wave length. I could not get through to him, and he definitely couldn't get through to me," I complained.

"That's normal," Paul said, trying to console me.

"Yes, but I'm supposed to know better. I'm supposed to be an expert in communication. I know about the *things that matter most* in the OPEN area of the Ladder of Commitment. I know I need to control my reactions if I want my son to commit to what I believe is important. I know I have to change the way I communicate until I get the response I want from my son. I know everything there is to know about how to get people up this Ladder. But do you think I did any of these things whenever a conflict arose between me and my son during his teenage years?"

"I would hope so," Paul expected.

"Well, guess what? I didn't. In stressful moments my brain went out the door just like everyone else's. Instead of using the vast knowledge I have within me, I, too, reacted the way most human beings react. I screamed rather than communicated. I threatened rather than explained. I told my son only once and expected him to understand. I sought compliance rather than taking the time needed to get my son's commitment.

"But then one day I got a brain," I said, having to pause as I tried to control the deep emotions stirring within me, still regretting my inadequacies at that time. "Finally, one day I realized my son didn't get the *major premise*."

Paul's eyes narrowed into a puzzled look.

"I realized my son didn't know the imperative behind my parental directives. He didn't understand my goal as I tried to steer him in a specific direction. He misinterpreted my role as a parent and fought against my expectations. Somehow, in all our interaction together, my son had misconstrued why I exist as a parent," I explained.

I asked Paul to tell me why parents exist from the perspective of most teenagers.

"To make their lives miserable," he immediately answered, as if he were playing back a recording of what one of his children had said to him.

"They actually tell us that don't they?" I agreed. "Our teenagers say: 'You just want to ruin my life. You don't want me to have any friends. You want to make my life miserable,'" I whined. "And is that why *you* exist as a parent, Paul?"

"No"

"So why do you exist? What is your purpose as a parent?"

"I'm here to teach my kids, to help them learn what they need to know to be successful. I'm here to protect them, to keep them safe. I'm here to love them," he declared.

"But our kids forget that sometimes, don't they? They forget the reason why we are here as parents. That's what I figured out one day when I finally got a brain after a huge argument with my son. I realized most of our arguments ignited because of a lack of role clarification which led to role ambiguity, role conflict, and role failure. I realized my son didn't understand my role as a parent. He didn't know why I exist. And that's when I came up with what I call *The Parental Major Premise*. I wanted to clarify my role in writing so my son would not be confused. I wanted to give him something to refer to whenever it looked like he and I were on opposite teams," I explained.

"The parental major premise consists of five assertions. The first assertion states very plainly: *We love you.*"

I wrote down each point of the major premise so Paul could see and remember it.

"If my son doesn't know we love him – if he can't see, hear, feel and sense our love – then nothing else matters. We will never get our son to do what we want him to do if he doesn't feel loved by us. If he doesn't think we love him, then it will be hard for him to accept our guidance and counsel because our intentions will always be questionable to him. But if he truly *knows* we love him, he can remove from his vocabulary the complaint that we don't love him because he knows it isn't true. And we can get past that argument once and for all and never have to hear that accusation again," I explained.

Paul nodded his head in agreement. Perhaps his children had questioned his love in the past.

"Of course, if you don't love your kids, you can't state this premise as true, can you, Paul?"

He shook his head slightly in affirmation.

I wrote down the second assertion of the parental major premise: *We would never do anything to purposely harm you.*

"When our kids say we just want to make their lives miserable or that we don't want them to have any friends, they act as if we are purposely trying to harm them," I explained. "But that isn't why we put restrictions on them. In fact, it's just the opposite. We restrict their actions because we *don't* want them to get hurt. We're trying to protect them. But they don't get it. And that's why I developed this premise so my son would finally understand our motivations whenever we say no to something he wants to do. Our purpose is not to hurt, but to help. We say no because we are trying to protect him from harm."

"This is so good," Paul said, shaking his head. "That's exactly why we say no to our kids."

Defining the Major Premise

"Of course, the same caveat applies to this assertion as the first one," I warned. "You can't make this statement if you're a child abuser. This assertion cannot be true if you purposely do or say anything that hurts your kids, makes them feel bad, degrades them, pushes them down, or in any way diminishes their self-worth. That's why parents have to stop yelling at their kids. That's why we have to get rid of sarcasm, cynicism, belittling, or any other degrading behavior toward our children. We can't do anything that we know will harm them. Not if we love them."

I wrote down the third and primary assertion of the parental major premise: *We want you to have a happy, successful, independent and self-sustaining life.*

"We want our son to know that our only desire is for him to be happy. We want him to be successful in his life. We want him to be independent, which means we want him to eventually go away. We want him out of our house. We DON'T WANT HIM TO LIVE WITH US FOREVER," I emphasized.

Paul smiled, knowingly.

"And the only way he can be independent is if he is . . ."

"Self-sustaining," Paul interjected.

"Exactly!" I said, writing down the last two assertions: *Everything we do as parents is designed toward that end. So don't fight against us; we are on your side.*

"The problem with many teenagers is they don't feel their parents are on their side. They think whatever the parents do is designed to make their lives miserable. Yet, for most parents, our only desire, contrary to how our teenagers may sometimes feel, is that we want our kids to be happy, successful, independent and self-sustaining. Unfortunately, during the teenage years a lot of kids don't get it.

"And that's why I created the parental major premise, so my son would get it," I said, sharing with Paul the complete premise: We love you. We would never do anything to purposely hurt you. We want you to have a happy, successful, independent and self-sustaining life. Everything we do as parents is designed toward that end. So don't fight against us; we are on your side.

The Parental Major Premise

We love you.

*We would never do anything
to purposely hurt you.*

*We want you to have a happy, successful,
independent and self-sustaining life.*

*Everything we do as parents is designed
toward that end.*

So don't fight against us; we are on your side.

Defining the Major Premise

"That major premise not only helped my son get it, it also helped remind me to stay focused," I explained. "It helped me think through my own actions and discard any behaviors that were contrary to the major premise. Interestingly the major premise helped me be a better parent while it was helping my son be a better teenager."

"Wow! That's great," Paul declared.

"But, just in case you got confused and thought I was only talking about my son, let me remind you that everything I'm sharing with you applies equally well to both home and work situations. Remember how we already agreed there isn't a whole lot of difference between employees and children. Employees can get confused about why a manager exists. They, too, can think the manager is only there to make their lives miserable. But you and I both know why a manager exists, don't we Paul?" I quizzed.

"You tell me," he said, not wanting to give the wrong answer.

"Don't you get it? The reason why I was so blunt in giving you feedback earlier about internalizing what you had read regarding employee motivators is because *I love you*," I said, switching to first person and speaking to him as if I were counseling him as one of my managers.

Paul winced and seemed to tighten up at my words. He had an uneasy look on his face. He either thought I was joking or he was uncomfortable with my having used the word "love" in a work situation.

"That word may not work for you, Paul. And if it doesn't, don't use it. But it works for me; I like it. I don't have a problem whatsoever using the L-word at work. And the reason why is this: Have you ever worked with a team of people you loved?"

He did not hesitate in his response.

"Yes. I loved the sales team I managed back in Ohio."

"That's why I have no problem using the word love," I explained. "I don't know about you, but I would much rather work at a place where I love going into the office in the morning. I want to work with people whom I love being around. I want to work with a team I love spending my time with as much as I love being with my own family, since I often spend a lot more time with my colleagues than I do with my family. I want to love my job, love my teammates, and love the company I work for because life is a whole lot better when I do."

Paul's posture seemed to soften with my explanation.

"Don't you get it, Paul? As your manager, *'I love you. I would never do anything to purposely harm you. I want you to have a happy, successful, independent and self-sustaining career. Everything I do as a manager is designed toward that end. So don't fight against me when I give you feedback, because I'm on your side.*

"'If I assign you a difficult task you feel is beyond your capabilities, if it makes you uncomfortable, causes you stress, or highlights your incompetence for awhile, don't fight against me. I'm on your side. If I do or say things that make you feel like we are on opposite teams, please remember that I want you to have a happy and successful career. Sometimes I let you struggle all alone out there in the workplace because I'm trying to get you to become more independent. Only when you are independent can you have greater self-sustaining control over your future. Remember, everything I do as a manager is designed toward that end. So don't fight against me; I'm on your side.'

"That's the problem in the workplace, Paul. Too few employees believe management is on their side. And that's why they fight against us."

Paul grabbed the paper upon which I had written the parental major premise. He placed the paper on his table tray, leaned forward in his seat, tapped the paper with his finger, and shook his head.

"This is the best thing you've shared with me so far. I definitely want this. I'm stealing this from you."

"You don't have to steal it. I'm giving it to you. It's a gift."

He folded the paper and put it in his shirt pocket.

"I know you already grasp the full value of the major premise, Paul, but if I were facilitating one of my management training seminars right now this is where I would be jumping up and down shouting: Don't you get it? Don't you get it?

"Don't you get the fact that the parental major premise (or managerial major premise, for that matter) is how I give my son *information* about my personal imperative? It's how I tell him *why* I exist. It states very clearly what my *goal* is as a parent and why I push my son in a certain *direction*. The major premise clarifies my *role*. It states categorically the *expectations* behind my actions," I said, pointing to the words on my Ladder diagram to make sure Paul had not forgotten the topic of our discussion.

"I created the parental major premise because I wanted everything I just said to be so clear to my son there would be no *ambiguity*. I didn't want there to be any *role conflict* or *role failure* in our relationship. I wanted the message that I am on his side to be so strongly implanted into his conscious mind he would never fight against anything I tried to do for him.

"And it worked," I exclaimed. "And it's still working, judging from an incident that happened a few weeks ago. About three weeks ago my son and I were arguing over something. He kept pressing his point and I continued to stand my ground. He wasn't accepting why I could not allow him to do what he wanted. And then, right when I thought the disagreement was coming to a breaking point, my son stopped in mid-argument and said, calmly: 'This is a major premise issue, isn't it?' When I confirmed that it was, he apologized, hugged me, turned around, and walked away. That was his response in the middle of a major argument."

"Wow!"

"Cool, huh? Isn't it amazing how powerful clear communication can be in the OPEN area of the Ladder?" I said, bringing us full circle back to what we had been talking about earlier.

"Every parent and every manager needs to realize that *clear communication gets clear understanding, and specific expectations get specific results.* The better parents and managers are at openly communicating the *things that matter most* at home and in the workplace, the better things will be. Confused minds accomplish nothing. Clear communication and specific expectations focus people on the *things that matter most.*"

"You've convinced me. I know I have a lot of work to do to improve my communication at work and at home. So what's the fifth thing that matters most?" Paul asked, pointing to the right side of the Ladder.

"I'll tell you in just a minute," I said, holding up my hand to signal I had one more point to make before moving on. "I just want to make sure you understand the power behind what I just told you. You see, Paul, there is an

*Clear communication
gets clear understanding.*

*Specific expectations
get specific results.*

'it' in every element of life. There is an 'it' that family members need to get if they want harmony in the home. There is an 'it' in marriage that, once discovered, will lead to a happy and enduring marriage. There is an 'it' at work that practically guarantees a successful career if an employee will just latch on to it and practice it. There is an 'it' at school, and those students who figure it out usually do much better scholastically. There is an 'it' in one's religion that indicates a true and faithful follower. And there is an 'it' in society by which we judge whether someone is a good citizen.

"The things I'm listing down the right side of the OPEN area are the 'it' that people need to get in whatever situation they find themselves. I believe that the people who are the happiest and most successful in this life are those who get 'it'. The people with the greatest advantage are those who figure 'it' out early in life. The key to happiness and success is to learn the *things that matter most* – whether at home, at work, at school, at church, or in the community," I suggested.

"I agree, wholeheartedly," Paul declared.

"Great! Now I'll tell you about the fifth element that matters most at work," I said, picking up my pencil so I could add another word to our list.

ELEVEN

Communicating the Things that Matter Most - II

"Now let's discuss the fifth item of the seven *things that matter most* in the OPEN area on the Ladder of Commitment," I continued. "Whenever you clarify the roles and expectations for your employees you establish the playing field on which your employees must work. Once the playing field is established you then need to define the *boundaries* around the field," I said, adding that word to my Ladder drawing.

"The boundaries define the parameters within which your employees must work. This usually includes the standards, policies, procedures, processes, practices and systems you want your employees to follow as they perform their tasks. If your employees don't meet your standards, abide by your policies and procedures, or use your processes, practices, or systems, they're out of bounds," I declared.

I went on to explain that workplace boundaries also include such things as where employees are supposed to take their breaks, where they can smoke or eat, what they should wear, whether they can leave the company property during work, and other workplace rules and regulations. All company norms need to be clearly outlined for the employees so they will not go out of bounds.

"Several years ago I worked with a company that wouldn't allow its employees to park in the company parking lot next to the corporate headquarters if an employee's car was more than five years old. Employees driving older cars had to park in a lot that was three blocks away."

Stepping Forward Together

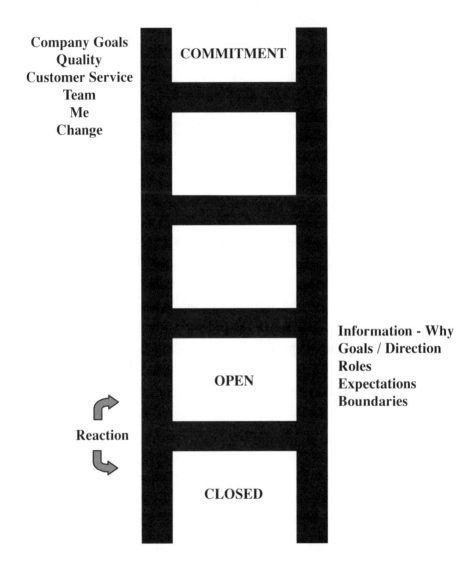

Company Goals
Quality
Customer Service
Team
Me
Change

COMMITMENT

Information - Why
Goals / Direction
Roles
Expectations
Boundaries

OPEN

Reaction

CLOSED

"You've got to be kidding!" Paul gasped.

"No, I'm not. The company also had a very strict appearance policy about what employees could wear. All male employees had to wear dark suits, white shirts, red ties, and black wing-tipped shoes. Women had to wear business suits, collared blouses, closed-toe pump shoes, and they could only wear flesh colored nylons."

"What was the purpose of that?"

"The company powers-that-be felt they needed to control the image of the company by heavily regulating anything regarding appearance."

"I think that's ridiculous. I don't think I'd do it if I worked there. I'd probably wear an orange tie and park my old car in the corporate lot anyway," Paul said defiantly.

"And you'd be out of bounds," I reminded. "And if you stayed out of bounds you wouldn't work there long."

"I wouldn't want to," he grumbled.

"And that's the point, isn't it? If people want to work at *your* plant in Las Vegas, they have to abide by your rules. They have to do things your way, not their own. If they don't want to do it your way, they can work for someone else, but they can't work for you or your company without adhering to your standards, policies, procedures, processes, practices and systems. That's the boundary. People who go out of bounds get penalized, and people who go out of bounds too often eventually get thrown out of the game."

Paul turned facing me directly and shook his head.

"Have you ever noticed how you have a sneaky way of telling me I'm wrong?" he said, nudging me in the arm with his elbow.

"I'm just trying to bring things to your consciousness. And if I have to gently smack you upside the head to do it, I don't have a problem with that," I smiled. "Remember, I love you and would never do anything to purposely harm you."

"Well, keep doing it. Maybe by the time we land in Vegas I might have some sense knocked into me."

"Oh, believe me, I'm sure I have one or two things I can teach you in the three hours we have left in our flight," I said, looking at my watch.

Stepping Forward Together

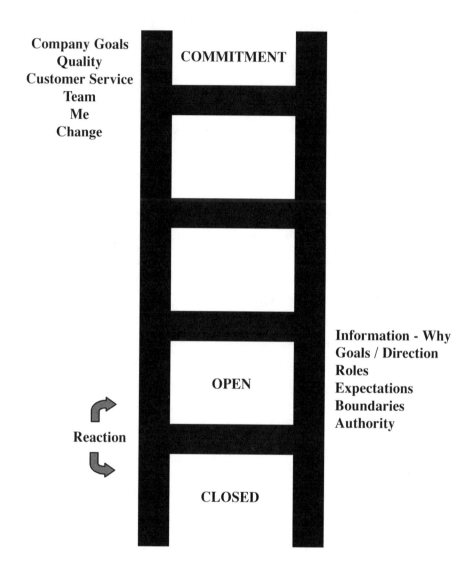

"So, are you ready for the next thing on the list of the seven things that matter most at work?"

"Please continue."

"After you've defined the boundaries of the playing field, you next have to clarify what authority your employees have for making decisions within those boundaries. Do they get to call their own plays or does the manager call the plays from the sideline? And if they do get to call the plays, do they call all of the plays or just some of them? For example, if they have a problem with a customer, what authority do they have to resolve the problem? Can they replace a product or refund the customer's money? Which decisions do they get to make on their own, and where do they need approval or input before proceeding?"

I added the word *authority* to our list.

"Another word for authority is empowerment. If you want your employees to do what you want them to do, you have to give them the authority and power to do so."

"That's logical," Paul concurred.

"So, if it's so logical, then how well do you feel you empower your managers and employees?"

"Well," he started hesitantly, "I know I gave a lot of power to my sales force back in Ohio. But I'm not as comfortable giving the managers at my plant the free reign I gave my sales staff."

"Why not?"

"I'm not sure. Maybe I don't have the confidence in them that I had in my sales people."

"Or, maybe, you don't have the confidence in *yourself*," I countered. "Maybe you're still trying to build your own confidence that you actually know how to run the manufacturing part of the business. People who lack confidence in their own abilities tend to question the abilities of others. Since they feel somewhat out of control themselves, they have a higher need to control others. Perhaps you're keeping a tighter reign on things at your plant than you otherwise would because you're still trying to find your footing as the general manager."

"That could be," he agreed.

Stepping Forward Together

"In a few minutes, when I tell you about the next rung on the Ladder, you'll learn that delegation and empowerment are really issues of trust, respect, and confidence. But I'm sure you already know that. The more trust, respect and confidence you have in your employees – and the more trust, respect, and confidence you have in yourself – the greater the level of authority you can delegate to others. Employee empowerment is nothing more than the degree to which there is mutual and reciprocal trust, respect and confidence between the manager and the employees."

I told Paul some of the biggest barriers to empowering employees are the internal beliefs or biases held within managers themselves. A lot of managers seem to have great difficulty empowering their employees. Some wrongly believe giving power to their workers will somehow diminish their own power. Perhaps these managers are the same ones who refuse to share information with their staff because they wrongly believe in the maxim that "knowledge is power."

"If you want to get your employees up this Ladder and gain their commitment, you have to give them the authority to act," I said. "It does employees no good to commit to an action if they cannot influence the outcome of that action by their own choices. If employees are simply carrying out the commands of another with no authority of their own to make decisions or take independent action, they are merely complying. And we already know compliance is a far cry from commitment."

"There's that compliance word again," Paul said, giving me a stern look and shaking his head. "You're just trying to rub that in my face, aren't you?"

"No, I just want it to be extremely clear that every point I make about the Ladder is connected to every previous point I've made. The Ladder is a tautology. Everything is connected because everything is true. If you want real commitment from your employees, you have to address every aspect of the Ladder because it shows the exact steps to create enthusiastic and committed employees."

"Well, your enthusiasm and excitement about the Ladder of Commitment really comes out," Paul added. "I'm getting excited just hearing about it."

"I hope so. But what's more important is that I practice what I preach. I use the Ladder in my own life. And I know it works. That's why I get so excited. I want other people to know what I know, think what I think, see what I see, hear what I hear, feel what I feel, and sense what I sense."

"I think I'm getting there," Paul said. He counted the words down the right side of the Ladder. "So that's six. What's the last one?"

"After you've set everything up by sharing background *information*, identifying *goals* and *direction*, clarifying *roles*, setting *expectations*, defining *boundaries* and explaining *authority*; the seventh thing you need to do in the OPEN area of the Ladder is give your employees *feedback*," I declared, adding the word to the list.

"Paul, in your opinion, how important is it to give employees feedback on their performance?"

"It's very important. People need to know where they stand."

"That's right. Employee feedback is the scoreboard that lets employees know whether they are winning or losing. It tells workers whether they are on target or off target.

"And just in case you missed the connection, you'll know whether they are on target or off target by how well they achieve the *business imperative*, accomplish their *goals*, and travel in the *direction* the company wants them to go. The list of the seven *things that matter most* are the areas where employees need feedback. Therefore, you also need to give employees feedback on how well they are fulfilling their *role*, meeting the *expectations*, staying within the *boundaries*, and properly using their *authority* as they perform their tasks."

"It all makes perfect sense," Paul exclaimed.

"Effective feedback is straightforward and unequivocal, leaving no doubt or confusion. Employees get confused when managers are wishy-washy or dance around the issues. Most people want clear feedback that is immediate, specific, objective and unbiased. The whole purpose of feedback is to give employees such a clear assessment of their performance they know exactly what they are doing right and what they are doing wrong. That way they can continue their good work and alter the bad.

Stepping Forward Together

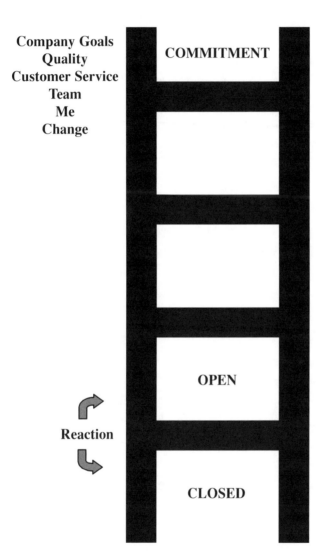

Company Goals
Quality
Customer Service
Team
Me
Change

COMMITMENT

Information - Why
Goals / Direction
Roles
Expectations
Boundaries
Authority
Feedback

OPEN

Reaction

CLOSED

"Remember how I said earlier that clear communication gets clear understanding and specific expectations get specific results? It's the same with feedback. The more specific you are in your feedback, the better your employees will be able to perform to your expectations. That's why managers should never hesitate to give honest feedback to their employees."

"Yet a lot of managers are hesitant to give feedback," Paul interjected. "Some managers seem to avoid giving feedback like the plague. Why is that?"

"What are they afraid of, Paul?" I asked, testing to see if anything I'd said so far had sunk in. He responded immediately.

"They're afraid of the reaction," he declared, pointing to the word on my Ladder diagram.

"You got it! They're afraid of the reaction they'll get when they give the employee feedback. If you knew, every time you gave feedback to your employees, that they would react well, would you hesitate to give feedback to them?"

"Probably not. I know I wouldn't be as hesitant."

"Fear of how employees will react to our feedback is the reason why we don't give it. We're afraid they will react poorly, so we hold back rather than be confronted with an ugly reaction we may not be able to handle well.

"So let me ask you something. Have you ever *not* given someone feedback even though you knew you needed to?"

"Yes."

"And did your not giving the person feedback help the situation? Did your avoidance of the issue actually improve the situation?" I asked.

"Of course not. In fact, in the situation I'm thinking of, it actually made the situation worse. The employee's behavior continued to deteriorate until it got to the point where I *had* to say something. And when I finally did say something . . . ."

Paul stopped mid-sentence. It just dawned on him, he said, that the very reaction he feared he'd get in the first place was the exact reaction he got when he finally did give the feedback. Only the actual reaction was a whole lot worse because he had delayed his feedback than what he had initially expected had he given his feedback earlier.

Stepping Forward Together

"Delaying or not giving someone feedback never helps the situation," I said. "It just makes the reaction worse. That's why managers need to get much better at giving feedback, particularly feedback that doesn't leave debris."

Paul looked at me quizzically.

"Have you ever given someone feedback where the feedback actually made the person's performance worse instead of better?" I pressed.

"Yes. I once had a sales guy who really wasn't very good at his job. He never made his quota. After I counseled him about his performance his numbers actually went *down*. I got rid of him about a month later."

"Now there's a success story," I said sarcastically.

I told Paul the best feedback is that which leaves people feeling positive and motivated to improve their performance as a result of the feedback. You can always tell whether your feedback methods are right by how people feel after the feedback. The worst feedback is that which figuratively blows people up, leaving body parts strewn about the office.

"Good feedback, even if it is negative, never leaves debris," I declared. "It leaves people's self-worth and self-confidence intact. It targets the performance, not the person. It focuses on the future, not the past. It offers suggestions on how to win, rather than chastises a person for losing.

"Most important, good feedback allows for a response. Effective feedback is a two-way communication process. My definition for feedback is simply this: Feed . . .," I said, extending my two arms out toward Paul as if I were handing him a baby, ". . . back, " I continued, pulling my arms back toward my chest.

"Feed . . . back," I said, repeating the motions. "Feed . . . back. Feedback is where I feed information to you and you give information back to me. It's where I speak and you listen, and then you speak and I listen. Feed . . . back. See how that works?"

Paul nodded.

"Have you ever been in a *feed* session, rather than a feedback session? You know, a feed session where someone just dumps a bunch of criticism on you, telling you what you did wrong, and then you're sent away without an opportunity to respond."

Paul grinned. "I've been in more than a few of those."

"That's not feedback; that just feed. Good feedback sessions are always a two-way interchange of thoughts and ideas. Good feedback always allows for a response."

Paul agreed.

"So there you have it Paul: The seven *things that matter most* in the workplace," I said, pointing to the list I'd written down the right side of the Ladder. "These are the seven things that must be addressed in the OPEN area if you want to get people to move up to the next rung on the Ladder."

"I like it. It's very clear and simple," Paul declared.

"So how soon do your employees need to be told these seven things?" I asked.

"Right away."

"Right away meaning what?"

"They need to know these things from day one."

"Yes, you're right," I agreed, "but may I submit you may want to address these things even earlier than that. I think you should share these seven things in the interview *before* a person accepts the job. I know in my own business I want a job candidate to know the business imperative, the performance goals and company direction, their role, my expectations, and the boundary and authority constraints before I hire them so there are no misconceptions about the job. I want them to know what they are getting into before they start the job. I don't want an employee finding out later the job is not what she expected. Nothing kills employee commitment more than a mismatch of expectations in one's job.

"This list of seven things actually provides a great outline for the job interview. Everything a new employee wonders about in an interview, but may never ask, is all right here in these seven things," I declared.

Paul jumped on that and added: "And by answering the unanswered questions before a person asks, it builds rapport with job candidates and lets them know they are important to you and the company," he said, showing he had internalized one of my major points.

"Thereby accelerating the commitment process by moving people up the Ladder of Commitment from the first point of contact with your company," I added.

I concluded this part of our discussion by reiterating the OPEN rung of the Ladder of Commitment is the most important rung on the Ladder. The extent to which a manager communicates the seven *things that matter most* is the extent to which people will move up the Ladder to COMMITMENT.

TWELVE

The Ethics of Success

I felt confident Paul had fully grasped everything we had just discussed, but I had one last point I wanted to make before moving on.

"So, Paul, what percentage of the companies you've encountered do you feel effectively communicate the seven *things that matter most* to their employees?" I asked, pointing to the list. "What percentage of companies do you think share vital *information* with their employees and explain the *whys* behind their business imperative? What percent clearly define the *goals* and *direction* of the company, clarify the employees' *roles*, share their *expectations*, set the *boundaries*, specify their employees' *authority*, and provide helpful *feedback* so their employees can perform well?"

"Not very many. Maybe ten percent," Paul guessed.

"Do you want to go higher or lower than ten percent?" I challenged.

"I don't know. It's probably lower than that. Maybe a lot lower."

"Well, I wouldn't know," I said with a mischievous grin. "I don't know the answer to that question. Maybe someday I'll do research on that very question and I'll write a book about my findings. Then I'll become famous, live off of the royalties of the book, and not have to travel so much anymore. That would be nice."

Paul smiled.

"Actually, I believe I know the answer, maybe not to that specific question, but to something that I think is directly related to it."

I told Paul I used to be a nationally recognized speaker during the Total Quality Management (TQM) craze. Actually, I was known more as an anti-TQM speaker than a TQM proponent. I was the person who countered the enthusiastic rhetoric of the keynote speaker at many TQM conferences. I came in and gave audiences a large dose of reality after they got all pumped up by the keynote address.

The reason why I was a TQM antagonist is because I witnessed far too many companies that got so heavily involved in the TQM *process* they forgot to get quality *results*. Their employees spent all of their time in TQM meetings trying to do the TQM process right, rather than spending time on the line getting quality right. When the process becomes more important than the results, something is wrong.

"You're right," Paul said. "I saw the same thing happen in our company back when we were doing the TQM thing."

"When I spoke at these TQM conferences I always started my presentation the same way," I explained. "I'd ask the people in the audience to stand up if their company was involved in a major quality initiative, customer service improvement program, team building effort, reorganization, re-engineering, re-alignment or other major change initiative implemented specifically to improve productivity or achieve better profitability.

"I'd then ask those standing to tell me how many people in their company were working full-time on the initiative and how much money and time had been invested in the effort so far. Some companies were just starting their intervention, but most had been involved in TQM or similar improvement processes for many years. Most had devoted a large amount of staff and countless man-hours to the project. Millions of dollars were being spent on these initiatives.

"Finally, I asked everyone standing to remain standing if their company had achieved significant performance or profitability improvement as a result of their initiative. In other words, I wanted to know whether the quality improvement initiative had actually improved the quality of the company's products. I wanted to know if the customer service initiative had significantly improved the level of service provided by the employees. Did product defects decline? Did customer satisfaction improve? Was the team more unified? Did the reorganization or re-engineered processes result in a much more efficient and effective organization? And, most important, was the company's bottom-line significantly improved as a direct result of the millions of dollars spent on the TQM initiative? And if not, they needed to sit down."

"I'll bet most of the people sat down," Paul surmised.

"You're right. According to the employees at the hundreds of conferences where I've spoken, only about 20 percent of the companies represented achieved significant improvement as a direct result of their change initiative."

"That's pretty sad, especially considering all of the money invested in those programs," Paul replied. "Why doesn't it work in the majority of companies?"

"What good does it do to spend millions of dollars on an initiative if you can't get your employees to OPEN up and share their ideas? What good are the buttons, banners, hats and coffee mugs handed out to every employee at the beginning of a customer service initiative if people don't understand the goal or agree with the direction the company is headed?"

I could have gone straight down the list of the seven things that matter most to answer his question, but I stopped.

"But that's not the question you should be asking. You shouldn't be interested in the 80 percent of companies that fail, but rather in the 20 percent that are successful! You should be wondering why the 20 percent succeeded," I exclaimed.

"So, do you know?"

"Of course I do. You don't think I'd ask a question if I really didn't know the answer, do you?" I grinned. "After speaking at these conferences, I followed up with the people in the audience who said their company's improvement initiative had succeeded. I wanted to know what made them so successful while so many other companies had failed.

"I discovered there are two common elements that stood out as contributing factors to why the minority group of companies achieved notable results from their initiatives. I believe these same two elements can be found in almost every profitable enterprise. It just might be that these two characteristics are the pivotal keys that determine whether a business will succeed or fail. They are so important I call these two factors *The Ethics of Success.*

"What do you think one of those ethics might be, since we've been talking about it for so long?" I asked, confident Paul would get the right answer.

"Open communication," Paul said, pointing to the OPEN area on the Ladder.

"You're absolutely right. Every one of the companies who achieved significant results through their company improvement initiative had a **high ethic of communication**."

I told him successful companies don't just communicate with their employees; they *over communicate*. They leave nothing to chance. They don't assume their employees will get the information they need to perform as expected; they make *sure* everyone receives the message. They go out of their way to ensure every employee knows what is going on in the organization. They define exactly what it takes to win, and they tell people how to do it. They put in place processes that allow for a free flow of information and coordination across functional lines. They communicate up the chain of command, down the chain of command, across, and outside the chain of command. They've mastered both the formal and informal communication channels. Everything in the organization is structured to enhance the flow of information. They use a multitude of communication methods so no one is left out of the loop.

"The best way I can say it is *successful companies communicate ten times using ten* different *methods*," I continued "And that probably only gets them half-way there.

"They don't just rely on one method of communication; they have a plethora of means to get the message out. And if communicating ten times using ten different methods doesn't elicit the results they want, they communicate 20 times using 20 *different* methods or 30 times using 30 different methods until everyone is on board. Successful companies know effective communication throughout the organization is so paramount to the success of the business they put just as much energy and effort into internal communication to their employees as they do on external marketing to their customers."

Paul raised his eyebrows in initial surprise to my last statement. Then, after thinking about it, said: "That's a good point. The employees should be just as important to the business as the customers. It makes sense to invest in communicating to them so they can perform better."

"Having said that, Paul, what's the primary method for communicating with employees in most businesses?"

"Probably by memo or e-mail."

"Yes. And the typical response when an employee or manager says he didn't know about something is: 'Didn't you get the memo?' And if the employee says he didn't get the memo, then what does the manager do?"

"Sends him the memo again," Paul chuckled.

"And if the employee again says he didn't know about something because he didn't see the memo, then what does the manager do?"

"Personally hands the person the memo and makes him initial that he received it."

"That's not communicating three times using three *different* methods," I declared. "That's communicating once and using the same method over and over. That's the problem with most people. When they don't get through to someone the first time they tend to say the exact same thing and use the same method again and again. Only each subsequent time they tend to get louder and enunciate their words.

"It's like when a parent tells a child to clean up his room, but the kid doesn't do it," I explained. "The parent says, 'Bubba, clean up your room.' And when Bubba doesn't do it, the parent gets louder and enunciates his or her words saying: 'Bubba, I SAID clean up your room.' And when Bubba still doesn't do it, then its, 'BUBBA! YOU CLEAN UP YOUR ROOM RIGHT NOW!!!' And you can always tell when parents are at the end of their patience because they call the kid by his full name, 'BILLY BUBBA! YOU CLEAN UP YOUR ROOM NOW!!!!'"

Paul chuckled. Like all parents, he'd done this with his own kids.

"What the parents somehow never seem to get is, instead of repeating themselves and enunciating their words, they ought to change the way they communicate. Whoom!" I said, swinging my arm like I was spanking a child. "That would get the little bugger to clean up his room."

*If you can't explain it
so other people can understand it,
maybe you don't understand it
that well yourself.*

Paul laughed harder.

"I didn't know smacking my employees was an option if they don't do what I want," Paul joked. Then quickly, lest I think he was serious, he added, "I know. I know. That's compliance, not commitment. If I want commitment I have to communicate 10 times using 10 different methods, or 20 times using 20 different methods, until they 'get it'."

"You're catching on, Paul." I praised. "I once had a client summarize what I just said this way: *'If you can't explain it so other people can understand it, maybe you don't understand it that well yourself.'*"

"I like that," Paul said. "So what's the second thing successful companies have in common?"

"They all had a **high ethic of accountability**," I explained. "Successful companies don't leave success to chance. They hold people accountable by making sure every worker performs as expected. They establish clear performance goals and specify exactly what results must be achieved. They measure and monitor the work, communicate how well or poorly people are doing, and take corrective action when deficiencies arise. They assign people their stewardship and require them to report regularly on how well they are progressing on their goals. They constantly checkup and follow through to ensure everything is done as required. The best companies acknowledge the accomplishments of their employees and tie compensation, recognition and reward to expected results. In other words, they *manage* their company and employees.

"Practically everything about management boils down to these two concepts," I suggested. "Literally every management competency hinges on how effectively or poorly a manager communicates. The textbook list of a manager's primary duties – planning, organizing, delegating, controlling, problem solving, and decision making – all require effective communication. Coaching, counseling and disciplining employees require effective communication skills. All performance management practices are primarily communication issues. I believe *the extent to which a manager motivates his or her employees is in direct proportion to the extent to which he or she communicates with those employees.*"

*The extent to which a manager
motivates his or her employees
is in direct proportion
to the extent to which he or she communicates
with those employees.*

"That's another good point. I totally agree with that," Paul exclaimed.

"However," I warned, "effective communication alone seldom results in high performance. Employees must also be held accountable for the work they do. When employees are held accountable for their performance, their performance improves. Effective communication is what starts workers moving, but accountability keeps them going.

"Consequently, Paul, if you want to create a successful enterprise at your manufacturing plant, you have to establish a high ethic of communication and a high ethic of accountability throughout your organization," I stressed. "That's why **the most important rung on the ladder is the OPEN area.** Managers need to get a lot better at communicating openly and honestly. Until they do, they won't be able to move their employees up to the next rung on the Ladder – which is where great performance happens."

THIRTEEN

Trust, Respect and Confidence

We had been talking for several hours. We both needed a quick break and a few minutes to stretch our legs. Unfortunately we were only half-way through the flight, but that gave Paul and me more time to talk about the Ladder of Commitment. When we were both back in our seats Paul said:

"OK, let's get back to our discussion. I'm anxious to learn what's on the next rung of the Ladder."

I continued where we left off by pointing to the seven *things that matter most* down the right side of the Ladder and saying: "If you communicate these seven things well in the OPEN area of the Ladder, you move up to the next rung, which is TRUST, RESPECT, and CONFIDENCE. These are three separate qualities, but they're all achieved on the same level on the Ladder."

I wrote those three words above the next rung on my diagram.

"When you get to this rung on the Ladder things really start to gel in your relationships with your employees," I said. "This is the level where people start stepping forward together as a team because there is mutual and reciprocal trust, respect and confidence among the members. This is the point where management trusts the employees; and the employees trust management. It's where management listens to and respects the perspective, opinions and ideas of the employees; and the employees respect the leadership, direction, and oversight of management.

"At this level management has confidence in the capabilities and actions of the employees; and the employees feel confident that management can lead the company or department successfully. Simply put, it is where

Stepping Forward Together

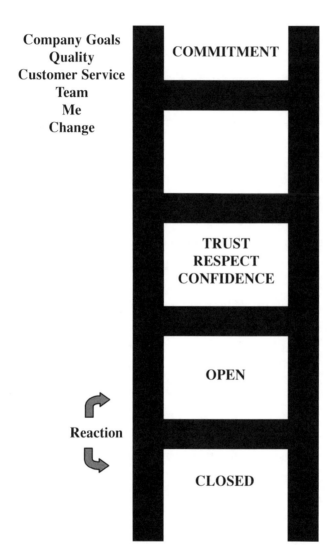

Company Goals
Quality
Customer Service
Team
Me
Change

COMMITMENT

TRUST
RESPECT
CONFIDENCE

OPEN

Information - Why
Goals / Direction
Roles
Expectations
Boundaries
Authority
Feedback

Reaction

CLOSED

everyone has trust, respect and confidence in each other's ability to get the job done right."

"Wouldn't that be nice," Paul said dreamingly, as if it were something he longed for but was not sure was actually possible.

I told Paul in order to avoid being monotonous and redundant, I would use the word "trust" to mean "trust, respect and confidence" unless I singled out one particular quality to focus on. I then told him I would explain how to develop trust in a person or team by first explaining how trust *cannot* be built.

"You cannot build trust by attending a trust-building seminar where you play trust-building games," I said, cynically. "Let me give you and example: have you ever attended a seminar where you had to do the trust fall?"

"Yeah, I did that at a management seminar at our corporate training center about a year ago," Paul said, apparently not impressed by the activity.

"Does it take trust – real trust – to be blindfolded and fall backward into the arms of a group of people?" I asked.

"I don't think so," Paul declared. "I don't think you actually have to trust the people who are catching you. They're not going to purposely let you fall on your head. Obviously they're going to catch you! No one is going to let you get injured."

"Unless they're evil," I joked. "That's probably why they have eight or ten people back there to catch you – just in case one actually *is* evil. That way if one person wants you to die, there are nine others who won't let that happen."

I gave another example by asking Paul if he'd ever participated in a training activity called the blind walk.

"Yep, been there done that, too," he said in disgust.

"And does it take trust to be blindfolded and then follow a leader through an obstacle course?

"Not really. Not real trust anyway, for the same reason," Paul declared. "Unless the leader is evil, he won't purposely run you into a wall or harm you. You don't have to trust the person; you just trust the fact that he's not evil."

"I agree, Paul. You cannot build trust by doing silly trust-building activities. At least not real trust, deep trust, long-lasting trust."

"So how do you build that kind of trust?" he asked.

"There are only two ways to build real trust," I declared. "And I submit to you that you already know what they are subconsciously; so now let me bring these two ways to your conscious mind. Once you know them, you can help people climb this Ladder faster in the future by consciously doing the two things you need to do to build trust, respect and confidence."

I asked Paul to think back to the moment when he and I started talking to each other when we first sat down on the airplane. I asked him if, at that moment, he trusted me.

"I didn't even know you," he replied.

"I'm not asking whether you knew me. I'm asking if you trusted me."

"Of course not."

"Why not?" I pressed. "I'm trustworthy, and I was trustworthy when I sat down next to you a couple of hours ago."

"But I didn't know that."

"But I just told you I'm trustworthy. If I had told you I was trustworthy when I sat next to you, then would you have trusted me?"

"I probably would have trusted you less," he declared. "Just because you say you're trustworthy doesn't mean you are."

"But I AM trustworthy," I persisted. "That's a fact. I am trustworthy."

"That may be a fact to you, but I don't know that. You have to prove it to me."

"Why do I have to prove it to you? I AM TRUSTWORTHY! Why can't you just accept that?"

"I don't know. That's just the way I am," Paul stated. "I don't trust people until they give me a reason to trust them. I've been burned in the past."

"But I'm not the person who burned you in the past. I've done nothing to you that would make you distrust me."

"And you've done nothing to make me trust you either," he insisted. "I'm not going to trust you until you prove you're trustworthy."

I told him we would talk in a few minutes about how I could prove my trustworthiness. Then I switched topics and asked if he respected me when we first met. I stopped him before he could answer so I could first clarify what I meant by "respect."

Trust, Respect and Confidence

"I don't want to know whether you respected me as a human being, but, rather, did you respect me professionally? Did you respect my professional expertise? Did you respect my professional judgment? Did you respect the fact that I know what I'm talking about and I'm good at what I do?"

"Again, how would I know that? I didn't even know you when you first sat down," Paul answered. "But I have some respect for you now."

"Really? You mean something has happened between the time we first met and two hours later that has impacted your respect for me?"

"Yes, I've been listening to you for the last couple of hours."

"And it's made a difference in how you perceive me, hasn't it?" I said, pointing my finger toward him to emphasize my point. "In just two hours you and I have already started moving up this Ladder, haven't we? And I'll tell you why in a few minutes."

I then switched to the third quality on this rung of the Ladder – confidence.

"OK, one more question. When we first started talking to each other tonight, did you have confidence, if you listened to what I had to say, that my comments would make a difference in both your professional and personal life? Did you have confidence that I would give you some helpful information to improve the productivity and profitability of your company? Did you know by listening to me and applying what I tell you, your life would be better because of it?"

"Well, when you said you were a consultant and you knew how to get employees to be enthusiastic and committed at work, I was interested in hearing what you had to say," he declared, "but I can't say I had confidence you knew what you were talking about. I *hoped* you would tell me something that would benefit me, but I didn't have *confidence* that that was true," he said, picking up on a point I'd made earlier.

"Dang it. And here I thought I could sell you some of my motivational tapes that would change your life for ever for only $19.95," I joked.

Paul smiled broadly. He, like many people, had probably been suckered into buying those kinds of tapes before.

Stepping Forward Together

"So what's it going to take for you to trust me, respect me, and have confidence in me, Paul?"

"Time," he offered.

"Time doing what?"

"Getting to know you. Finding out more about you."

"Oh, so that's it?" I asked. "You don't trust me because you don't know anything about me," I feigned as if this were the key to building trust. "I guess I screwed up by not introducing myself properly when we first met tonight."

I pretended we had just sat down on the airplane together back in Philadelphia. I stuck out my hand and reintroduced myself saying: "Hi. I'm Mac McIntire. I'm from Las Vegas. I've been married for 33 years. I have a 24-year-old son. I like to camp, hike, and Jet Ski. Oh, and I'm a Scoutmaster," I said holding up my right arm and showing the three-finger Scout Sign while repeating the Scout Law:

"I'm TRUSTWORTHY, loyal, helpful, friendly, courteous, kind, obedient, cheerful, thrifty, brave, clean and reverent. Did you hear that first word, Paul? TRUSTWORTHY!" I said strongly. "Now do you trust me?"

He smiled, huffed and simply said no.

"But I'm holding up my hand in the Scout Sign," I protested. "Don't you know what this Scout Sign means? It means 'on my honor'. On my honor I am trustworthy!"

"I don't know that," Paul shot back. "I can hold my arm up and swear to anything, too. But that doesn't make it so. I still don't know you are trustworthy."

"So I guess you didn't really mean it when you said you needed to get to know me in order to trust me, because I just told you some personal things about me and it didn't seem to make any difference," I said. "So what did you mean when you said 'get to know me'? Maybe you meant you needed to get to know me professionally?" I pressed.

"Hi. I'm Mac McIntire. I'm the owner and president of Innovative Management Group," I said, pretending again to introduce myself properly instead of ignoring him like I had when we first met. "We're a training and consulting firm based in Las Vegas. I've been in the training and consulting business for over 30 years and I've owned my own company for 18 years. I've consulted with major Global 500 companies throughout the world and helped them achieve significant results. I've worked with numerous Fortune 100 companies in the United States, and all of my clients agree that I am really, really good at what I do. Now do you trust me?"

"No," he said flatly.

"No? You mean my resume doesn't impress you? Because, believe me, I'm really, really good!"

"You say you're good. But I don't know that," Paul reemphasized.

"Maybe not now. But what if I showed you my credentials and resume; you'd have trust, respect and confidence in me then, wouldn't you?"

"No."

"Why not? Everything I said is true. I've done some great things to improve productivity and quality at manufacturing companies throughout the United States and across the globe."

Paul shook his head indicating he was not impressed.

"To be honest with you – I really don't care what you've done for other companies," Paul said truthfully. "I only care about what you can do for *me*."

"What I can do for you *where*?"

"At MY plant."

"When?" I pushed.

"NOW!" he said adamantly. "I want to know what you can do for me in my situation. I'm really not interested in what you've done for other companies because their problems might not be the same as mine. Just because you helped them doesn't mean you can do anything for me," he declared.

"Now hold on, Paul," I countered. "If someone else told you I was a great consultant, wouldn't that influence your trust, respect and confidence in me? Doesn't a person's or a company's reputation or word-of-mouth advertising count for something?"

Paul thought about that for a second.

"Yes, I think it does impact trust, respect and confidence," he said. "But only to a small degree. For example, I might go to a new restaurant based upon someone else's recommendation, but I'm not going to trust the food and service is good until I've tried it for myself. It's the same with using your services as a consultant. If someone else recommends you to me – particularly if it's someone I trust – I might meet with you based upon the recommendation. But I'm not going to hire you until I determine for myself whether I can trust you."

"You've just made a very important point, Paul, and I want to make sure it gets grounded in your conscious mind," I said. "What you've just described is what I call 'peripheral' trust. When someone recommends my services to you, you don't actually trust me; you trust whoever recommended me. Although it's not real trust in me, your trust in someone else's recommendation gives you a modicum of trust in me and puts us just a little bit higher on this Ladder."

I explained that person X might be more receptive to person Y if person Z trusts person Y and person X trusts person Z. People tend to put their faith and trust in people whom other people trust. This is why product endorsements and opinion polls are used so heavily. People are swayed by the opinions of others. Employees generally will trust upper management if their direct supervisors trust the executives. This is why it is so important that mid-level and front-line managers communicate their trust in upper management: so their employees will also trust top management.

"So, other than a little bit of peripheral trust, what does my reputation, experience or resume get me?" I asked, getting back to what we had been talking about.

"It gets you in the door. It gets you a meeting with me. But that's it."

"You're exactly right. My years of experience only get me into a sales meeting. Likewise, a job candidate's resume only gets them an *interview*, nothing else. It's what happens at the sales meeting or during the job interview that determines whether you will hire me as a consultant or offer a job candidate a position with your company."

Paul agreed.

"Does the fact that you hired us mean you now trust us, respect us, or have confidence in us?" I challenged.

"No, it only means I'm willing to give you a chance to prove yourselves," Paul rightly surmised.

Trust, Respect and Confidence

Paul just uncovered another key point about trust, respect and confidence. Just because someone has been successful in the past, doesn't automatically mean they should be trusted now. Success in past situations doesn't necessarily mean someone will be successful in a current or future situation, even if the conditions are similar. A past situation might have some bearing on how well a person will perform in the new situation, but a person's past knowledge and experience doesn't guarantee future success.

When a manager hires a new employee, he or she takes a risk, even if the new employee comes with a great resume showing years of experience. The hiring manager *hopes* the job candidate's credentials are a true indicator of that person's future potential, but the manager will not trust or have confidence that it is true until the new employee proves that his past experience is relevant to the new job.

"So how do we as consultants or new employees prove ourselves?" I asked, knowing the answer to that question is the first of the two ways to build trust, respect and confidence.

"By getting results!" Paul declared.

"Getting results where? At a past client or former job?"

"No. You need to get results at MY plant in Las Vegas."

"That's right! You will trust people when you see they can produce RESULTS. You may listen to their WORDS telling you they are trustworthy; but you will know whether it is true when they show it in their ACTIONS and BEHAVIORS," I declared writing the words *results, actions, behaviors* and *words* to the left of the TRUST, RESPECT and CONFIDENCE rung on the Ladder.

"These four things indicate whether you can trust someone or not," I declared. "You will trust people who produce the right results, do the right actions, model the right behaviors, and say the right words. Therefore, if you want to get up this Ladder faster with new employees, you need to get them working as soon as possible so they can start producing the results and modeling the actions, behaviors and words necessary to earn your trust. New employees cannot rely on their past successes or rest on their laurels. They need to produce results at *your* manufacturing plant, carry out their job

Stepping Forward Together

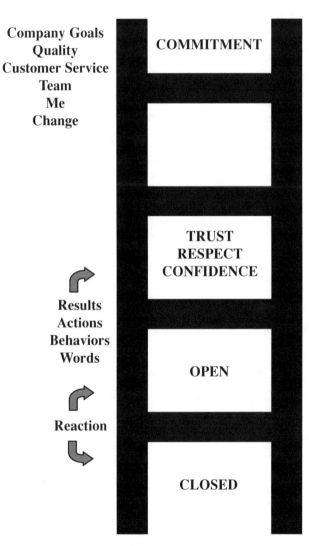

responsibilities to *your* standards, and do their work to *your* complete satisfaction to earn *your* trust, respect and confidence."

"That's true," Paul affirmed. "The people I trust are those who do their jobs well, and I don't trust those who slack off."

"The same thing applies when you hire me as a consultant," I continued. "It doesn't matter what results I have achieved with other clients. You will not trust that I know what I'm talking about until I start producing results at your company."

"Agreed," he said.

"Remember when I told you there are two ways to develop real trust?" I asked, reminding him that trust-building exercises seldom develop real, lasting trust. "Although it's true you will trust people when they start producing results, there is another way to get up to the TRUST, RESPECT and CONFIDENCE rung on the Ladder even before someone starts producing," I explained. "And you already know what it is, Paul, because you identified this way in your first response when I asked you if you trusted me when we met. Do you remember what you said?"

"Yes. I said I didn't trust you because I didn't know you."

"That's right. You didn't know me. You will trust people when you *know* them. But, remember, we've already established that you didn't mean 'know things about me personally' – like I'm married, have a son, and I like to jet ski. Nor did you mean 'know me professionally' – that I've been a consultant for 33 years and have owned my own company for 18 years. This information may be interesting, but it has little bearing on whether or not you will trust me.

"So what did you mean when you said you need to get to *know* me?" I pressed.

"I need to get to know *YOU*. I need to know who you are. I want to know about your values and your beliefs. I need to know who you are inside," Paul declared, knowing as the words came out of his mouth that what he was saying was true.

"You got it!" I confirmed. "You see, what you really meant when you said you need to get to know me is: you want to get to know my character. You want to know the qualities and attributes that make up who I am deep down

You will develop trust, respect and confidence
in people when you hear
how they think,
how they reason, and
how they come to conclusions.

in my core. You want to know what drives me; what moves me. You see, it's not what we have *done*, but who we *are*, that counts when it comes to trust, respect and confidence.

"Therefore, consciously or subconsciously, whenever we come into contact with a person for the first time, our trust-detecting antennae search to pick up signals of whether a person is trustworthy. Our eyes, ears, and intuitive senses are fine-tuned to discern clues about a person's character. And the greatest clues are how a person thinks, reasons, and comes to conclusions," I announced.

I told Paul that, long before a person starts producing results, *you will develop trust, respect and confidence in someone when you hear how they think, how they reason, and how they come to conclusions.* You trust people when their thinking, reasoning and conclusions are sound. You trust people who are rational, logical, or sensible; while distrusting those whose thinking is weak, reasoning is flawed, or conclusions are questionable.

You have respect for and confidence in people who think like you, reason like you, and come to conclusions that are similar to your own. But that is not all. You'll also trust and respect people who expand your thinking and reasoning or who help you come to conclusions that are far better than your own. You trust people who raise your thinking and reasoning to the next level.

"We tend to trust people who are philosophically aligned with our way of thinking," I suggested. "We feel amenable to individuals who have similar values, principles, beliefs and attitudes to ours. We gravitate toward people who are of our ilk. Conversely, we are less trusting and generally exhibit less respect for people whose views are vastly divergent from our value system or beliefs."

Paul had gone inside himself so I paused to let him ponder what I had just said. No doubt he was testing my hypothesis against his own experiences. He probably was thinking about people whom he trusts and those he doesn't. When I thought he had concluded his contemplation, I continued.

"Now let me see if I can prove my premise," I suggested. "Do you have an employee in whom you really trust, really respect, and really have confidence?"

"Yes," he said, smiling and nodding his head affirmatively.

"I'm going to ask you a question about that individual that will help you realize why you trust, respect and have confidence in him or her. Does this person in whom you have trust, respect and confidence get *IT*?" I said, knowing I would not need to explain my question.

"Yes she does."

"OK. Do you also have an employee in whom you do not trust, do not respect or do not have confidence?

"Yes," he replied in disgust.

"Does this person get *IT*?

"No"

"Does he even have a clue?" I chided.

"No, he doesn't."

"So what is the difference between these two individuals? How can you tell one employee gets it and another doesn't?" I asked, again having confidence Paul would know the right answer.

"I can see it in their *results*," he said, pointing to the left side of the Ladder. "I can tell by their *actions* and *behaviors*. I can hear it in their *words*."

"That's true," I commended. "But the truth is you can tell which people you can trust long before they start producing results or carrying out assigned tasks. You'll know if they are trustworthy when you hear how they think, reason, and come to conclusions. You'll know whom you can trust by listening to the thoughts and comments of your employees. Those who get it will be philosophically aligned with your thinking, reasoning and conclusions. This is the second way to develop trust. You can tell fairly early who is getting it and who isn't because you can hear it, see it, feel it, and sense it. Can't you?"

"You're right," Paul said, telling me it doesn't take him long after he's hired a new manager or employee to tell who gets it and who doesn't.

Now I wanted to put all the pieces together to make sure Paul understood how everything we'd been talking about fits. I was about to make one of the most major points about the Ladder of Commitment.

"So tell me, Paul, what is the *IT* that some people get and others don't?"

Trust, Respect and Confidence

Paul did not hesitate. He looked at the Ladder, pointed to the seven *things that matter most* in the OPEN area, and said: "They know *why* they are here. They understand the business imperative. They know the *goals* and *direction*. They fulfill their *role*, meet my *expectations*, stay within the *boundaries* and never overstep their *authority*. The people I trust get these things and the people I don't trust don't get them."

"Man, you are good, Paul! But, of course, I knew that from the second we started talking," I said, winking and flashing my most mischievous smile.

"Baloney! You didn't even know me."

"See. You *are* good," I exclaimed, impressed at how much he had assimilated in just a few hours. He got it.

"You're absolutely right. When we first met, you didn't know me and I didn't know you. We knew nothing about how each other thought, reasoned or came to conclusions. You had no idea whether I'm good. And I didn't know whether you knew what you were talking about, either. And yet we're already starting to climb up this Ladder, and we are beginning to step forward together, aren't we?"

"Yes, we are," he agreed.

"So now let's find out why. I'm sure you already know the answer, but I want to make sure it is very conscious to you," I said. "Do you remember earlier when you said you did not respect me when we first met, but you have gained some respect for me since then? What has happened between then and now?" I asked.

"I've been listening to you explain the Ladder of Commitment, and everything you've said so far makes sense," he answered. Then, realizing he knew the real reason, he added, "I now know a little bit about how you think, how you reason, and how you come to conclusions. Everything you've said so far sounds good to me. It makes sense. I like what I'm hearing and what I'm learning. I like the way you think."

"That's it exactly!" I said, tapping the Ladder model with my finger to emphasize the point. "You see, I haven't achieved a single result or taken any action to prove myself to you, yet you're already starting to trust me, respect me, and have confidence in what I say. You like the way I think, reason, and come to conclusions. That's what gives you the confidence to trust what I say and respect my professional judgment. We're moving up this Ladder already and I haven't even been out on the shop floor at your manufacturing plant. I've started building your trust without producing a single result for your company."

I told Paul that although he will definitely trust his employees when he sees the results of their actions and behaviors, the trust-building process actually begins as he listens to them talk. As he interacts with his staff, he hears how they think, reason, and come to conclusions. Consciously or subconsciously, he senses those on his team who get it, and those who don't. This is why it's so imperative for him to get out among the workers on the shop floor so he can quickly climb up the Ladder with him employees by interacting with them. Personal contact and communication are critical to building commitment.

I also suggested getting out among the workers would help the employees develop trust, respect and confidence in his leadership. The employees are looking to see if he, too, can produce *results*. They are monitoring his *actions* and *behaviors* to determine whether he is someone they can trust. They are listening to his *words* to hear how he thinks, reasons and comes to conclusions.

I told him his employees started judging his leadership capabilities from the very first day he took over as general manager at the plant. They listened for clues about what kind of manager he would be. They expected him to present a logical, reasonable and rational plan to move the organization forward. They listened to the thinking, reasoning and conclusions behind his operational initiatives. They watched his every move and listened to his every word to determine if they could trust him, respect him, and have confidence in him as their leader.

"People will not commit to follow you, as the leader, until they know the thinking, reasoning and rationale behind your actions and behaviors," I suggested. "That's why you need to start talking to your people – so they can know *YOU*. You can climb this Ladder and create enthusiastic and committed employees, even if you haven't achieved any results yet, just by having a well thought-out plan. People will trust your plan long before they start trusting you."

Paul placed his elbow on his tray table and leaned against his hand, which was covering his mouth. He had gone inside himself and was seriously pondering what I had just said.

"I've never thought about this stuff this way before," Paul said, "but it all makes sense. When I was a sales manager I could tell, when I was interviewing job candidates, which ones were going to be good sales people because the good ones already had a plan for what they were going to do. They'd studied the company's products and mapped out the approach they might take if they got the job. The thinking, reasoning and conclusions exhibited by the good candidates set them apart in the interviews and gave me the trust and confidence to hire them.

"Now that I think about it," he continued, "this is true of a lot of people I interact with at work. I have trust, respect and confidence in people who produce results, but I also trust those who have a plan to get things done. I trust those who offer solutions, rather than problems. I trust those who think through every situation and come to the right conclusions. You're right! It isn't just what people do, it's how they think, reason and come to conclusions that makes me want to climb all the way up the Ladder to COMMITMENT with them."

I went on to explain that the best way for managers to accelerate the climb to the TRUST, RESPECT and CONFIDENCE rung on the Ladder with their employees is to be OPEN with them about the *things that matter most.* Managers can hasten the process by sharing the thinking, reasoning and conclusions behind the business imperative, goals, direction, roles, expectations, boundaries and authority outlined for the employees. The level of enthusiasm and commitment of the workforce will be in direct proportion to how strongly they trust the thinking, reasoning and judgment of their leaders. Employees will become committed when what is being asked of them makes sense to them. Managers can get their employees to do the right things for the right reasons when the employees know the reasoning behind what is being asked of them.

Stepping Forward Together

As usual, I switched to a personal example to show how trust, respect and confidence are built at home.

"Paul, one of the best ways to gain the commitment of your children to your parental teaching is to share the thinking and reasoning behind your words, behaviors and actions – particularly any commands you give to your children. As we discussed earlier, it does little good to tell your children *what* to do, if you don't explain the *why* behind your directives so they can validate in their minds the need for action. Children will never learn from a parental dictum unless they know the rationale behind the order. Parental demands delivered with no clarifying information may get children to blindly comply, but it will not teach them how to think or reason for themselves in similar situations in the future. The thinking behind an order provides the understanding necessary to make the right choice when they have to make decisions on their own.

"A major part of your parental role, Paul, is to teach your children how to think, reason, and make the right decisions to succeed in life. If you want your children to assimilate your values, philosophies, beliefs and characteristics, you have to share the thinking, reasoning, and conclusions behind your behaviors, actions, and words. Modeling the right way entails more than just acting a certain way; it also requires explanations as to why that way is important. Parents need to spend less time telling their children what to do and, instead, spend more time teaching them how to think, reason, and judge for themselves. Parents should discuss – rather than dictate – the qualities they wish their children to acquire."

I told Paul I believe the primary role of parents is to teach children about the "its" of life. Parents need to help their children understand that there is an "it" in every situation, and those who understands the "its" of life are the ones who usually are the most successful and happy in life.

"You mentioned just a few minutes ago there are some people at your company who get it, and some who don't. Is that right?" I asked.

"Yes."

"Which employees are the most successful at work: those who get it or those who don't?"

"Obviously, the ones who get it," he answered.

"And how about at home? There's probably an 'it' in your home, too, that you wish your children would get. Isn't it true that the sooner your children get the 'it', the better their lives will be at home?"

Paul chuckled. "That's right. I'm still waiting for my kids to figure that out so my wife and I can stop nagging them."

"And how about at school? There's an 'it' there, too, isn't there?" I continued. "There are certain behaviors that are acceptable at school and other behaviors that are totally unacceptable. The students who get it, and model the acceptable behaviors, tend to do better scholastically than those who buck the system. Sometimes in school, and particularly in college, how the teacher feels about you can be the difference between a C grade and an A. This, too, is something you hope your children will get, isn't it?"

"Getting 'it' seems to be a reoccurring theme in our discussion," Paul pointed out.

"You're right. That's because everything on the Ladder of Commitment is designed to help people get 'it'," I confirmed. "There are certain actions, attitudes, words, behaviors, and qualities by which one is deemed to be a good worker, a good husband, a good wife, a good child, a good student, a good church member, a good neighbor, a good citizen, etc. These conditions may not be the same in every company, marriage, family, school, church, neighborhood or community, but there are criteria by which people are judged in every element of life. These criteria comprise the norms, or the 'its', of a specific situation. Those people who understand, accept and abide by the norms of a company, home, church, neighborhood, etc., are those in whom we have trust, respect and confidence. Those who don't get 'it' – or who violate 'it' or fight against 'it' – are the people we do not trust, respect, or have confidence in."

"I agree completely," he said, shaking his head affirmatively.

"Paul, I mentioned earlier that I'm a Scoutmaster. As you can imagine, having me as a Scoutmaster is a little different for my boys since I always feel a high need to teach them correct principles. I really like it when we talk philosophically, so we spend time around the campfire talking a lot about the meaning of life. One night I asked my 12- and 13-year-old Scouts this question without any explanation: Generally speaking, at what age do people tend to get 'IT'?"

"What did they say?" Paul asked, wondering if the boys knew what I was talking about.

"These kids are very sharp. They knew exactly what I was asking because they're used to this type of question from me. They agreed that, sadly, some people never get it. Some adults reach the age of maturity without ever maturing. The boys also said some people get it late in life, coming to a death-bed understanding of what is important. They suggested some people get it after a significant emotional experience, such as a divorce, death, tragic event or termination from a job. Some people catch on when they graduate from college, get married, or have kids of their own. And some people, the kids agreed, figure it out very early in their lives when they are yet young."

"Your Scouts are pretty astute," Paul praised. "I have an older broth-er who is almost 50 years old who hasn't figured it out yet. Everything in his life is a struggle because he just doesn't get it. My 15-year-old daughter seems to understand life better than he does."

"And *that's* the whole point, isn't it," I declared. "Life is a struggle for those who don't get it, whereas life is much easier for those who do. You see, the follow-up question I asked my Scouts in that discussion is much more important than the original question. The follow-up question I asked my boys was: Who is happier, who is more successful, and who has the greatest advan-tage in life – those who get it, or those who don't?"

"That's it, isn't it?" Paul exclaimed. "The ones who get it at work are the ones who have successful careers. The ones who get it at home have happy marriages and a wonderful family life. The kids who get it at school get the best grades. Getting it is the key to everything."

"Yes it is," I confirmed. Then, wanting to pull all the pieces of our discussion together, I said: "The best workers, the best students, the best neighbors, the children who please us the most are the ones who get it. The ones who get it are the ones in whom we have trust, respect and confi-dence. And we know who we trust by how they think, reason and come to conclusions."

"I get it!" Paul acknowledged.

I was impressed by how well Paul had been tracking everything I had been telling him. So, while we were on this topic, I wanted to explain a couple of other key points about building trust, particularly regarding the interview process when hiring new employees. Since the purpose of the Ladder is to get people to COMMITMENT as soon as possible, I wanted him to know that the commitment process with an employee begins in the initial interview.

"Paul, how soon do you want your employees to get it?" I asked.

"Right away."

"What does 'right away' mean?" I pressed.

"From day one. I want them to start catching on to the way we do things as soon as they can," he answered.

"Wouldn't you like to know if someone gets it *before* you hire them?"

"That's true," he agreed, "but is that possible?"

"Do you remember when we said earlier that a person's resume doesn't get them trust, respect and confidence – all it gets them is an interview?" I asked.

"Yes."

"I think it might be helpful if I tell you how I interview potential new employees at my company. You see, I don't know about you, but I want to be up this Ladder to TRUST, RESPECT and CONFIDENCE in that employee on the very first day they start working for me. I'm not going to send a new consultant into the field to work with one of our clients unless I can trust, respect and have confidence in their judgment."

"Isn't that why you pair up new employees with experienced employees, so they can learn from them for awhile?" Paul asked.

"Yes. That's what many companies do, and it is a helpful tool until both the company and the new employees have achieved the trust and confidence needed to have the employees work on their own. But in my company I don't want to do that. If I hire the right people – employees I already know I can trust – I don't have to have two employees doing one job while one is being trained. Instead I can let the current employee continue with his clients and assign the new employee to new clients. That way I have two people doing twice as much work instead of two people doing the work of one."

Stepping Forward Together

I agreed Paul needed to train new employees on how to work on the assembly line at his tool manufacturing plant, but I suggested he should be looking to hire workers who can learn the tasks quicker so they can work on their own as soon as possible. The key to hiring new employees is interviewing them in such a way you can determine which candidates will be able to earn your trust, respect, and confidence quickly.

"I want to make sure you really understand this point, Paul," I said, pausing to check if he was tracking what I'd been saying.

"The *conscious management* and *managerless management* process starts in the interview. I want to know in the interview before I hire people whether they will be able to do the job consciously without close supervision. I want to know in the interview whether I will be able to trust, respect, and have confidence in the candidate to the point where I can trust him to manage himself. The people I want to hire are those who can climb this Ladder quickly so I won't have to manage them."

"So how do you determine that in an interview?" Paul asked.

"By hearing how the job candidates think, reason, and come to conclusions. I want to know if they understand how to do *this* job at *my* company," I declared. "I'm not interested in their resumes; I'm interested in *them*. I'm not interested in their past; I want to know what they can do for me now and in the future. That's why I quickly set aside the candidates' resumes when I'm interviewing them for a position with my company. Their resume got them the interview. I've already read what they've done, so we don't need to talk about their past in the interview. What I want to know now is what they can do for me and my company in the future. The interview should focus on what the job candidates intend to do in the positions they are applying for, not rehash what they've accomplished in past positions. The only relevant information from their past experiences is those things they have done that will make them successful at my company in the future."

I told Paul that just as he can tell which of his current employees get it by how they think, reason and come to conclusions, so too can he tell which job candidates get it by hearing how they think, reason and come to conclusions in the interview.

Trust, Respect and Confidence

"You see, the key to a good hiring interview is to get the *interviewee* to talk, rather than listen to the interviewer," I said. "Too many hiring managers spend too much time talking in the interview when they should be listening. The interviewer should be drawing out the thinking, reasoning and conclusions of the job candidate, rather than sharing their thoughts or making statements. My mantra is: *don't put in, draw out.*"

I showed Paul how the seven *things that matter most* in the OPEN area of the Ladder provide the outline for the interview.

"During the interviews you want to determine whether the potential new employees get it. You need to engage them in a dialogue about your business rather than discuss their past employers. You want to know whether they understand the *business imperatives* at your company. You want to ask them about the *direction* they would take once they are in their new position and what *goals* they would hope to accomplish in their first year of employment. You want to assess if they understand what their *role* will be and what will be *expected* of them in that role. You also should ask what *boundaries* and *authority* they expect to be given in their new role. And, finally, you should determine whether they will be receptive to your *feedback* in the future should they be hired.

"During the interviews you shouldn't *tell* prospective employees about the goals, roles, expectations, etc., at your company. If you do they will just repeat back what they heard and tell you what they think you want to hear," I cautioned. "Instead, you should *ask* them what they think these things might be. During the hiring interview you want to determine whether the candidates get YOUR business. You want to discover whether they understand what it will take to be successful at your company. You want to hear how they think, reason and come to conclusions about your business so you can have trust, respect and confidence in them *before* they are hired."

I reminded Paul that when I hire people I want to be as far up the Ladder of Commitment with them as I can be before they start. I want to discern during the interviews whether they are someone in whom I can have trust, respect and confidence. I don't want to hire someone based upon their past experiences and then find out their character is not in harmony with what I'm looking for in an employee.

Stepping Forward Together

"The point is, a person's resume tells you what they have done, but it doesn't tell you who they are," I declared. "The whole purpose of the hiring interview is to determine who the people are and whether they are aligned with the values, beliefs, philosophies and principles of your business. So put the resumes aside, stop focusing on what they have done, and start finding out who they are. A good interview builds trust, respect and confidence in people long before you see their results, actions or behaviors," I said, pointing to the left side of the Ladder.

Paul nodded his head and agreed.

I further suggested that when I hear managers complain they have had to suffer the consequences of a "bad hire," the truth is they probably conducted a bad *interview*. I believe managers who focus heavily on a person's resume and past experience during an interview tend to complain more about bad hires. The manager trusts what he read on the candidate's resume or what the interviewee said about her work experience during the interview, and then the manager is shocked later when the new employee cannot perform as the manger expected from the interview.

On the other hand, managers who focus on the job *candidate* during the interview, rather than the candidate's resume, will get a greater understanding of what the individual is capable of doing in the future.

"Wow!" Paul marveled. "This is just amazing how everything fits together on the Ladder."

I asked Paul if he had any questions about how to build trust, respect and confidence.

"Actually, I do," he said, somewhat hesitantly. "I've been sitting here wondering if it's possible to have trust, respect and confidence in someone you don't like. I've been thinking about a guy I have to interact with back at Corporate. I trust he will always get the right results, I respect his professional expertise, and I have confidence in his decision making capabilities; but I really don't like him as a person. He's obnoxious and real difficult to work with."

"I think you answered your own question, Paul. Obviously the answer is yes you can have trust, respect and have confidence in someone you don't like. And you just proved it."

Trust, Respect and Confidence

Paul's question gave me an opportunity to explain how one leg of the Ladder of Commitment can represent the *personal* side of a relationship and the other leg one's *professional* qualities. Similarly, the legs of the Ladder could represent a supervisor's *managerial* abilities on the one side and her *leadership* qualities on the other. One leg describes how good people are when working on *tasks*, while the other leg identifies how well they handle *process* issues. Finally, the two legs can represent how one is perceived at *work* versus how one is viewed at *home*.

"Paul, as you've discovered, it's possible to trust someone's professional capabilities, but not like him personally," I explained. "On the other hand, it's also possible to like a person personally, but not have confidence her professional abilities. A salesperson, for example, could be very charismatic and well-liked by potential customers, but also be totally incapable of selling. Similarly, an employee who is a computer wizard could be highly competent as a technician, yet also be socially inept and completely unable to get along with his peers at work."

"I agree," he said.

"The same is true regarding a person's leadership versus management abilities," I suggested. "A manager could be a highly competent administrator, yet also be a very poor leader. She could be good at paperwork, but bad at people work. She could be excellent at holding people accountable, but fall short where it really counts – in getting along with people.

"Similarly, a good leader may not be a good manager. He may be effective at inspiring the troops to 'take the hill', yet be poor at putting a plan together that would allow the troops to take the hill with the least amount of casualties. He could be very in tune to the needs of the employees, yet also be incapable of meeting the needs of the business. He could have plenty of followers, yet not be able to organize those followers to achieve the desired results.

"Some people are very adept when it comes to working on tasks, but their process skills are lacking," I continued. "Others are more process oriented than task oriented. Process-oriented people become frustrated with task-oriented individuals because they often focus on getting the work done with little regard for the impact on the people. Task-oriented workers are annoyed by process-oriented employees because they often have a high need to ensure everyone is comfortable with the process. Consequently, task-oriented people may be slower to develop trust, respect and confidence in process-oriented people, and vice versa.

"Finally, as I said earlier in our conversation, a person could be well trusted and respected at work, but not be trusted and respected at home. Conversely, she could have the utmost confidence of her family members, but not have the backing and support of her employees, colleagues or boss at work."

Paul sat quietly in his seat. He apparently had gone inside himself, thinking about his relationships with people at work and home. While he was being introspective, I wanted to make one last point.

"Paul, unfortunately, some people are what I call 'one-leg-ladders.' They can be trusted or respected personally *OR* professionally, but not both. Something in their words, actions, behaviors and results keeps people from trusting them on one side of the Ladder or the other. They may be a good person, but a bad worker. They may be a wonderful manager, but a horrible leader. They may be great at tasks, but lousy with processes. They may be loved at home, but despised at work. They may have some character or behavioral flaw that keeps them from being trusted or respected on both legs of the ladder."

"Whoa!" Paul exclaimed. "You just described another situation I'm dealing with. I have a friend who is an alcoholic. But he doesn't accept he's an alcoholic. Everyone around him knows he has a drinking problem, but he doesn't believe it. No matter what we say to him about his drinking, he doesn't get it. He won't accept he has a problem.

"The point is he's a great husband and father when he's sober. He's an absolutely superb businessman when he hasn't been drinking. But once he takes a drink, he turns into a tyrant. When he is sober he is well liked. People trust and respect him. But when he's been drinking, no one can stand to be around him. No one can trust or respect him when he's been drinking. It's amazing that people can be at the TRUST, RESPECT and CONFIDENCE level with him when he's sober, and be CLOSED when he is drunk. How can such a good person not see that his drinking is destroying people's trust, respect, and confidence, both at work and at home?"

"Although your friend doesn't realize it, he only has one leg to his ladder. One-leg-ladder people live a precarious life that is wobbly and unstable," I cautioned. "Your friend will never find balance and true success in his life until he accepts and resolves his character flaw. His family, friendships and job will always be in jeopardy until he alters his course. One-leg ladders cannot stand forever. There will come a day when the good leg of his ladder will collapse if he doesn't overcome his personal flaw."

"I agree. I wish there was something I could do to get through to him," Paul said sadly.

"The best thing you can do is continue to move toward him, stay OPEN, and try to get him to a point where he will be receptive to your feedback," I offered. "He will only accept the truth from someone in whom he has trust, respect and confidence."

FOURTEEN

The Tangible Indicator
of Trust, Respect and Confidence

By now pretty much everyone on the plane was asleep. There were a few passengers reading. Their overhead lights provided the only light in the dark plane. Paul and I seemed to be the only people engaged in conversation. Neither of us was tired. We both became more energized the more we talked.

"When people achieve the TRUST, RESPECT, and CONFIDENCE rung on the Ladder," I continued, "there is a tangible indicator that proves they have reached this level in their relationship. I submit this tangible indicator is what every human being craves. It is what every manager wants from his or her employees. It is what all employees want from their manager. This tangible indicator is what every husband wants from his wife and every wife wants from her husband. It is what every parent wants from children and every child seeks from parents. The tangible indicator of trust, respect and confidence is what every person wants from every other person in a relationship, whether it is in their professional or personal life."

I could see the wheels turning in Paul's head as he tried to determine what the tangible indicator might be. I was confident he would eventually figure it out, but I wanted to facilitate his understanding by giving him a hint.

"Paul, imagine I am your boss and you have proposed for my approval an absolutely wonderful new idea on how to produce power tools better, easier, cheaper, or faster at your plant in Las Vegas. If I trust that you fully understand the needs of the customers, if I respect your professional judgment and expertise, and if I have confidence that you have the company's

Stepping Forward Together

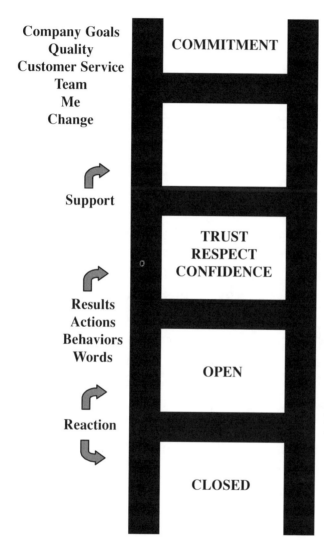

Company Goals
Quality
Customer Service
Team
Me
Change

Support

COMMITMENT

TRUST
RESPECT
CONFIDENCE

Results
Actions
Behaviors
Words

OPEN

Information - Why
Goals / Direction
Roles
Expectations
Boundaries
Authority
Feedback

Reaction

CLOSED

interests at heart – what should my answer be when you propose your idea, since I trust you, respect you, and have confidence in you?" I asked.

"You should say yes."

"Why would I say yes when I don't know whether your idea will work?" I pressed.

"Because you trust me, respect me, and have confidence in me," Paul knew.

"Paul, you will *know* when someone trusts you, respects you, and has confidence in you because they will SUPPORT your actions and decisions. This is the tangible indicator. It is what every manager and employee wants from his or her boss," I declared. Then, attempting to model how Paul might feel regarding the need for support from his corporate boss, I said:

"Dang it! If you trust me as the general manager of the Las Vegas plant, then support me! Support my decisions! Support my actions! Stand behind me and support what I am doing at the plant. Trust that I know what I am doing. Respect my professional judgment. Have confidence that I know how to bring profitability to the business and I won't do anything stupid to damage the brand."

Paul nodded his head vigorously to indicate this expressed his true feelings.

"That IS what I want," he sighed. "That's it exactly. I want my boss to trust me as the leader of my business unit. I am the eyes and ears of the company in Las Vegas. My boss needs to trust that I am in the best position to judge what is right for the business. He should support what I am doing because I'm doing what I feel is right for the company."

"Might I suggest," I added, giving him other examples, "that the company also needs to trust and support the salespeople who are in the field talking to the customers. The salespeople are the ones who should know best what the customers want. Similarly, management, including you, should trust and support the people working on the front line when they make suggestions for improvement, because they are the ones closest to problems. Support up and down the chain of command and across functional lines is critical to the success of your business."

I added the word *support* to the Ladder model.

Everything *is a*
trust, respect and confidence issue.

The Tangible Indicator

I wanted Paul to know that people literally yearn for support from others. Senior executives want the support of the company's board, shareholders, and employees regarding their strategic and tactical initiatives. Managers want their decisions and actions to be supported by their senior leaders. Supervisors want their subordinates to support the policies and procedures of the company and perform their job duties the way they were trained. Employees want the backing and support of their managers, particularly when differences arise between a customer and the employees. Husbands and wives want to be supported as they fulfill their home and family responsibilities. Married couples with children want each other's support whenever they interact with or discipline a child. And, of course, children – especially teenagers – crave the support of their parents and friends.

"That may cause a problem," Paul suggested. "I can see where there might be a clash between the support a person wants from one group and the support the person seeks from another group. While trying to gain the support of one group the person may lose the support of the other group."

"What are you thinking about?" I asked, not sure where he was going.

"I was just thinking that a teenager, for example, might do things that are contrary to her parent's wishes in order to gain the support of her peers. She may violate the trust, respect and confidence of the parents in order to gain the trust, respect and confidence of her friends."

"That's insightful," I said.

"Similarly, an employee might do things that are detrimental to his career by acting in such a way that gains the respect of his coworkers, but loses the respect of his boss," he continued. "I've seen new supervisors, for example, who try to gain the respect of their employees by acting like a friend, and, in so doing, the supervisor loses the respect of his boss for not managing his people properly."

I smiled broadly and nodded my head in agreement.

"That's very insightful, Paul," I commended. "You have intuitively picked up on what I consider to be the most important point of everything we've been talking about tonight. You see, **everything is a trust, respect and confidence issue.**"

Stepping Forward Together

I repeated my statement three times so Paul would know how important this point is.

"Paul, if you learn nothing else from our discussion tonight, learn this one thing: everything is a trust, respect, and confidence issue," I emphasized. "There isn't a single situation in life that is not a trust, respect or confidence issue. Every contact and interaction we have with another person either moves us up this Ladder toward TRUST, RESPECT and CONFIDENCE, or it pushes us away from it. There is no neutral ground. The sooner people realize this fact, the better off they will be because they can consciously do everything in their power to build trust, respect, and confidence in every relationship they have, both personal and professional."

I wanted to give Paul several examples so he could fully grasp this extremely important point.

"You see, Paul, sometimes, as husbands, we don't know what is expected of us until we come home and hear our spouse exhale forcefully in a huff as soon as we walk through the door."

Paul smiled broadly. Obviously he, too, had had this experience in his home.

"*'Is something wrong?'* you ask," I said, playing both parts again in a role play.

"*'No!'*" she says in a CLOSED response.

"*'There must be something wrong. I heard you huff and puff. What is it?'*"

"*'It's nothing!'* she says, still remaining CLOSED.

"*'Did I do something wrong? What did I do?'* you plead, trying to get to the bottom of the problem.

"*'You don't get it, do you?'* she sighs in another CLOSED response.

"*'Get what? What did I do?'* you wonder, not having a clue to the problem.

"Finally, after a big fight, you find out your wife wanted you to wash the dishes. That's what all the huffing and puffing was about," I explained.

Paul smiled broadly. "I think you've been to my house," he quipped.

I returned to the role play, pretending to be Paul. I pointed to the OPEN area on the Ladder.

"*'Honey, if you wanted me to wash the dishes, why didn't you just ASK ME or TELL ME to do it?'*"

"*'Because if I have to tell you, it doesn't count,'* she says."

Paul roared with laughter.

I waved my hand over my head in the sign that indicates a concept is way over a person's head.

"We don't get this part, do we, Paul?" I smiled. "Count for what? If our wives want us to wash the dishes, all they have to do is ask us or tell us to do so. We don't get the 'doesn't count' part, do we?"

Paul agreed.

"So what do you do to fix this problem, since she wants you to wash the dishes?" I ask.

"Wash the dishes," he rightly concluded.

"And does the fact that you are now washing the dishes make her happy?" I pressed.

"No!"

"You're right. She's probably in another room still huffing and puffing and mumbling to herself: *'Why do I have to tell you . . . I tell you and tell you . . . I am sick and tired of having to tell you . . . .'*"

Paul couldn't stop laughing. My role play was apparently spot on. He'd been here before, as have a lot of husbands. Sometimes the only way people learn about an expectation is when they violate it. Then all heck breaks lose.

I returned to a serious tone so he would know what I was about to say was no joke.

"Paul, if this was a *dishes* problem, what would fix it?"

"Washing the dishes."

"Therefore, the fact that she is still upset, even though you are now washing the dishes, should tell you this is not a dishes problem," I explained. "So what kind of a problem is this?" I asked pointing to the Ladder.

"It's a RESPECT issue," he rightly surmised.

I continued the role play, pretending to be his wife: "*'If you respected the fact that I work hard all day, too . . . If you respected the fact that maybe I'm tired and I'd like to sit down and relax . . . If you respected the fact that maybe I'd like to watch the news or read the newspaper, too . . . you'd do SOMETHING around here . . . and you'd do it NOT because I asked, but because you respect the fact that I'm tired and I don't want to wash the dishes, either.'"*

Paul confirmed my premise by nodding his head in agreement.

"But this isn't just a RESPECT issue, Paul, is it?" I added, pointing again to the Ladder. "What else might it be?"

"It's also a TRUST issue," he knew.

"I'm sure your wife would like to trust she could come home after a tough day at the office, if she works, or from dealing with your two kids and her other responsibilities at home, and find that someone else had done something around the house to lift some of the burden off of her shoulders."

Paul silently nodded his understanding.

"This is also a CONFIDENCE issue, isn't it?" I continued. "Your wife would like to have the confidence that people will help out around the house without having to be told."

"You're right," he confirmed, seeing how trust, respect and confidence are connected.

"Everything is a trust, respect and confidence issue," I over-emphasized on purpose. I then switched to a second example to make sure Paul saw the connection at work.

"Prior to your becoming the GM in Vegas and the manager of the sales force in Ohio, were you ever a supervisor of front-line employees?" I asked.

"Yes, I once worked at a call center in Omaha. I supervised over 100 reservation agents."

"Did you ever have an employee who came back late from breaks?" I asked.

"Yes!"

"Is this problem a *tardiness* issue?"

"No. It's a trust, respect, and confidence issue," he said, surprised at how obvious this was now that he understood the Ladder.

"If you want to get people to do the right things for the right reasons, you have to focus on the right issues," I explained. "If you argue about the dishes at home, you will never resolve the problem because the dishes are not the issue. Likewise, if you counsel an employee about his attendance, that won't solve the problem because attendance is not the issue. The key to moving people in the right direction is to talk about the real issue – which is trust, respect and confidence."

I told Paul if a manager tries to counsel an employee about his attendance – instead of focusing on trust, respect and confidence – it usually results in an argument from the employee where he defends his punctuality. When managers talk about an employee's attendance, the employee tends to argue the facts. He protests he was not late, he argues about the number of times the manager claims he was late is wrong, or he offers some other defense to counter the manager's feedback.

"In reality, does it matter to you how many times the employee has been late?" I asked.

"Not really, because, if I were the manager, I'd want him to be on time, every time."

"Yes, that's true. But the real reason it doesn't matter is because you know this is not an attendance issue – it's a trust, respect and confidence issue." I reminded. "I'm going to show you how I would counsel an employee who comes back late from breaks so you can see how to focus your feedback on the real issue."

I turned toward Paul and acted as if he was the employee I was counseling.

"Ah oh! Looks like I'm the bad guy again," he joked.

I smiled and confirmed that he was.

"Before we begin, Paul, do you think employees typically know why they are being called into the manager's office for counseling?"

"Yes, I'm pretty sure they do."

"That's why I don't spend a lot of time in a counseling session talking about an employee's attendance (or whatever the problem may be), because he already knows why he is there. So I quickly discard any discussion about the employee's attendance, just like I quickly set aside a job candidate's resume in a hiring interview. The attendance problem, like a resume, is in the past. What we need to focus on in the performance improvement session is the future."

Paul smiled, apparently impressed with how everything I had shared with him so far fits together. I checked to see if he was ready to be counseled for his "attendance" problem, and then started the role play.

"Paul, you know I brought you into my office to discuss your coming back late from breaks, don't you?" I began.

He nodded.

"That's what you know. What you probably don't know, is your coming back late from breaks is not just an attendance issue – it's a TRUST issue," I explained. *"And do you want to know how I know? Because every time you go on a break I look at my watch. And every time you come back from a break I look at my watch. Every time I look at my watch it sends me the message that I don't trust you."*

I paused the role play and asked Paul to remember back to when he was a front-line supervisor. I asked if he had some employees working for him back then who, when they took a break, he felt he needed to look at his watch when they left or when they came back. I also asked if he had some people who, when they went on a break, he never felt the need to check his watch. He said he had both kinds of employees working for him.

"What was the difference between the employee whom you always checked your watch and the one you didn't?" I asked.

"Trust"

I returned to the role play.

"Paul, every time I look at my watch it sends me a message that I don't trust you. And I need to tell you it is not to your advantage to send a message to your boss that you are not trustworthy. You're going to want me to trust you in the future, and I will tell you why in just a minute.

"Paul, you need to realize your being late from breaks isn't just a trust issue. It's also an issue of RESPECT. Every time you come back late from break you send a significant message of disrespect to your fellow workers. Your being late says to your colleagues that you don't care about them – you don't care if they are tired, too – you don't care if they get their breaks on time.

And let me tell you, it is not to your advantage to send a message of disrespect to your co-workers because they will not respect you in return.

"But you don't just send a message of disrespect to your colleagues, Paul. You also send a message of disrespect to me. Your continuing to be late says you don't respect my authority as your boss, since I've counseled you about this before. It also says you don't respect the company or its policies. And you obviously have no respect for our customers, since they are the ones whose service you are neglecting when you are late.

"I have to warn you it is not to your advantage to send a message to your boss that you have no respect for me, the company, our policies or our customers. It is not to your advantage to send a message to your fellow workers that you do not respect them. I'm telling you now that you need to fix this problem, Paul, and I will tell you why in just a minute.

"But you also need to understand that this isn't just a trust and respect issue – it is also one of CONFIDENCE. When I schedule the breaks for our department I line them up so I know everyone will be able to get their breaks at the appropriate time according to the labor laws. But when you come back late, you throw my schedule off and I no longer have confidence that everyone will get their break on time. That's also why I look at my watch whenever you go on a break – because I don't have confidence you will come back on time. And if I can't have confidence in you, Paul, that is not good for you. And now let me tell you why . . ."

I paused for dramatic effect.

". . . because **there will come a day!**"

I paused again, just as I would in a performance counseling session, so the emotional impact of those words could take effect inside Paul.

I wrote the words down on my notepad to emphasize how powerful these words are in motivating people to do the right things. I explained that the statement "there will come a day" is not a threat. It is a promise, or guarantee, that something will happen in the future if the employee does or does not change his behavior. I also clarified that the phrase should never be used as a negative, punishing, or threatening statement. However, my brief pause after saying the statement was done consciously as a means of gaining the employee's attention. It's all right for the employee to think, for a very brief moment, that the statement is a threat, so long as the person doing the counseling erases that perception quickly. If "there will come a day" ever carries a negative connotation, it will lose its value to move people in a positive way.

"Paul, you will want to come back from breaks on time in the future so you can earn my trust, respect and confidence because 'there will come a day' when you will want my . . ."

I stopped the role play to see if Paul could figure out the next word. He paused for just a second, then, confidently said:

"SUPPORT!"

"Exactly!" I said pointing my index finger at him to reinforce his right answer. "'*There will come a day*' is a powerful phrase you ought to use whenever you counsel someone because this phrase causes people to do what you want.

"The more you know about a person the more you can motivate him or her to do what you want because 'there will come a day' for everyone," I explained. "'There will come a day' for every parent when she will want to be at home with her child rather than at work. 'There will come a day' when an employee with a pet will need to miss work to take his animal to the veterinarian. 'There will come a day' when a NASCAR enthusiast will want to be at the races. 'There will come a day' when a hunter will not want to miss the opening of deer season. 'There will come a day' when a tri-athlete will want time off to run in a big race. Every single employee has a special need he or she will want the boss to support when that 'day' comes.

"The same is true at home," I added. "Paul, 'there will come a day 'when your children will want your support. 'There will come a day' when your son or daughter will want to borrow your car, go to a dance, stay out late, or attend some special event. And on that day they will want you to say yes. So do what I do with my son. I tell him he needs to behave *today* because 'there will come a day' in the future when he will want my support. And on that day he will wish he had minded me now."

"That's great!" Paul said.

I returned to the role play.

The Tangible Indicator

"'There will come a day' when you will want my support. 'There will come a day' when you will need to be home with a sick child. 'There will come a day' when your son or daughter will want you to attend a special event at school. And on that day, Paul, when you ask for special time off, what do you want my answer to be when you ask?"

"I want you to say yes," Paul answered.

"And how quickly do you want that yes to come out of my mouth?"

"Right away."

"That's exactly right. The truth is, Paul, there are some people on my staff to whom I immediate say yes when they ask for special time off. And there are other people – and you happen to be one of them – who, when they ask for special favors, I hesitate and have to think about the request before answering. You know this is true, don't you? You can feel it. You can sense it. You know I respond differently to different people, don't you?"

Paul looked like he had a question, but he didn't want to interrupt the role play. I was pretty sure I knew what the question was and would make sure I answered it later. I did, however, interrupt the role play so I could help Paul understand what I had just said.

"I want you to go inside yourself, Paul, and answer truthfully the question I'm about to ask," I proposed, wanting to bring to his conscious mind something that happens subconsciously in most managers. "Be honest. Back when you were a front-line manager, did you have some employees who, if they came and asked you for special time off, you gave your permission without hesitation or even checking the calendar?"

"Yes"

"I'll bet you even would have gone so far as to personally cover their shift for them if you had to?" I pressed.

"Yes, that's true. I would."

"On the other hand, did you also have some employees who, if they asked for special time off, you first had to ask them a whole lot of questions before giving them the time off?"

"That's true, too," he answered.

"And, I'll bet it would have irritated you if you had to come in and cover the shift for these people?" I challenged.

He confirmed this, too, was true.

"What was the difference between these two groups of people?" I asked.

"Trust, respect and confidence," he said confidently.

I started to continue with the role play, but Paul interrupted me.

"You want to hear something interesting?" Paul asked. "I actually think there are three different types of people rather than the two you mentioned. There are people I trust, who I automatically support. There are people I don't trust yet, where I have to ask a lot of questions before I give them my support. And there are people who I know I don't trust, who will never get my support."

"You're absolutely right, Paul. You just taught me something tonight because I hadn't ever thought of that. There *are* three different levels."

"I'm not completely clueless," Paul joked.

Returning to the role play, I said: *"Paul, 'there will come a day' when you will want my support. 'There will come a day' when you will want me to say yes to your request. And on that day my answer will be determined by how much I trust you, respect you, and have confidence in you. You already know you are not in the instantaneous yes group. But what you probably don't know is that you COULD be. All it takes to get into the instantaneous yes group is for you to earn my trust, respect and confidence.*

"So, Paul, since we're talking about your attendance, how can you guarantee my support when you need it in the future?"

"By coming back from breaks on time," Paul answered.

"Correct! How often?" I pressed.

"All the time."

"Did you hear what you just said, Paul? If you want to earn my trust, respect, confidence and support, you will come back from break on time, EVERY time from now on."

I paused for effect, just as I would in a real counseling session.

"You see, Paul, I don't really care if you've been late seven times. I don't care if you've been late six, five, four, three or two times. If you want me to trust you in the future, you will come back on time . . . ."

"Every time," Paul confirmed.

"That's right! You see, Paul, don't come on time for ME. Don't do it for the COMPANY. Don't do it for the CUSTOMERS or your FELLOW EMPLOYEES. You're going to come back on time from breaks every time from now on for whom?"

"For me," Paul answered.

"You're going to come back on time every time from now on because 'there will come a day' when YOU will want my support." I paused again, just as I would in a counseling session. *"You get that now, don't you, Paul?"*

"Oh, wow! I get that very clearly. That is cool!" Paul declared. "I wish I had recorded it because I definitely want to use that approach in any future counseling sessions I have."

"Everything is a trust, respect, and confidence issue," I reminded. "The sooner you start using those words in your feedback sessions – rather than talking about dishes or attendance – the sooner you will start moving people in the right direction."

I reminded Paul that much earlier in our discussion I mentioned that the first of the seven *things that matter most* on the OPEN rung of the Ladder is the need to explain the business imperative. The business imperative explains *why* a specific action is necessary. Back then I also said the best way to get people to commit to do what you want them to do is to link the business imperative with a person's personal imperative. It is much easier for a manager to get people to accomplish the goals of the business when the business goals and the employees' goals are the same.

"In the role play of the counseling session that I just did, I linked the company's business need of having an employee come back from break on time . . ." I said, holding up my right index finger, ". . . with the employee's personal need of wanting the support of the manager in the future," I explained holding up my left index finger. I then interlocked my two index fingers and said: "I linked the business imperative with the personal imperative. I made sure the employee understood the chances were higher he could get what *he* wanted in the future by doing what *I* wanted now."

"That's very powerful," Paul praised. "But if you say yes to one employee and no to another, isn't that favoritism. If I did that with an employee, he would run complaining to Human Resources in a heartbeat."

"So what are you afraid of?" I asked, wanting to check if he had fully grasped the major premise we'd been talking about.

"I'm afraid Human Resources won't . . . ." he paused for just a second before he got it.

"I'm afraid Human Resources won't *support* my actions."

"And of course they won't," I declared, "unless you've already developed a relationship of trust, respect and confidence with Human Resources *before* the 'day' comes. Don't you get it? 'There will come a day' when you will want Human Resources' support. 'There will come a day' when you will want your bosses' support. 'There will come a day' when you will want the support of another department. So the key is to do everything you can *now* to gain their trust, respect and confidence so you will have their support when you need it in the future."

"Like, duh!" Paul said, slapping his head.

"Now let me address the favoritism issue," I offered, getting back to his legitimate concern. "I need you to go inside yourself and answer truthfully again. Do you have favorites at work?"

He did not hesitate in saying he did.

"If I had you in a court of law and accused you of have having favorites, how would you plead, if you were not a liar or a perjurer?" I pressed.

"I would have to plead guilty . . . with an explanation," he said trying to weasel out of the offense.

"And I'll bet I know what the explanation is. So tell me, who are your favorites?"

"The people in whom I have trust, respect, and confidence," he declared forcefully. "My favorites are the ones who 'get it'. I favor those who are committed to the job the way I want them to do it."

"In other words, your favoritism is based upon *performance*," I clarified.

"Yes."

"So what's wrong with that?" I asked.

"Now that you mention it, nothing is wrong with that. It should be perfectly OK to reward people for their performance and to withhold rewards from those who don't perform," he said, obviously feeling better about his actions.

I explained that legally there is no problem favoring employees who perform better than others. I stressed, however, that he would face legal challenges if his favorites were certain members of the opposite sex, his drinking buddies, his friends, members of his car pool, or any other criteria that might be used to curry his favors other than performance.

"It is perfectly OK to treat employees differently, as long as the treatment is performance-based," I emphasized. "And I know Human Resources will support you on that. I believe there is a common misconception of what consistency, fairness and favoritism mean in the workplace. At first brush one might think employees want managers to treat everyone equally. But when the concept is explored deeper, equal treatment really isn't what employees want. That's because, deep down, most people know in some situations there is nothing more unjust than the equal treatment of unequals."

"Amen to that!" Paul said.

"If being consistent actually did mean treating employees equally, then management would have to treat the poor performer exactly the same as the exemplary performer," I added. "If consistency means equality, then management should reward the lazy and indolent worker the same as the diligent and industrious laborer. Likewise management should respect those they do not trust, as if they are trustworthy and respectable. Or, worse yet, management should treat workers they trust as if they are untrustworthy and those they respect as if they are not respected."

I got up on my soapbox because this is a topic that is hotly contested in the workplace. I believe this is an area managers need to raise to their conscious level because their actions are usually done subconsciously. Favoritism and inconsistency at work are NOT wrong, if they are used properly.

"The Declaration of Independence declares 'all men (and women) are *created* equal' and endowed 'with certain unalienable rights'," I affirmed. "This is true. All men were *created* equal and all should have certain rights by birth. But then something happens. *After* birth men become unequal. Differences arise as people travel divergent paths based upon their own ambitions, desires, beliefs, understanding and opportunities. Some people do well in life, while others do poorly. Some people progress while others remain dormant. Some people succeed where others fail. The choices people make and the actions they take throughout the course of their lives determine their position and status in society. This is part of the 'it' that every person needs to get.

"Similarly, all employees are equal the day they are hired. They are entitled to certain basic rights outlined in the core values and policies of the company. However, it's what the employees do *after* they are hired that determines how employees should be treated beyond the basic rights of employment. Each employee should be treated differently – I might even say inconsistently – based upon how he or she performs and behaves in the organization. Individual treatment of individuals and situational responses to situations is the only fair way to manage."

"I wish my Human Resources Department felt the same way you do," Paul whined.

"I wouldn't assume they don't," I challenged. "I'll bet they agree with what I just said. However, the reason why Human Resources exists – their business imperative, goal, role, expectation, boundaries and authority – is to protect the company from litigation by making sure all managers do what is legally right," I said, pointing to the the *things that matter most* from the OPEN rung on the Ladder. "They may error on the side of treating everyone exactly the same in order to stay as far away from the edge of liability as they can."

I returned to my soapbox to make a couple more key points.

"Those who profess and practice the equal treatment of all employees will soon find all incentives to perform well, and all penalties for not performing, vanish. Where there is no incentive to excel, there is no excellence. Where there is no consequence for failure, people fail to perform. Equality often breeds mediocrity.

"Good managers who are honest or introspective know they should *NOT* treat employees equally because employees are not equal. Some people have greater skills and talents than others. Some are wiser, more insightful, and capable of making profound decisions, while others are more limited in their scope of understanding. Some workers are fast, producing twice as much as their colleagues. Some are creative thinkers or great problem solvers, capable of designing next generation products for their employers. Some employees have more value than others because they accomplish more at less cost to the company. Therefore, those who do more deserve more, while those who do less deserve less.

"Good managers know treating every employee with the same consistency can be grossly *UN*fair because employees have different needs in similar situations. One employee, for example, may need great compassion from one's manager while grieving over the loss of a loved one. Another employee may desire just the opposite, wanting the manager to apply more pressure and make her work harder in order to keep her mind off of her grief.

"Good managers who are honest or introspective admit they have favorites. Good managers favor those who perform well. Good managers favor those who they can trust over those who work only when the manager is present. Good managers favor those who do their jobs to standard and disfavor those who willingly or spitefully perform poorly. Good managers unhesitatingly provide special favors to those who perform favorably."

"Finally!" Paul rejoiced. "It's wonderful to hear someone who thinks exactly as I do."

"Yeah? But I'll bet you try to hide the fact that you have favorites because you're afraid of the repercussions if this becomes known," I challenged.

"That's true."

"But I'll also bet people can tell that you actually do have favorites, even if you think you are hiding it," I proposed.

"That's probably true, too."

"I believe most managers cannot hide the fact they have favorites – unless they're really good at controlling their reactions," I said, pointing to the CLOSED rung on the Ladder. "I'll even go so far as to say it probably is very obvious you have favorites. So, *when the obvious is obvious, make it obvious*," I proposed.

He looked at me quizzically.

"When the obvious is obvious, make it obvious," I repeated. "It's obvious you have favorites, so rather than trying to hide it, make it obvious.

That way it will be conscious. Everyone knows you have favorites, so admit it by shouting it from the rooftops.

"And the other thing you should be shouting from the rooftops is what ISN'T obvious – the reason WHY you have favorites. Everyone knows you have favorites; what they don't know is why. So make it obvious. Make it obvious why some people are treated better than others. Explain why you treat good performers one way and poor performers another. Declare boldly that those who are trustworthy are trusted, those who are respectable are respected, and those who are supportive are supported. Tell everyone how they are treated is a direct reflection of what *they* do and how *they* act."

I told Paul I discovered long ago that people who are friendly usually have the most friends. Those who love others are loved by others. Those who are kind receive kindness in return. That which one sows, one reaps. This is true in life, and I believe it ought to be true at work.

"I have a special name for this reap and sow truism," I continued. "I call it my *Life is a Mirror Principle*. Life is a reflection of who one is and how one acts. What a person gets out of life is what he or she gives. Grumpy people tend to see the world as a grumpy place. People with negative attitudes generally see the world in a negative light. Happy, optimistic people, on the other hand, usually see the world as upbeat and positive.

"Managers sometimes need to be very OPEN with employees and explain that life is a mirror. I believe, contrary to the Golden Rule of treating people as they *want* to be treated, managers should treat employees as they *deserve* to be treated. Employees who perform and behave well ought to be treated well, while those who perform and behave poorly ought to be treated less well. The message from managers to employees should be this: If you don't like the way you are being treated, then change *your* behavior. I'm just mirroring the way you act. I'm treating you the way you deserve to be treated based upon your actions and reactions. Therefore, all you have to do to be treated better is to act better."

"I'll tell you, Mac, I'm really starting to like this *conscious management* stuff," Paul smiled.

"Then do everything consciously," I declared. "This includes making your actions conscious to everyone whose support you will need. You should make the fact that you have favorites obvious to Human Resources. You should go down there first thing Monday morning and tell them you WILL have favorites and you will NOT treat everyone the same. Tell them you will reward those who perform well and you will withhold rewards from those who don't. Earn HR's support in advance by being upfront and declaring the obvious. Earn HR's trust, respect, and confidence by showing them your favoritism is based upon performance rather than some illegal action that HR cannot support. Show them you will not violate any laws or policies in your favoritism. Be sure to document that your words, actions, behaviors and results are in harmony with your values, beliefs, principles and philosophies. Do this consciously and I am confident HR will support your decisions and actions."

"I should be gaining the support of every department within my company now before I need it," Paul suggested. "That's the key, isn't it? Gain their trust, respect and confidence in advance so I will have their support later."

"You got it! And the way to gain their trust, respect and confidence is to talk about the *things that matter most* – the background information, the goals and direction, roles, expectations, boundaries, authority and feedback," I said, pointing to the things listed down the right side of the OPEN rung on the Ladder.

I apologized for stating so adamantly my personal bias about the myth that managers should not have favorites and should treat everyone the same. I then went back to what we had been discussing before.

"Prior to this slight tangent, we had been talking about linking the business imperative with a person's personal imperative in order to get them to do what you want," I reminded. "Remember my role play of the employee who needed to return from break on time to earn my support? The fact is every person has imperatives that influence their decisions and actions. And the more you link their personal imperatives with the business imperatives the greater the odds you can get them to do what you want them to do."

"It sounds great," said Paul.

"That's how you gain the support of Human Resources, Paul. You need to understand it is imperative that Human Resources protect the company by not allowing managers to do anything that is illegal. They cannot support an unlawful action. Favoritism is a common complaint among employees. Human Resources must be able to trust that everything you do is proper when you treat people differently, particularly in granting favors. Therefore, the way to earn HR's trust, respect, confidence, and support is to make sure you stay within the policies and guidelines of the company. That's all HR wants. They want to feel confident you can be supported should your actions be challenged in court. Consequently, you will accomplish what *you* want when you link your imperative with *HR's* imperative."

"I've got the point. I think I understand it, but could you give me one more example so I can see how you link the two imperatives?" Paul asked. "This is so important I want to make sure I really get it."

"Sure. Let me give you a home example this time so you can see how to link the parental imperative with the teenager imperative because, believe me, they are not always the same, are they?" I quipped.

"Oh, this ought to be good," Paul said, as he leaned closer to make sure he could hear.

"Your daughter is 15, is that right?" I asked.

"That's correct."

"Paul, very shortly *'there will come a day'* when your daughter will turn 16, and on that day what will she want?"

"She'll want to borrow the car," he answered, grimacing at the thought.

I reached into my pocket and pulled out my car keys. I asked Paul what the car keys represent to a 16-year-old. Very quickly we concluded the car keys represent freedom, independence, status, coolness, and friends.

"A kid can be the biggest nerd in the school, and, if he gets a car first; all of a sudden he has friends, doesn't he?" I proposed.

Paul knew it was true.

"Of course, when those friends get their own cars, the nerd loses the friends. But for a while there, the nerd with the car was cool," I joked.

I then asked him what the car keys represent to parents. We agreed the keys represent fear, worry, concern, increased car insurance rates, death, destruction and mayhem.

The Tangible Indicator

"And that's the problem," I proposed. "The reason why parents are so afraid to give the car keys to the teenager is because the car keys *don't* represent fear, death, destruction and mayhem to a 16-year-old. If the 16-year-old was as afraid as her parents are that she might die in the car, maybe we wouldn't be so frightened. But the teenager is so focused on being free, independent, cool, and having friends, dying in the car never enters her mind. And that's what scares us. We are afraid that in trying to be free, independent and cool in front of her friends, she will do something stupid in the car and get herself killed."

Paul let out a big sigh. Apparently this was something he had been thinking about and dreading in his very near future.

"But this really isn't a car issue, is it Paul?" I said purposefully to see if he had learned anything yet.

"No. It's a trust, respect, and confidence issue," he rightly declared.

"And support!" I added making sure he connected all four elements together. I then switched again to my role-playing mode and pretended Paul was his daughter so he could she how to apply this concept at home.

"What's your daughter's name?" I asked.

"Cami."

"You see, Cami, 'there will come a day' in the very near future when you will want to borrow the car. And on that day you will want me to say yes. But I'm telling you now, I will only feel good about giving you the car if I can trust you, respect you, and have confidence that you will do the right thing in that car.

"So let me tell you how to earn my trust, respect, and confidence so you can guarantee my support in the future.

"If you borrow my car and I tell you to be home at midnight, what time will you be home if you want me to trust you in the morning?" I asked Paul expecting him to answer as if he were his daughter.

"Midnight?" he replied.

"Good guess. 11:59 would be better, 11:58 would be even better, and 11:57 would be even better than that. But I'm telling you now, 12:01 is not acceptable. NO EXCUSES!"

Stepping Forward Together

"But what if . . . ," Paul started to protest as he knew his daughter would.

"See! You don't even have the car yet, and you already can come up with 'what if' excuses. If you can make up excuses now before you have the car, how will I know later when you do have the car that whatever excuse you have for being late isn't also made up? I'm sorry. I'm not going to take that chance. So I'm taking away ALL excuses from you now so I don't have to wonder in the future if you are telling me the truth.

"Therefore, if you're afraid you might run out of gas, get gas. If you think you're going to get lost, get on MapQuest and get directions. If you think you may get a flat tire, leave early so you'll have time to change it. If you think traffic might be bad, leave early. Whatever reason you feel you might be late, you figure out the solution now before it happens, because 12:01 is not acceptable – NO EXCUSES."

Paul nodded his understanding.

"Cami, out of respect for your need for freedom, independence, and coolness, I'm giving you permission to have your friends in my car. I know that's a major reason why you want the car. But I also expect you to respect the fact that it is MY car, not yours. Therefore, when you are in my car you will respect my values and do nothing in my car that is against my values. I hope your values and my values are the same – since that is what we've taught you for 16 years of your life – but I don't know whether that is true or not. What I do know, however, is if you want me to respect you by letting you use my car, you need to show respect for me by not doing anything in my car that is against my wishes. Nor will you allow any of your friends, whom you want to be cool in front of, to do anything in my car that violates my values. Do you understand?"

Paul said yes.

"Cami, if I am to have confidence that my car will come back undamaged and my insurance rates will not go up, how will you drive my car?"

"Carefully," Paul answered for his daughter.

"And when your friends, who you want to be cool in front of, are telling you to 'punch it', to race, or to do anything that is reckless in my car, who will you listen to when there is all that peer-pressure in the car – me or

your friends? Cami, you better decide today, before you ever get the car, who you will listen to and what decisions you will make if you want to earn my trust, respect and confidence regarding the car."

I paused to gauge Paul's response to the role play.

"This is good! I'm going to use this with Cami when she turns 16," Paul said.

"One more thing, Cami," I said continuing the role play. *"If you want me to respect your need for independence, what will my gas tank look like in the morning and who will have paid for that gas, oh independent one? You need to understand I will not be paying for your gas because you cannot ask for independence and then act dependently. Out of respect for your desire to be independent, I will NOT be giving you any money. I would never disrespect your need for independence by allowing you to be dependent on me. So don't ask for any money; I won't be giving you any."*

Paul was smiling broadly and shaking his head.

"You are really good, Mac. I like the twist at the end."

"It's a great little twist, but it's true," I affirmed. "Many teenagers cry for their independence, but they are not willing to shoulder the full responsibilities of that independence. They demand to be treated like adults, but they continue to act like children. I just want to make it conscious that what a teenager says and how she acts are often at odds. And this conflict of behaviors definitely impacts trust, respect, and confidence between the teenager and the parents. I have no delusions that teenagers will behave maturely in every situation. But, I find when parents talk about the real issues – trust, respect and confidence – it is much easier to get children to do what you want them to do – particularly if you link the parental imperative with the teenager's imperative."

I returned to the role play to make my final point.

"You see, Cami, 'there will come a day' . . . and you ought to be thinking about that day before it gets here so you will already have gained my support in advance. I'm telling you this now, honey, so you won't do what is right for ME. Don't do it for your MOTHER. Don't do it because we tell you to. Do it for YOU, because 'there will come a day' when you will want me to say yes with no hesitation."

Stepping Forward Together

"I love how this Ladder works both at home and at work," Paul marveled.

"Now, just to make sure you get it, let me again put all of the pieces together for you," I offered. "Remember how earlier I said there is an 'it' in everything in life? This is the ultimate 'it'. The key to everything in life is earning the trust, respect and confidence of those around you so you will gain their support. Trust, respect, confidence and support are the key to a happy marriage. They are the key to a successful career. They are the key to building customer loyalty, to achieving a cooperative union-management partnership, and even the key to peaceful foreign relations.

"People need to stop talking about dishes, cars, customer service, union contracts or foreign policy, and, instead, focus on how they can build lasting relationships of mutual and reciprocal trust, respect, confidence and support."

Paul fell back in his seat. He had gone inside himself and was pondering something. After a few seconds he said:

"That's it, isn't it? That's what a successful job interview is: gaining the trust, respect, confidence and support of the hiring manager. Likewise, getting your ideas accepted and implemented requires gaining the trust, respect, confidence and support of those who will approve it and those who have to implement it. Building customer loyalty is merely the result of having gained the trust, respect, confidence and support of your customers. It's so obvious! How come I didn't get this before?" Paul lamented.

"Oh, I think you did get it before, but maybe not consciously," I suggested. "I've just made the subconscious conscious so it's more apparent. And now that it's conscious, you can consciously do something about it. And the good news is it is very easy to gain other people's trust, respect, confidence and support because every single person can tell you how to do so. You see, Paul, you know exactly what the managers and employees at your plant can do to earn your trust, respect, confidence and support, don't you?"

"Yes, I do."

"And you know exactly what your wife and kids can do to earn your trust, respect, confidence and support, too. Is that true?" I continued.

"Yes."

The Tangible Indicator

"Don't you get it, Paul?!" I exclaimed, almost coming out of my seat with excitement. "It's so easy to get the 'its' of life because all we have to do is ask someone what it is. Every boss can tell her employees how to succeed at work. Every teacher can tell his students how to be successful at school. Every husband knows what he wants from his wife. Every wife knows what she wants from her husband. All children know what they want from parents; and parents know what they want from their kids. Every person, in every relationship, can tell exactly what he or she wants in that relationship and what it will take to earn their trust, respect, confidence and support.

"And the thing everyone needs to realize, Paul, is you can't argue it. It's not open for discussion or disagreement. If you want to gain the support of someone, you have to do the things that will build their trust, respect and confidence," I declared. "Your daughter cannot declare to you what she will do to earn your support when she wants the car. You set the parameters. You know the behaviors that will earn your trust, respect and confidence.

"Likewise, the boss decides what the employees must do to gain the boss' support. If the employees behave or perform contrary to the boss' expectations, they lose the trust, respect and confidence of the boss. The employees, too, can tell their boss how to earn the trust, respect, confidence and support of the employees.

"Wise students realize teachers decide who the model student is. Teachers grant or withhold special favors based upon who conforms to their expectations. Those students who get it are the ones who get on the good side of the teacher so they can get what they want."

I went on to explain that there are certain conditions of which people must be aware if they are to succeed in various aspects of their lives. There are specific *imperatives* at work, school, home, marriage, parenting, and other elements of life that must be achieved. There are *goals* that need to be accomplished. There is a *role* one must fill and *expectations* that must be met. There are *boundaries* that cannot be crossed and *authority* that cannot be overstepped. And one must be receptive to *feedback* at work, in school, at home, in a marriage, and as a parent if one wishes to be successful.

"The thing I try to get people to understand is it's useless to argue with someone who knows what they want," I suggested. "When a manager,

You cannot argue philosophies;
you can only argue tactics.
Once the company's philosophies have been established,
such as its vision, values and strategies,
these things are no longer open
for disagreement or argument.
However, the tactics of how
the vision, values or strategies are carried out
can be argued until a decision is made.

teacher, or parent is committed to his or her values, beliefs, principles, or philosophies, there is no way someone can argue or rebel against those elements and gain the trust, respect, confidence and support of the manager, teacher or parent.

"Let me say it another way: *You cannot argue philosophies, you can only argue tactics.* What this means is, once the company's philosophies have been established – such as its vision, values and strategies – these things are no longer open for disagreement or argument. The managers and employees need to just accept them and move on. The philosophies cannot be argued; however, it's perfectly acceptable for the managers and employees to argue the *tactics* of how the vision, values or strategies are carried out; they just can't change the core philosophies.

"Paul, once the corporate executives have made a philosophical decision about where they want to take the company, you can't argue whether it is the right thing to do. At least not if you want to maintain the trust, respect, and confidence of your superiors. If, for example, your company has decided to implement a cost-cutting initiative, you can't declare you don't want to cut costs. Not cutting costs is not at option available to you. The philosophical decision has been made by the company and you must support that decision by cutting costs. *How* you cut costs and *where* you cut costs is open for discussion, but not *whether* you will cut costs. You can argue tactics, but you'd better not argue philosophies."

Paul was still mulling this over, so I gave him another example.

"Let me use my own company as an example and pretend you work for me," I continued. "Once I know where I want to take my company – Innovative Management Group – you cannot argue with my vision if you want to work for me. Once I have determined the core values of my company and I know what it takes to win, you cannot tell me these core values are wrong when I've already declared they are the values I believe in and want. Once I know the business imperative, the goals, direction, roles, expectations, boundaries and authority levels for the company, you cannot declare that you don't agree with the conditions I have set. At least, you cannot argue against them or remain in disagreement and still expect to work for me."

Stepping Forward Together

Paul looked like he was in agreement. But I wanted to clarify something before he agreed with my comment without understanding another critical element of this point.

"So you don't misunderstand me, let me be clear," I cautioned. "I don't mind people arguing with me *before* these things are decided. I welcome input on the vision and values of the company. I want people to help me discern the business imperatives, goals, and the direction for the business. They even can provide input on their roles, expectations, boundaries and authority. But once these elements have been established, I expect employees to carry out their job duties without argument. I expect them to accept and abide by the philosophical agreements regarding their position. Once these things have been determined I am perfectly willing to listen to contrary views about our tactics – *how* we do it – but they cannot argue philosophically whether they *should* do it."

Paul was listening attentively. I could see he had gone inside himself and was making some mental notes.

"It's the same at home," I continued. "If you want to have a happy home and successful marriage, there are certain imperatives that must be met. To have unity in the home, you, your spouse and your children must be going in the same direction toward the same goals. Each person in the family must fulfill his or her individual role and meet the expectations of the other members of the family. Both parents and children must operate within set boundaries and not overstep their authority. And, of course, to be really happy, each person must be willing and able to give and receive the feedback needed to strengthen relationships.

"You see, Paul, your daughter or son cannot earn your trust, respect, confidence, and support by arguing against your deeply-held principles, values, beliefs, or religious convictions. These things are not open to disagreement philosophically. The *tactics* of how you administer these things, such as your religious convictions, may be open for discussion and disagreement, but not the convictions themselves. Very few people will easily support those who wholly disagree with or disregard their deepest convictions. Nothing infuriates parents more than kids who behave contrary to the principles and values the parents have been trying to instill in the home. A child's rebellious behavior sends a significant message of disrespect for the parents."

"You've got that right," Paul affirmed.

"The people who succeed in life, both at work and at home, are the ones who figure this out early in life and live accordingly. Success is simply a matter of whether a person is willing to do what is necessary to gain the trust, respect, confidence and support of those with whom they interact in whatever situation they may be."

"It sounds so simple and so obvious," Paul said. "Yet there are some people who never seem to get it. There are workers who never catch on. There are people who fail in marriage over and over. There are parents who never earn the respect and support of their children because they are lousy parents. What happens if someone never gets it? What do you do with them?"

"You're a great straight-man, Paul," I said. "You just set me up perfectly for my next major point."

FIFTEEN

What to Do When Someone Doesn't 'Get It'

Paul asked what should be done with those people who never get it. Since the consequences of the worst-case scenario can result in drastic measures having to be taken – such as a termination, divorce, or some other form of banishment – I wanted to make sure he was philosophically grounded before I gave him the final answer. If he had any subconscious biases or beliefs that might influence his actions and cause him to respond inappropriately, I wanted to bring those to the surface before addressing such a potentially difficult subject. I didn't want him to misinterpret or misuse my advice.

"Paul, by now you should know that the obvious answer to your question of what you do with people who don't get it is to keep explaining it until they do?" I stated strongly. "You need to do everything in your power to help them understand. Share the background *information* and explain the imperative. State the importance of the *goals* and why the person must go in the right *direction*. Clarify the person's *role* and your *expectations*. Explain the *boundaries* and *authority*. Give as much *feedback* as necessary to help the person get it.

"You need to stay OPEN and keep changing the way you communicate. Explain it 10 times using 10 different methods, or 20 times using 20 different methods, until the person finally catches on. Find a way to get through to them," I stressed.

"Yes, but aren't there some people who will never get it no matter how many times you explain it?" Paul persisted. "There has to be a point where it becomes futile to keep trying."

"Well, let's test your assumption to see if you are right," I proposed. "Is there ever a point where you might give up trying to improve an employee's performance and just terminate the person?"

"Yes."

"Is there ever a point where you might rightfully give up on your marriage and get a divorce?"

"Yes, but I would hope we'd try to work it out first. We should go to marriage counseling and try to save our marriage before giving up," Paul suggested.

"OK. Is there ever a time when you should give up on a wayward child?"

"No! Never!" Paul stated adamantly.

"So it's OK to give up on an employee or a spouse, but not on your children? Why is that?" I wondered.

"You should never give up on your kids," Paul repeated. "You should keep trying, no matter what. There's always hope that a bad kid will turn around. Parents need to love their children, no matter what. They need to do everything they can to help their kids to get it."

"But isn't there also always hope that a bad employee or bad marriage will turn around? Why would you give up on them? Shouldn't you be as equally committed to fixing those relationships as you are to maintaining relations with a child?"

Paul was silent for a moment. I could tell he was trying to figure out the difference between the way he felt about his children and the way he felt about his spouse or an employee.

"I'm not sure I have an answer," he admitted. "I just feel a different level of commitment between me and an employee and me and one of my kids."

"And what about your wife?" I pressed. "You said there was a difference there, too."

"That's a good question," he said shaking his head. "I don't know why I feel a difference there. I probably shouldn't!"

"I don't know whether you should or shouldn't," I counseled. "I just wanted to raise it to your consciousness that there is a difference in the commitment you feel toward your children, your spouse, and your employees. That level of commitment will make a difference in how patient you may be and how far you are willing to go when someone around you is not getting it. You may, for example, be very patient with your children, be less patient with your spouse, and be even less patient with an employee."

"You're probably right," Paul affirmed.

"We could sit here all night and force you to go inside yourself to discern the philosophical reasons why you feel differently toward your children, spouse or employees, but I'm not sure it matters. The fact is that *IS* how you feel. So, now that you are consciously aware of your biases, you need to keep those biases in mind as you judge whether your actions are appropriate when dealing with people who don't get it," I cautioned.

"And now that I've exposed your bias, let me tell you one of mine," I interjected. "I believe there should be no difference between the commitment you feel toward a child, a spouse, or an employee. I believe your first desire should always be to *save* the relationship, rather than end it. You should be willing to do whatever it takes to resolve the issues that are damaging the bond. If fixing the relationship *isn't* your first desire, then I think you need to go inside yourself and reassess your role as a father, a husband, or a boss."

"I agree," Paul said quickly, probably wondering whether I thought he might disagree.

"My personal belief is that 'divorce' from a spouse, child, or employee should only be acceptable in extreme circumstances," I proposed. "There may be situations where one party abuses the relationship so significantly that the other party has to go to CLOSED in order to protect the company, one's children, or oneself from physical, psychological, emotional, spiritual, or financial harm.

"But I wish to stress that it's imperative that the parties in these relationships remain OPEN for as long as they can," I continued. "They must do everything in their power to salvage the relationship before going to

CLOSED. To prematurely harden one's heart not only makes it impossible to continue in the relationship, it often damages a person's ability to be OPEN in future relationships. If someone closes too quickly, he may never gain the introspection necessary to learn how his behavior or actions may have contributed to the demise of the relationship. That can cripple his future relationships. The negative impact of lessons not learned usually continues until learning takes place."

"On the other hand, there also is great danger in remaining in a bad relationship too long. The longer one stays in a bad relationship the more damaging the effect can be on that person's ability to build future committed relationships. I'll explain this more fully in a minute."

Paul had been listening tentatively. He probably wasn't sure where all of this was leading.

"My point is this, Paul: Have you ever gone to CLOSED with someone and stayed there?" I asked.

"Yes, I have."

"Tell me about the situation, if you don't mind."

"Well, two situations come into my mind immediately," he answered. "I went to CLOSED and stayed there with my first wife. And I went to CLOSED with one of my managers at the plant several months back."

"Did your going to CLOSED help?"

"Help what?" Paul asked.

"Did it improve the relationship? Did it fix the situation?" I pressed.

"Well, I divorced my wife and fired the manager. So, yes, I guess it did improve the situation!" Paul smirked.

I wasn't laughing.

"Did it ever cross your mind that your being CLOSED might be the reason *why* those relationships failed? Did you ever think that maybe *you* are the one who doesn't get it?" I assailed, knowing I was hitting him pretty hard with what might be an unjustified attack.

Sometimes I come on pretty strong to get people to go inside themselves to find the truth. People cannot learn and grow until they confront their values, philosophies, beliefs, biases, and other issues that influence the way they think, reason and come to conclusions. I didn't know whether Paul was at fault in the termination of his marriage or the firing of the manager, but I knew *he* knew. I just wanted him to think about that as we continued our discussion.

"Paul, I'm sorry for stating that so bluntly. But I want to anchor into your conscious mind that it is only right to go to CLOSED with someone and stay there *after* you have done everything you can to remain OPEN. If you did do everything you can to fix the relationship, then you shouldn't feel any guilt about ending the relationship and you can respond just as bluntly back to me that you have been wrongfully accused."

"I wish I could say I did everything I could, but after learning about the Ladder, particularly these things in the OPEN area," he said, pointing to the seven *things that matter most,* "I realize there are some things I could have done differently. Looking back I would react a lot differently now than I did then."

"The reason for my challenge is this, Paul. It has been my experience that, for some reason, people tend to go in the opposite direction from that which is right. Let me give you an example. Typically, when an employee is failing on a team, how do the other employees treat the weak member? Do they move toward the struggling employee and try to help her out? Do they usually go to her and try to warn her of her shortcomings?" I asked.

"Usually not. I would say they usually move away from the bad employee and ostracize her."

"And when a new employee joins the team, what's the first thing the employees say to a new employee about the failing employee?" I continued.

"They say to stay away from her."

"They tell the new employee to clear the area around the failing employee because she's going down," I added. "In other words, they tell the new employee to *not* trust, respect or have confidence in the struggling employee. Consequently, the new employee moves away from the bad employee, too. And now that everyone on the team has withdrawn their support from the failing employee, what happens to that employee?"

"She fails. She either quits or gets fired," Paul rightly surmised.

"It becomes a self-fulfilling prophecy. The failing employee fails because the team let her fail. The other employees could have kept the

*People seem to be programmed
to go in the opposite direction
from that which is right.*

employee from failing if they had stepped toward the employee and helped her instead of moving away from her," I suggested.

"That's a good point," Paul agreed.

"The same is true in marriage," I continued. "When a marriage is failing, does the couple usually move *toward* each other? Do they spend *more* time with each other? Do they go out on more dates with each other? Do they talk to each other more and draw closer together in an effort to save their marriage?"

"No, they spend less time with each other."

"Then they wonder why the marriage fails. How can the marriage survive when the couple is doing just the opposite of what is necessary to save the marriage?" I exclaimed. "I don't know why it is, but *people seem to be programmed to go in the opposite direction from that which is right.* They go to CLOSED at the very time when they need to be OPEN the most.

"Paul, may I submit it is impossible to fix a marriage, help a troubled child, or resolve an employee problem if the people involved are CLOSED toward each other. Therefore, if you go to CLOSED and stay there, you've already made a decision to *NOT* fix the situation. When people get to a point where they won't talk to each other, the relationship is over."

Paul leaned against the window and let out a big sigh. "I wish I had known this a few months ago. You're absolutely right. I went to CLOSED with the manager long before I fired him. I had given up. I wasn't even trying to fix the situation; I just wanted him gone."

He stopped talking and went even deeper inside himself. "And that's what I did with my first wife, too. After a while I knew it wasn't going to work out. I tried to make it work, but there came a point where it just wasn't worth it anymore."

"Worth what?" I jumped in, wanting him to get the main point of our entire discussion.

"Worth the hassle. Worth the pain. It wasn't worth staying in a miserable marriage," he bemoaned.

"You see, Paul, ''there will come a day'' when it is no longer worth it," I proposed. "'There will come a day' when you have done everything in your power to make the relationship work, and there is nothing else you can do. 'There will come a day' when you know your relationship with a person has come to an end. And on that day you should end it and do it quickly.

"But," I warned, "never end a relationship prematurely. Therefore, you need to know how to recognize when the day to end it has arrived. When is that, Paul?"

"I don't know," he said with a perplexed look on his face.

"Yes, you do know, Paul," I prodded looking him directly in the eye to see if he was getting it. "You know the answer because you know this isn't a question of whether someone gets it or not. It's an issue of what . . . ?"

Paul racked his brain. He knew he knew the answer. He just couldn't put his finger on it. He looked at the Ladder drawing on my pad of paper. I watched as his gaze narrowed in on a specific point on the Ladder. Suddenly he got it. He slammed his finger down on the notepad and exalted loud enough to disturb the sleeping couple in the row in front of us: "It's a trust, respect and confidence issue!"

"Yes! Everything is a trust, respect and confidence issue," I reminded. "And now recall that the way to build trust, respect and confidence is to hear how people think, reason and come to conclusions. Sometimes it becomes very obvious that a relationship is not going to work out because the parties involved are so disparate in their thinking, reasoning, and conclusions. It is difficult to have a meaningful and lasting relationship with someone who is not aligned with your values, philosophies, beliefs, perspectives or personal biases. The strength of the bond in a relationship is in direct proportion to how closely aligned the people are in their thinking, reasoning and conclusions. People feel a much closer bond to people who are like them."

"But isn't it true that opposites attract?" Paul questioned.

"Yes. Opposites do attract; then they repel," I suggested. "The characteristics and qualities that someone initially finds appealing in their opposite, usually end up being irritants later in the relationship. For example, the outgoing, talkative nature of an extrovert may be attractive to an introvert because the less gregarious individual sees the other's extroversion as a quality she wishes she had herself. The introvert latches on to her extroverted opposite to provide a dimension that is missing in her life. However, far too often, the high energy of the extrovert eventually overwhelms the introvert and drains her energy, thus damaging the relationship. The initial attraction gets wiped out by the irritation caused from the very behavior that attracted her to her opposite in the first place."

Paul interjected he had witnessed similar conflict between couples he and his wife socialize with. He said he often wondered what attracted the people to each other since their opposite qualities seemed to grate on each other.

"The same is true in the workplace," I suggested. "I've witnessed, for example, where a company hired young people just out of college with the expressed desire that eager, inexperienced workers would bring fresh ideas to the company. I've watched as these novice employees lose credibility within the organization because their ideas are too naïve, too radical or too divergent from the norms of the company. Quite often the ambitious new employees eventually quit or get fired because they never quite fit the company mold. People in a relationship cannot be too different in their thinking, reasoning, or conclusions or that divergence may eventually lead to dissolution of the relationship."

"But what about valuing diversity within a company?" Paul quizzed. "That's a major topic of discussion at my company right now. It's one of our corporate initiatives. Shouldn't managers welcome divergent thinking?"

"Don't get confused, Paul," I warned. "There is a difference between valuing the diversity of the workforce (meaning valuing the different contributions people bring to the table based upon their diverse gender, ethnic, cultural or other perspectives) and valuing divergent thinking at work. While it is perfectly acceptable to be diverse in some things, there are other things that cannot be compromised or altered regardless of a person's diverse background."

"Such as . . . ?" Paul wondered.

"Such as punctuality issues," I offered. "There are some cultures where punctuality is not the norm. There are countries where maintaining strict schedules and delivering on time is not as highly valued as it is here in the United States. But I'll bet punctuality and timeliness are important to *you* as the general manager of your plant? I imagine you expect your workers on the production line to be at their work stations on time regardless of their cultural prerogative. I'll even go so far as to say punctuality is *imperative* if one wishes to remain employed. The employee must come to work on time if he wants to keep his job, even if it violates his diverse nature. And if he cannot, or will not, do what is required of him, the employment relationship cannot continue."

"That's true."

"Likewise, there are rules and conditions at school that determine what is and is not acceptable behavior," I continued. "Any student who violates the rules, regardless of her personal perspective or diverse nature, will suffer the consequences for her violation. Similarly, certified professionals who violate the conditions of their certification risk being decertified or disbarred from practicing their professions. Likewise, any member of a specific church or religious sect faces excommunication for violating the doctrines or tenets of that faith.

"There are laws, regulations, rules, values, principles, and conditions that everyone in every relationship must abide by in order to remain in that relationship. This is true whether at work, at school, at church or at home," I proposed. "There are things that employees must 'get' if they wish to remain employed. There are things couples must 'get' if they want to remain married. And may I suggest that even though you say people should never give up on their children, contrary to what you may believe, there may come a day when your son or daughter might violate your values, beliefs, or principles so deeply it becomes necessary to remove him or her from your home for the sanity or safety of the other family members."

"I hope that never happens," Paul said, shuddering at the thought.

"As do I," I consoled. "But, unfortunately, sometimes there comes a day in a relationship when you realize a person has lost your trust, respect or confidence, because he has gone too far. He is at a point where you must withdraw the tangible indicator of your trust, respect and confidence. You must withdraw your . . ." I paused, pointing to the Ladder diagram.

"Support," Paul pronounced.

"Yes. Sometimes there comes a day when a person no longer *deserves* your support because they've so severely damaged the relationship there is no reparation," I declared. "Sometimes for the good of the company you have to fire a bad manager. Sometimes for your own sanity you have to end a bad marriage. Sometimes you even have to remove a child from your home to protect the other members from the child's disruptive or dysfunctional behavior. Sometimes you just have to say 'we are done' and end it."

Paul nodded his head in silent affirmation.

"So now we know the answer to your question. When is it appropriate to permanently go to CLOSED with another individual?" I asked.

"When you've done everything you can to build trust, respect and confidence and it's obvious you're never going to get there," Paul rightly answered. "Or, I suppose, when someone has violated your trust, respect and confidence to the point where the relationship is no longer salvageable."

"Exactly! And now I'll tell you how you will know when you are at the point in a relationship where there is nothing else that can be done. I'll tell you how to know when it is time to end it."

I told Paul many years ago I held a position where I provided marriage counseling to couples who were struggling in their marriages. I confessed to him that I eventually became known as the 'divorce counselor' instead of a marriage counselor. The reason for the label was not because I recommend divorce *frequently*, but because I recommend divorce *quickly*. I then explained why.

"Have you ever known a couple who went to marriage counseling and then ended up getting a divorce anyway?" I asked.

"Yes. My first wife and I did. And I know other couples who also went to counseling and still got a divorce," he answered.

"And have you also known couples whose marriages were actually saved through counseling?"

"I can think of only one couple," he offered.

"That's been my experience, too. Whenever I ask people those two questions, most are aware of far more couples who went through counseling and ended up getting a divorce than couples whose marriages were saved by the counseling. In fact, from my unscientific survey, I would say 80 percent of the people who go to marriage counseling end up getting a divorce anyway.

"That's why I was such a bad marriage counselor," I exclaimed. "I'm an efficiency expert. I don't want to waste my time counseling the 80 percent who are going to get a divorce anyway. I figure if they are going to get a divorce anyway, they might as well get it before wasting their time and money on marriage counseling. Besides, I'd rather focus my energy on the 20 percent who want to fix their marriage."

Paul seemed amused at my comments.

"So I came up with a way to determine which couples who came to me for counseling would eventually get a divorce and which couples could salvage their marriage. And I could figure it out in the first ten minutes of meeting them. All I had to do was ask them four questions. Their answers told me whether they were in the 80 percent or the 20 percent."

Paul turned sideways in his seat so he was directly facing me. He leaned forward so he would not miss anything. "Maybe I should take notes," he joked.

"Maybe you should, Paul, because I think I'm about to explain why you got a divorce from your first wife. I'm also going to tell you whether there is a divorce in your future from your current wife. And if your marriage now is stable, I will tell you why it is solid."

"I'm all ears," Paul said

I switched to role playing mode and said: "The first question I asked a couple when they came to me for marriage counseling was, '*Do you LOVE each other, and is your love mutual and reciprocal?*'

"What do you think the typical answer was from the couple since they were struggling in their marriage?" I asked.

"I would hope they would say yes. But they probably said no,"

"Normally they said something like 'I don't know,' 'I don't think so,' 'the spark is gone,' and sometimes they'd say a flat out no. My response to their answer was always the same. '*Who cares?*' Then I paused for dramatic effect. '*Who cares whether you love each other? What's love got to do with it?*'" I said, pumping my hands above my head and doing my best Tina Turner imitation.

"Paul, do you know people who have remained in their marriage and kept their marriage commitment even though they didn't love each other?" I asked.

"Yes."

What to Do When Someone Doesn't 'Get It'

"Why would people stay in a marriage where there is no love?" I challenged.

"For lots of reasons," Paul responded. "They stay together for the kids. They do it for financial reasons. They stay married because they don't want to be alone. They do it out of comfort or convenience. Some people stay in a bad marriage just because they don't know what else to do."

I added, "Or they may stay together for religious reasons. They may stay married because they made a vow of commitment or because they don't believe in divorce regardless of the circumstances.

"There are many reasons to stay in a marriage even though there is no love in the relationship," I continued. "Love is a *benefit* of marriage; not a *requirement*. I hope there is love in a couple's marriage. It makes the relationship much more pleasant. But love is not a mandatory requirement in order to stay married. However, there are three things that *are* requirements if one wishes to stay together. And you already know what they are."

Paul looked at the Ladder and nodded. He knew the answer. I went on without waiting for a response.

"The second question I asked the couple was, *'Do you TRUST each other, and is your trust mutual and reciprocal? Do you trust, when your spouse says he or she will be at a certain place, at a certain time, doing a certain thing, that this is truly what he or she is doing? Is your spouse a truth-teller or does he or she lie, exaggerate or distort the truth? Can you trust the thinking, reasoning and conclusions of your spouse? Can you trust your spouse in public, or does he or she say or do things that embarrass you? Can you trust your spouse in private, or does she or he do things behind closed doors that would embarrass you if it became known to others outside your home? Can you trust your spouse with your money? Can you trust him or her with your children? Can you trust your spouse when he or she is with the opposite sex? Is your spouse someone you can trust regardless of the situation?'"*

I went on to explain the implication of their answers. If the wife, for example said she did not trust her husband, I then asked her if *she* would do everything in her power to develop trust in the marriage. Normally that elicited an emotional protest from the wife saying she was not the one who had violated the trust – her husband had. She would ardently complain that her husband had committed some egregious act that had sullied her trust; therefore, her husband was the one who had to mend the relationship, not her.

"*'I'm not asking who did what to whom,'*" I would respond. "*'I'm asking you if you will do everything in YOUR power to develop trust in this relationship. I will ask your spouse if he, too, will do everything in HIS power to develop trust, but right now I'm only asking you. Will you do everything you can to re-establish trust in this marriage?'*"

I explained that that's when the wife usually said something like, "I don't think I can ever trust him again after what he did."

"I would respond to her comment by saying, *'I'm not asking you if you can EVER trust him again. I'm asking you if you will do everything you can to TRY to develop trust in him again.'* And if she said she was unwilling to do that, I told the couple, *'That's one strike. You have two left.'*"

I told Paul it only takes one person in a relationship to refuse to try to make it work in order for the relationship to fail. He agreed.

"The third question I asked was, *'Do you RESPECT each other, and is that respect mutual and reciprocal? Do you respect each other's beliefs, values, views, opinions, ideas, counsel, and input? Do you respect each other's time, space, needs, wants, desires, hopes, dreams, wishes, fears, and concerns? Or is one person's opinion more valuable than the others? Is one person's time and space more respected than the others? Do one person's needs and wants supersede the needs and wants of the other? Is it acceptable for one person in this marriage to achieve his or her dreams, while the other partner has to forego his or her aspirations? For example, does one person have a "career", while the other one has only a "job"; therefore, if you ever have to move, you will move for one's career because the other one can always find another job? Is one person more important than the other in this marriage? Is one person in this relationship superior and the other subordinate? Again, is there mutual and reciprocal respect in this marriage?'*"

I explained that the lack of mutual respect in the relationship is a common complaint in marriages. Infidelity, for example, is a respect issue as much as it is one of trust. The disrespect or disregard one shows for his or her partner by having an affair is often just as damaging, or even more so, than the violation of one's trust.

"If either party confirmed there no longer was respect in the marriage, I would ask the offended party (in this case, the wife) whether she would do everything in her power to try to re-establish respect for her spouse," I explained. "That's when I again would get the normal argument that she was not the one who did anything to destroy the respect, and I should be talking to her husband instead. And I would reply, *'Once again, I'm not interested in who did what to whom. I'm asking if you will do everything in YOUR power to develop respect in this relationship. I will ask your spouse if he, too, will do everything in HIS power to earn your respect, but right now I'm asking you if you can respect him. Will you do everything you can to reestablish respect in this marriage?'* And if she said she didn't think she could ever respect her spouse after what he did, I would say, *'That's two strikes. You have one left.'* And you know what the last strike is, Paul."

"Confidence."

"*'Do you have CONFIDENCE this marriage can be saved?'*" I would ask. *'Do you have confidence your marriage will ever get better than where it is now? Do you have confidence your spouse can change, if a change is required, to save your marriage? Do you have confidence your spouse will WANT to change and WILL change if needed? Do you have confidence YOU can make whatever changes are necessary to salvage your relationship? Can your spouse have confidence in you that you will want to change and will change?*

"*'Do you have confidence your spouse will speak the truth in these sessions and not lie or exaggerate? Do you have confidence that whatever we talk about in these counseling sessions will be the way your spouse truly believes and feels, or are you concerned your spouse might say things just to hurt you or get back at you? Are you confident both of you will honestly work toward fixing this marriage, or are you afraid one or the other of you will drive a greater wedge between you by saying mean or spiteful things during the counseling sessions?*

"*'And finally, do you have confidence both you and your spouse will keep everything that is said in these counseling sessions confidential? Or are you afraid your spouse might use what is said in these meetings against you in some other setting? Are you concerned he or she might tell others of the problems in this marriage?'"*

I told Paul marriage counseling often fails because the couple violates trust and respect by involving third parties in the problems of the marriage. The lack of confidentiality drives a further wedge in the relationship and often becomes a "last straw" offense that dooms the marriage.

"I'm very adamant about this point in counseling sessions, Paul," I exclaimed. "I insist on confidentiality. In fact, I am so dogmatic about confidentiality I warn the couple that, once we start the counseling, I will take away every one of their support networks. I demand they no longer talk to their mothers, fathers, brothers, sisters, friends, confidants, or even their pastor about the problems in this marriage. They will only talk to each other or to me about their differences. I demand they agree to go to no one else for advice or help with their marriage problems!"

"Why is that?" Paul asked, furrowing his brow in puzzlement.

"Because it is a major violation of trust, respect and confidence!" I declared in a tone of finality. I switched the story slightly to make it a little more personal to Paul. "Don't you get it? If your marriage is struggling and your wife goes to her mother to tell her about the problems in the marriage, what kind of stories do you think your wife is telling her mother about you? Do you think she's saying how wonderful you are? And when her mother hears all of these horrible things about you, where does your wife's mother go on the Ladder of Commitment regarding you?"

"She goes to CLOSED!"

"Unless, of course, the mother likes you more than her own daughter," I said, offering another possibility. Paul smiled, knowing this might be true in some marriages.

"In that case, the mother may go to CLOSED toward her daughter because she doesn't agree with her daughter's negative assessment of you. Either way, the mother goes to CLOSED on someone. And that can't be helpful. Unfortunately this could also be the case if your wife goes to her father, brother, sister, friends, confidant, or pastor. Whenever someone complains to a third party about someone else, the third party invariably has to choose sides. Even a pastor, who is supposed to remain neutral, often chooses sides. And once that happens, the third party ends up closing down toward the allegedly guilty person.

"Here's the real issue, Paul. When non-involved parties become involved in your marriage problems, it's a lot harder for you and your spouse to climb back up the Ladder to COMMITMENT. Now you not only have to deal with getting your wife back up the Ladder, you also have to repair your relationship with everyone else who has become CLOSED toward you because they think you are the problem in the marriage. That, by itself, can be the death knell to the marriage. You and your spouse may go through counseling and end up resolving your grievances and fixing your problems, but, after all that time and effort, who *ISN'T* fixed if there are third parties involved?" I pressed.

"Her mother, father or anyone else my wife complained to," Paul responded.

"Right. The others aren't fixed because they didn't go through the counseling with you. They weren't in the sessions where they could hear the comments or experience the process the two of you went through to resolve your differences. They didn't hear the thinking, reasoning and conclusions the counseling session solicited that eventually got you to trust, respect and have confidence in each other once again. All the third party people have for justifying their opinion of you is what they heard when your wife was complaining about you. And, unfortunately, even if she tells them everything is now all right, they often harbor lingering doubts because they did not go through the cathartic counseling experience. In other words, you and your wife may now be up the Ladder, but mom, dad, brother, sister, friends, pastor and everyone else are still CLOSED."

I told Paul the involvement of third parties in the problems of a marriage establishes a formidable Catch-22 scenario. On the one hand, third party involvement can provide solace, comfort and support to a person who is hurting from a failing marriage. But this involvement causes the third parties to go to CLOSED regarding one or the other partner. Third parties seldom remain neutral. They pick sides and ostracize the alleged offending partner. Estranged relationships with third-parties can often damage the marriage even more by removing the extended relationships that may be needed to help the couple fix their problems.

For example, when a pastor or members of a church congregation are aware that a couple's marriage is failing, they often chose sides in the conflict. This makes it difficult for the couple to attend church together without one of the partners feeling awkward around the pastor or congregants. But continued church attendance may be the very thing the couple needs to strengthen their marriage. Consequently, a major component of the healing process is no longer available to them as a couple because of third-party involvement.

Similarly, the best therapy for the couple may be to continue socializing together with their friends. But, if they've involved those friends in the marriage problems, the couple may no longer feel comfortable associating with past friends who now think ill of them.

And, of course, damaging one's relationship with in-laws or extended family can also make it difficult to salvage the marriage.

"Paul, I'm convinced that many marriages fail because too many people know the marriage is failing. I submit some marriages that otherwise could be saved, end in divorce because, consciously or subconsciously, one or both of the married parties realize that even if they did everything in their power to develop trust, respect and confidence between them and their spouse, they may never regain the trust, respect, and confidence of the spouse's parents, siblings, friends, or pastor. Deep down in their subconscious processes they realize they may be able to turn their spouse's ill-feelings around, but it would take an insurmountable effort to turn around everyone else who has knowledge of the marriage problems. Sensing it would be a futile waste of time and energy to change everyone's negative opinion of them, they jettison the marriage rather than go through the pain and hassle of trying to fix a multitude of individuals. If they had to deal only with their spouse, they might be able to fix the problem. But the burden of having to fix everyone else, too, makes it impossible to save the marriage.

"Sadly, my experience has shown, when confidentiality has been violated and third parties have become involved in the marriage problems, the situation is often irreparable," I offered. "Once someone's confidentiality has been violated, the offended partner invariably feels his back is against the wall. Knowing the marriage is now over, he often becomes defensive in the counseling session and does everything he can to shift total blame for the marriage failure to his spouse. Since he feels he cannot fix the marriage, or fix all of the people who are involved in the marriage problems, he has to attack his spouse to justify his reasons for wanting out of the marriage. He has to show he is the one who has been wronged."

I switched to a work example to show Paul that the violation of confidentiality and the involvement of third parties in problems at work is also a major breach of trust, respect and confidence. Often, a disgruntled employee leaves a performance counseling session and immediately goes to her fellow workers to complain about the counseling she received. She does this to vent or to gain solace and support from her peers. She often wants to justify why she is right and the manager is wrong. She wants her fellow employees to side with her and be against the manager. This violation of confidentiality usually results in the third parties going to CLOSED on the Ladder toward someone. They either close down toward the manager if they agree with the employee, or they close toward the employee and side with the manager. Either way, relationships on the team become strained and the team no longer steps forward together.

I returned to my story about the marriage counseling session to make my last point before pulling all of the pieces together so Paul could see how this analogy applies to his work team.

"If either person says he or she lacks confidence that the marriage can be fixed, I then asked if that person would do everything possible to develop the confidence necessary to save the marriage. And, of course, if the person said no, I told them: *'That's three strikes. You are done! Get a divorce. Get it NOW. Get up from your seats and let's go see an attorney because this marriage is over.'*"

Paul was shocked that I was so blunt.

"Here's the reason why." I explained by asking a series of questions. "Can you remain married and live with someone you do not *love*?"

"As I said earlier, yes. You do it for the kids, the money, and so forth.," he answered.

Stepping Forward Together

"That is right. People do it all the time," I explained. "But, can you live with someone whom you do not *trust*? Can you live with someone who is not trustworthy or trusting?"

"No!" he said resolutely.

"Can you live with someone whom you do not *respect*, who is not respectable, or who is disrespectful to you?

"No!"

"Can you live with someone when you have no *confidence* that your marriage will ever improve and you believe your situation is hopeless?" I asked. "Can you live with someone who violates your confidentiality by blabbing outside the walls of your home everything that happens within those walls? Can you live with someone who feels a need to bad-mouth you when you are not around? Can you live in a relationship where there is no confidence or confidentiality?"

"No way!" Paul declared.

"May I submit to you that the answer to these questions is actually yes," I offered. "It happens all the time. There are thousands of marriages where couples are living in a relationship where there is no trust, respect or confidence between them. It *IS* possible to stay in a marriage where these things don't exist. The question is not whether a couple can live together without trust, respect, and confidence; the question is for *how long* can they live together without it?"

I asked Paul if he had ever known a couple who got a divorce after 20, 30 or more years of marriage. He said he had. I told him he could confirm the truth of what I just said by asking the divorced couple this question: "I know the date when you got a divorce, but when did you *separate*?

"They may be confused by the question and tell you they never separated," I suggested. "They'll probably tell you they lived together until the day one of them filed for divorce. But that's not true. Believe me, they started living separate lives long before they left the house. Although they lived in the same home together, they were living alone long before the divorce. The divorce only brought finality to a marriage that had ended much earlier."

Paul let out a mournful sigh. The entire time we had been talking about this subject I could tell he had gone inside himself. It seemed he was reliving his own personal experience with this situation. His eyes were teary as he listened.

"People can try to stay together for the kids, for financial reasons, or any of the other reasons we mentioned earlier, but, eventually, 'there will come a day' when they just can't take it anymore." I continued, facing Paul to see if he would know the answer to the question I was about to pose. "What won't they be able to take anymore, Paul?"

"The lack of trust, respect and confidence," he said softly with the pained look of someone who had just gained insight into a hurt he thought was behind him.

"There comes a point where the marriage can't go on if the couple is unwilling to do everything they can to develop trust, respect and confidence in the relationship. They must end it even if the kids are still young, even if they don't have the money to live separate lives, even if they don't know where they will go or how they will support themselves. They must end it because they just can't take the overwhelming lack of trust, respect and confidence in their relationship and the resentment they feel because of it. They must end it because it is impossible to continually support a spouse who cannot be trusted or respected. There comes a day when being divorced is far better than living in such a horrible and debilitating relationship. There comes a day when the façade must end.

"That's why I recommended divorce so quickly," I explained. "I knew if the couple held out too long in a hopeless marriage, the situation would be worse for them in the end than if they had gotten a divorce earlier. That's why I recommended divorce after the first ten minutes of the first counseling session for the 80 percent of couples whom I knew would eventually get a divorce anyway. I recommended divorce to *save* the relationship, because I knew if they didn't get a divorce the relationship would be totally destroyed."

Paul obviously did not know what I meant.

"In my experience I discovered most couples, at the beginning of marriage counseling, usually are at the point in their relationship where they don't *like* each other anymore. They have grown apart, feel they are no longer compatible, and they believe they cannot live happily together any more. At this stage there is no deep animosity between the two; there's only deep disappointment that things aren't working out.

"This is the best possible time to end a marriage for those who are going to end it anyway. People who don't like each other can move on in their lives and have a happy and successful divorce. People who don't like each other can still talk to each other civilly. If there are children involved, they can politely interact with each other whenever they share the kids because they have no ill feelings toward their former spouse. They don't detest their ex; they just don't want to live with that person anymore. That's why I recommended they skip the marriage counseling and go right to the divorce. I wanted them to get a divorce while they simply didn't like each other.

"On the other hand, my experience has also shown that if the couple has no intention of resolving their differences and they go through the façade of marriage counseling, the counseling sessions are much more volatile," I explained. "Since, deep down they know the marriage is over, the couple spends the counseling sessions attacking and accusing each other. They find fault in everything their spouse does. This, I believe, is a subconscious ruse to place blame for the demise of the relationship directly on the shoulders of their spouse. This makes the person feel better because they can assume the role of the victim in the divorce rather than the perpetrator.

"I soon found out that people who have no intention of fixing their marriage, who are forced to go through marriage counseling, usually end up *hating* each other by the end of the sessions. They have been attacked so vehemently during the sessions – and attacked back with equal intensity – that all hope of civility in the relationship is lost. By the time the counseling is over, they can't stand to be around each other. Their hatred for one another becomes so strong they carry that hatred into the courtroom and beyond.

"Unfortunately, people who hate each other tend to play evil games to get back at each other," I explained. "They play games with the money. They play games with the assets. They play games with the children. They use the children as pawns to get back at their ex. They feed their children horrible stories about their ex to try to win the children over to their side. They also grill their children after a parental visit for information about the ex they hate so they have more ammunition in the ongoing battle.

"People who hate each other have a miserable divorce. They make life miserable for everyone around them. It would have been far better had they got a divorce earlier when they just didn't like each other."

"Fortunately my situation never got to that level," Paul said gratefully. "So, did any of the couples believe you when you told them to get a divorce?"

"Of course not. But I knew it was just a matter of time. I knew there would come a day when they would learn I was right. So I gave them a piece of advice to remember when the day arrived, as I knew it would. I told them whoever files first, wins!"

"What does that mean?" Paul asked.

"It means the one who files first for divorce is the one who is the most prepared for the divorce. The one who files for divorce usually has hired the best lawyer in town. He's already decided what he wants out of the divorce. He has his list and knows exactly what he will demand in the divorce settlement. He may have even stashed money away or hidden the assets in preparation for the divorce. The person who files first knows where he is going after the divorce and what he is going to do. Since he knew the divorce was coming, he got his ducks in a row long before he filed for the divorce.

"On the other hand, the one who gets filed upon is often taken by surprise. She either didn't see the divorce coming or she hid her head in the sand hoping it wouldn't come. Consequently, she isn't ready when the day comes. In reactive mode she goes out and hires a lousy attorney. She hasn't thought through her position in the divorce settlement so she ends up with the short end of the stick. She doesn't know where she will live or what she will do after the divorce. Her life becomes a mess as she tries to sort through what just happened to her."

"You're right," Paul marveled. "Wow! That's so true!"

"Now, just in case you got lost in this very long analogy, let me remind you why we started down this path," I said, wanting him to realize everything I had been telling him was connected to his initial concern, which was how to get the managers and employees at his manufacturing plant in Las Vegas to step forward together as a team.

Stepping Forward Together

"So what does that story about marriage counseling have to do with your team? You asked what you should do with someone who doesn't get it," I reminded. "You now know the real issue is not just whether this person gets it, but rather whether there is mutual and reciprocal trust, respect and confidence in the relationship. And if the answer is no, the answer to your question should now be abundantly clear."

"Get a divorce!" Paul eagerly suggested.

"Not so fast, Paul. First you have to answer a couple of questions," I interjected, curbing his enthusiasm. "Do you have any managers or employees at your plant whom you do not trust, do not respect or in whom you have no confidence?"

"Yes. Unfortunately, I do."

"Will *YOU* do everything in your power to develop trust, respect and confidence in these individuals? Will you step toward them, rather than away from them, and try to build your trust, respect and confidence in them? Will you go out of your way to try to make the relationship work? Will you do whatever it takes to fix the relationship?"

Paul thought for a few seconds and said, "To be honest, there are some people I'm willing to do that for and others I'm not. I think I have a few people on my team who are not salvageable."

"That's what I expected you to say. Now you can honestly and rightly say you need to get a divorce from the few individuals you are not willing to work with. And I would suggest you get the divorce now! Here is the reason why: Do you have to *love* the people you work with in order to step forward together as a team?"

"No," he answered.

"Do you even have to like them? Is it possible to step forward together at work with people you don't like?"

"Yes. I do it all the time," Paul explained. "There are some people I don't like in the corporate office, but I still work well with them. Just because I don't like their behavior doesn't mean I don't like their results. They are good at what they do. I just don't like the way they do it. But I still work with them fine."

What to Do When Someone Doesn't 'Get It'

I continued, saying, "It would be wonderful if everyone loved the people they worked with. It makes for a much better work environment. But loving or liking your colleagues at work is not a requirement of the job. Loving your teammates may be a *benefit* of having a good team, but it is not a *requirement* to work as a team. But three things are necessary if you want to get people to step forward together," I declared.

"Trust, respect and confidence," Paul joyfully exclaimed.

"Can you work with someone whom you do not *trust*?" I asked. "Can you work with someone who is not trustworthy or who is not trusting of others? Can you work in an organization where distrust prevails?"

"No."

"Can you work with people whom you do not *respect*, who are not respectable or who are disrespectful to each other?"

"No."

"Can you work with people who give you no *confidence* they will ever get it? Can you work with people in whom you lack the confidence that they can or will improve? Can you work with people who violate your confidentiality and talk about you behind your back?" I pressed.

"No, I can't," Paul declared.

"The answer is actually yes," I proposed. "People do it all the time. People work in organizations where there is no trust, respect or confidence. They do it because they have a mortgage payment. They do it because their kids are in college and they need the income to pay the tuition. They do it because they have no where else to go. They stay in a bad work relationship because, even though the 'marriage' is failing, it is better than being unemployed."

"Yes, but for how long?" asked Paul.

"That's the question, isn't it?" I proposed. "They can try to work at a place where there is no trust, respect, or confidence. But, eventually, 'there will come a day' when they won't be able to handle it any more regardless of the mortgage payment, college tuition, or lack of another job. The lack of trust, respect and confidence will tear at them and eventually drive them out of the organization. It's just a matter of time."

"You're right!" Paul agreed.

Stepping Forward Together

"Yeah? So let's see how right I am. You said you have some people whom you don't trust, and you are not willing to do whatever it takes to build trust between you and them."

"It's not that I'm not willing," Paul corrected. "I think I've already done everything I can to trust them, respect them, and have confidence in them. But it didn't work. They still don't get it. I just think it would be a waste of my time to continue trying. They're never going to get it."

"Then get a divorce. Cut them loose. Because I'll bet you 'separated' from these individuals a long time ago. You probably stopped talking or listening to them. No doubt you spend as little time with them as possible. You're still living together at the same workplace, but you're living separately. The divorce is coming. It's just a question of when and who files first."

"That's what I realized as I was listening to you," Paul confessed. "I realized I gave up on them – I stopped stepping toward them – months ago. I don't trust, respect or have confidence in anything they do or say, so I just ignore them."

"And I'll bet they can feel it," I submitted.

"Oh, I'm sure they can," he agreed.

"So, the only question is 'who is going to file first'? Remember, whoever files first wins, even at work."

"How so?"

"Think about it, Paul. There may be employees working at your plant right now who have already separated from the company, they just haven't left yet. If they already know they are leaving they're probably getting their ducks in a row right now. They've already put a resume together. They may even have typed the resume on your computer and made copies of it on your copy machine. They've been looking for another job – also perhaps on company time. They may have even gone so far as to have copied whatever work files or databases they think they might need in their next job. Perhaps they already have acquired another job and they're just waiting for the right time to declare they are leaving your company.

"When an employee files first and the manager didn't have a clue it was coming, the manager is often shocked and in a bind. If the organization is small, the boss may have to cover the vacant shift until a replacement is found. The manager now runs around, totally unprepared, looking for a replacement – any replacement – just so she doesn't have to work the shift. Consequently, she often hires a poorly suited replacement – any warm body – just to have someone in the position. The next relationship the manager enters into can be worse than the relationship with the initial bad employee when the manager searches for someone else while on the rebound from a soured relationship.

"On the other hand, if you know you are going to fire an employee, usually you've already started the search for his replacement. You've also begun documenting everything so you will have your ducks in row when you fire the individual. You've talked to HR. You've consulted your lawyers. You've already decided what you will and will not offer the employee in a severance package. The future is a clear and easy choice for *you*.

"Then, of course, there's the terminated employee. If he didn't see his firing coming, he often goes through a lengthy period of shock, anger and depression as he mopes around trying to figure out why this happened to him. He doesn't have a clue as to where he will find another job. Before he can start looking for a new position he has to get his resume together, and he may not have easily available resources to do so. The ex-employee's life is a mess because he was filed upon first by his boss."

Paul was nodding his head vigorously. "He who files first, wins. I've got to remember that."

"It's also helpful, Paul, if you think of your action as *setting someone free* rather than a divorce or a termination," I said.

Paul was amused at the euphemism.

"Paul, if you've already decided you can't trust, respect or have confidence in someone, there is no way he will ever be successful with you. He can never meet your expectations or fulfill his role in a way that will please or satisfy you. There is no way he can have a *happy, successful, independent or self-sustaining career* as long as he works for you," I said, referring back to the third and most important point of my Parental Major Premise that also applies at work.

"Paul, if you've already decided you're not going to trust the employee, set him free so he can go work at a company where he *can* be trusted and respected. Just because he can't be successful with you, doesn't mean he can't be successful somewhere else."

"Set them free," he repeated. "I like that, too. That is a lot more palatable than firing someone or getting a divorce."

"This is the important differentiation between good terminations versus bad terminations. When you set someone free – and you do it sooner, rather than later – the parties involved often realize it was in everyone's best interest to end the relationship because it was not working out. In many cases the employee eventually looks back and sees the termination as a positive step that allowed him to move to the next stage of his life.

"Bad terminations are the ones where the parties remained in the relationship too long and got to the point where they started hating each other or the company. Bad divorces or terminations usually result in lingering feelings of resentment and animosity. Confrontational separations can create dysfunctional scars that plague people's lives long after the relationship has ended," I warned.

I re-emphasized that sometimes the best thing that can happen for everyone concerned is to get out of a bad relationship early. If a manager terminates a person soon after determining the employee will never be a fit for the company, in most cases the manager usually can still give the employee a good recommendation because the manager realizes the issue was only one of trust, respect and confidence at *this* company or in *this* position. Since the manager has no ill will toward the employee, she can recommend the employee to another company without hesitation knowing there is a possibility the employee can be successful somewhere else.

However, if the bad employee stays at the company too long where the off-purpose behavior causes ill will between the manager and employee, it often becomes difficult for the manager to be supportive of an employee she doesn't like. Since she "hates" the employee, she has no intention of helping the employee after he leaves the company. Consequently, it would have been much kinder to let the worker go when it was still possible to be civil toward the departing employee.

I expressed my belief that far too many managers delay an inevitable termination out of a false belief they are doing what is best for the employee by giving him more chances. However, when those chances lead to a further decrease in trust, respect and confidence, the relationship becomes even more estranged. By the time the worker has "blown" his chances, the manager is completely disgusted. Postponing an inevitable action only makes the situation worse.

"Amen to that," Paul agreed. "I've seen that happen over and over again in my career."

"So let me give you one last piece of advice," I offered. "If you have come to the decision that a work relationship is over, the key to a successful termination is to end it without hurting anyone. No one wants to terminate an employee and make that person's life miserable. That's why the employer puts the action off as long as possible. But, as I've explained, any unnecessary delay could make the situation worse and cause even greater pain and misery.

"The best divorces or terminations occur when both parties agree ending the relationship is the best solution. When this occurs, the conversation should switch to a discussion about how best to end the relationship without hurting anyone. How can the couple end the marriage without hurting each other, the kids, the extended family or anyone else involved? How can an employee be let go without hurting the employee, the employee's family, the boss, the co-workers, or the company? How can the parties involved lessen the pain and grief when a relationship ends?"

"This discussion has been very helpful to me," Paul beamed. "I've been able to go inside myself and resolve the conflicts I've had with some of my employees. In some cases I can see I am the person who is at fault. I'll have to go back and fix those relationships. But in other cases, I now think I've done everything I can to rectify the situation. I feel I can now get a 'divorce' without feeling guilty. If I handle the termination right – and stay OPEN with the employee and control my *reactions* – I should be able to help the individual realize being set free is in his own best interest. All I have to do is link his personal *imperative* with my business imperative. I need to help him realize he will never achieve his *goals* or be successful in his *role* at my plant because he cannot meet my *expectations*. Consequently, I am setting him free to pursue success somewhere else where he can be successful. "

I smiled a huge grin and applauded quietly. "Very impressive, Paul. You are a fast learner. You definitely get it!"

"Hey! I had a great teacher, Mac!"

When the mutual admiration ended, I wanted to make one last minor point before we moved on to discuss the next level on the Ladder of Commitment. I pointed to the Ladder and asked: "Speaking of divorce, when people are dating, where are they on this Ladder?"

"They're OPEN," Paul answered.

"I doubt it," I retorted. "Normally dating is one giant façade. That's when people put their best foot forward. They are on their best behavior. They act unnaturally as they try to impress their date. Dating is a time when people say things they may or may not actually feel or believe because that's what they think their date wants to hear. Dating is a dance where people dance on the surface and seldom go deep. Dates are usually CLOSED."

Paul agreed that sounded right.

"So what about when someone is courting or engaged? Where are they on the Ladder then?" I insisted.

"Uh, I would hope they would be OPEN then," Paul said, not quite sure if he had the right answer.

"Yeah, right! They're totally open," I said sarcastically. "That's when the couple opens up to each other and one says: 'I thought I should tell you before we get married that I am a spouse abuser.'"

Paul laughed at how funny that sounded.

"Or they say: 'I thought I should let you know *before* we get married I'm a child pornographer, so don't leave me alone with our kids,' or 'Honey, I just want you to know before we stand at the altar that I like to charge my credit cards way over the limit and never pay my debts,' or 'I should tell you now that I intend to make you support me through college and then I will do nothing to support you when you want to go to school.' Why is it that no one mentions this kind of stuff *before* they get married?" I asked.

"Because they're CLOSED," Paul said, changing his original position.

"So when do you find out the hidden secrets that were kept from you during the dating and courting years?" I asked.

"*After* you get married," Paul bemoaned.

"That's a little late, don't you think?" I chided. "Likewise, it's a little late to discover the flaws in a job candidate after you've hired her or after the 90-day probationary period is over."

"So how do you flush that kind of stuff out before tying the knot? he questioned.

"By talking about *the things that matter most* early in a relationship," I responded. "When a dating relationship starts to get serious, it's time to talk seriously about the *things that matter most*. If it looks like a relationship may be headed toward a long-term commitment, the couple should discuss the *imperatives* in their relationship. They should identify whether they are interested in the same *goals* and are going in the same *direction* in their lives. They should discuss the *roles* each will play when their bond becomes permanent. They should share their *expectations* of one another now so they will know what will be expected of them in the future. They also should agree on the *boundaries* of their relationship and what *authority* each will have in making decisions and choices in their future together. And, finally, they should establish ground rules now for how they will give each other *feedback* when problems arise in their marriage.

"And, of course, you remember, Paul, that I already told you the seven *things that matter most* are my recommended outline for all job interviews," I reminded. "It's how you change a CLOSED façade in an interview into an OPEN discussion of the candidate's true character and qualities."

"I'll just say it again, Mac. Wow! I think there would be far fewer divorces if that conversation took place before people got married. In fact, it ought to be a requirement that couples have that discussion before they can acquire a marriage license."

"I'm afraid that requirement would negatively impact one of Las Vegas' major industries if people had to think before they got married," I joked.

SIXTEEN

Beyond Belief to Commitment

Our plane had begun descending toward McCarran International Airport in Las Vegas. Although it was pitch black outside I knew exactly where we were without looking out the window. I'd been on this late-night flight many times and knew we had just over 30 minutes to finish our conversation. I picked up the tempo so I could get Paul all the way up the Ladder to COMMITMENT before we were forced to part ways.

"Paul, you learned earlier how relationships really start to gel and people begin stepping forward together more effectively once they've developed trust, respect and confidence in each other," I continued. "The longer you work with someone the more you understand how this person thinks, reasons and comes to conclusions. Eventually you get to the point where you trust her judgment, respect her knowledge and expertise, and have such unwavering confidence in her abilities; you just *believe* what she says and does. Your history of hearing her words, watching her actions, assessing her behaviors, and benefiting from her results allows you to easily accept that she knows what she's talking about and she can do what she says she can. This takes you to the next rung on the Ladder which is the level of BELIEF."

I wrote the word *belief* on the next rung of the Ladder.

"The BELIEF rung on the Ladder is significantly higher than TRUST, RESPECT and CONFIDENCE," I stressed. "At this point, you have so much trust, respect and confidence in your Marketing Director, for example, you just believe him when he says you ought to market your company's tools a certain way. You believe your Production Manager when she says you can increase productivity by adding another punch-press to your assembly line.

Stepping Forward Together

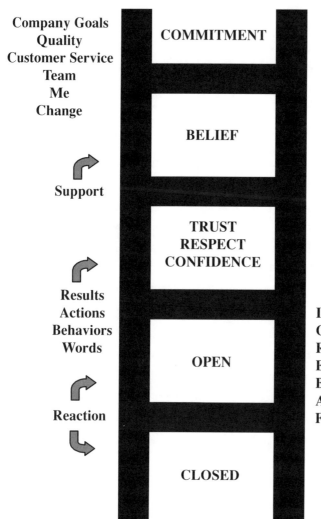

Company Goals
Quality
Customer Service
Team
Me
Change

COMMITMENT

BELIEF

Support

TRUST
RESPECT
CONFIDENCE

Results
Actions
Behaviors
Words

OPEN

Information - Why
Goals / Direction
Roles
Expectations
Boundaries
Authority
Feedback

Reaction

CLOSED

"You also believe your wife when she gives you feedback about a weakness you have, and you do everything you can to overcome the weakness. When you reach the BELIEF level on the Ladder, you believe people so strongly you accept what they say, and you do as they suggest."

"Really?" Paul questioned. "Is there such a level where you just believe and do what a person says without question?"

"I didn't say you believe without question," I corrected. "Clearly, people who are at the BELIEF level in their relationship still ask questions. But their questions have a much different purpose, tone and feel to them. I want to come back to this and explain it further in a few minutes, but, if you don't mind, I want to talk more about getting to the point where you just believe what people say and do. That's the main purpose of climbing the Ladder of Commitment. That's what *conscious management* and *managerless management* are all about.

"How can you leave your employees to manage themselves if you don't believe they will do the right things while you're gone? How can you delegate to your employees if you don't believe they will think what you think, see what you see, hear what you hear, feel what you feel, or intuit what you intuit when they are working on their delegated tasks? How can you accept people's suggestions and feedback if you don't believe their input is valid?

"BELIEF always follows TRUST, RESPECT and CONFIDENCE; it never precedes it," I explained. "Before you believe someone you first have to trust what he says. You have to respect his opinion and input. You have to have confidence he knows what he's talking about. Your belief in someone is based upon your history with that person. Your belief in others only emerges after they have proven themselves."

I told Paul there does come a point in a relationship where people willingly do what others tell them to do without question.

"When you are at the top of the BELIEF rung on the Ladder, versus just entering a state of belief, you do get to the point where you will do things without question. I'm definitely at that belief level with my wife," I declared. "I'm not there on everything she says or does, but on the areas where I do believe her, I do whatever my wife says without question. That's how much I trust and respect her.

"I'm also at that level of BELIEF with many of my work colleagues. I've worked with people who, if they say we ought to do something at Innovative Management Group, I just do it. Experience has taught me to listen to them and do what they say because I know they are a whole lot smarter than I am. I don't just trust, respect or have confidence in them; I'm to the point where I just believe them."

Paul had a puzzled look on his face. I asked what he was wondering.

"Is it true BELIEF never precedes TRUST, RESPECT and CONFIDENCE?" he asked. "I know we discussed earlier how you need to know someone before you trust that person. But I'm wondering if it's possible to believe people whom you don't really know."

"Give me an example," I pressed.

"How about obvious authority figures? Aren't there some authority figures people just automatically believe?" Paul asked.

"I hope you're not thinking of authority figures like politicians," I joked.

Paul smiled. "No. I was thinking of people like ministers, newspaper columnists, scientists, professors, doctors, lawyers, and people like that. I think a lot of people believe what their doctor or lawyer says because they yield to that person's professional judgment. Some people accept what another person says because they view that person as an authority on the subject."

"Does that mean you will believe everything I say, because I'm an authority on business management practices?" I asked. "After all, I am a consultant. I get paid big bucks for my advice and expertise. Therefore, based upon your premise, you should believe everything I say."

"I wasn't talking about me being the one who believes the authority figures. I was talking about other people who might believe them," Paul smiled.

"Oh, I see. This is one of those situations where you're supposed to say 'I have a *friend* who has this problem,'" I chided.

"Exactly."

"So let's take a look at the examples you gave and see if people will believe ministers, scientists, columnists, etc., without trusting them first," I offered, wanting to test if his hypothesis was true.

"You say people might believe these authority figures, such as an attorney or doctor, and accept their pronouncements as true because they are deemed to be experts on a particular subject. Is that right?

"Yes, I think that's true."

"And you suggest they accept the advice or direction of these authority figures without first having developed trust, respect and confidence in that person. Is that also correct?"

"Yes."

"May I submit to you the reason some people go church-hopping is because they are looking for a minister whose preaching is aligned with their beliefs and philosophies," I suggested. "I don't think people just automatically accept what their pastor says. I think they weigh the preacher's comments against their own values, beliefs, and predispositions. In other words, they are more apt to believe a minister whose thinking, reasoning and conclusions are aligned with their own."

Paul didn't protest my assumption.

"I think the same is true when people read newspaper articles or a columnist's essays. If a reader adamantly disagrees with an author's views, I doubt the reader will believe the author even if he or she is an assumed authority on the subject. People often reject authoritative pronouncements that are not in harmony with their own way of thinking. Conservative college students, for example, may have a hard time accepting a liberal professor's views if they are in conflict with the students' values – even if the professor's views are true. People even align themselves with scientific facts that support their personal perspective, as can be seen in the polarized debate over whether the earth was created by natural evolution or 'intelligent design.' It seems to me people only believe the opinions of the experts in whom they already have a modicum of trust, respect and confidence."

Paul looked like he wasn't convinced yet, but he was OPEN to what I said.

Stepping Forward Together

"My point is this, Paul. I believe people accept what *certain* authority figures say because they like the way those figures think, reason, and come to conclusions. At the same time, they reject the words of contrary authority figures because they don't agree with their thinking, reasoning or conclusions.

"What that means is, before people *believe* an authority figure, they have to go through some process, either consciously or subconsciously, that allows them to gain some semblance of trust, respect and confidence in that person or their position. I propose, for example, that people who believe what a physician tells them have already gone through a process, again either consciously or subconsciously, where they have learned to trust doctors. They listen to their minister because they have already gained trust, respect and confidence for either that particular minister, or for ministers generally."

"That seems to make sense," Paul proposed, "but I'm not sure I fully agree with you, yet."

"You just proved my point!" I submitted. "I'm considered to be an expert on this topic, but you don't believe me. That's because, when it comes to this particular point, you don't trust my knowledge, respect my expertise, or have confidence in my viewpoint. You don't believe me because we are not *there* yet," I said pointing to the TRUST rung on the Ladder.

"Touché. You got me on that one," Paul admitted. "But what about blind faith? Aren't there some situations where you just have to believe and accept things as true without getting all the way up the Ladder to BELIEF?"

"First of all, I doubt people will blindly believe something if they're CLOSED to it. So BELIEF has to be above the CLOSED rung on the Ladder. Would you agree, Paul?

"I agree."

"Therefore a person would have to be OPEN to the possibility that something is true before she will blindly believe it. Would you agree with that?"

"Yes."

"So BELIEF obviously is higher on the Ladder than OPEN," I offered. "And, in fact, I submit a person even has to reach the level of TRUST, RESPECT and CONFIDENCE before she can have blind faith. In other words, blind faith may not be as blind as it appears."

"How so?" Paul wondered.

"Let's use faith in God as an example," I suggested. "That's certainly an area where someone might practice blind faith. But is it really blind? First of all the person must be OPEN to the idea that God exists. He must harbor some sort of conviction (trust), reverence (respect) and assurance (confidence) that God is real or I doubt he would continue down a path of obedience. Therefore, a person's faith is not blind, but, rather, based upon a conscious or subconscious trust and confidence that God is real. It is this sure foundation that allows an individual's faith to ultimately rise above mere TRUST, RESPECT and CONFIDENCE, to a level where one's BELIEF in God is based upon his personal relationship with God."

I didn't want to continue down this path lest I offend Paul if he was not religious, so I switched to a business example to make the same point.

"I think recent events in the business world have raised people's consciousness about what happens when people blindly follow their corporate executives. That's why we now have laws like the Sarbanes-Oxley Act that protects people against the unethical actions of rogue company executives," I suggested. "I think it would be wonderful if workers could blindly believe what their leaders say and do. To get there, however, the employees have to be OPEN toward management. People will not follow anyone they are CLOSED toward.

"Although they don't need to know their leaders personally, I believe the workers will decide whom they will follow based upon how their leaders think, reason and come to conclusions. If the employees do not TRUST their leader's thinking, RESPECT management's judgment, or have CONFIDENCE in the executive's plans, I seriously doubt they will believe or commit to what they are being asked to do. They may comply with the leader's directives, but they will not do it out of wholehearted commitment.

"I again submit, therefore, that BELIEF always follows TRUST, RESPECT and CONFIDENCE," I exclaimed. "But I could be wrong."

"I won't argue with you," he said, raising his hands in a surrender posture.

"Don't go to CLOSED on me now!"

Stepping Forward Together

"I didn't go to CLOSED. I BELIEEEEEEVE you," he said raising his hands up again and doing an impersonation of a televangelist.

"So now let me go back and address your question about whether people still ask questions once they reach the BELIEF level on the Ladder. I mentioned just a few minutes ago people do ask questions initially at this rung on the Ladder, but the tone and feel of those questions is quite different than at the lower rungs," I suggested.

"Let me give you an example. You recall from our discussion of the OPEN area that the first question people wonder whenever a change is proposed is why the change is necessary. We agreed people will not commit to something unless they have a reason why they should. Remember?"

"I remember."

"So, to commit to something, you have to ask *why* questions. Would you still ask *why* questions even though you've reached the BELIEF level?" I questioned.

"Yes," he said confidently.

"Why would you ask *why* questions at BELIEF? You already believe it's the right thing to do."

"Yes, but I still need to understand it," Paul declared. "I still need background information about the proposal. I need to understand the business imperative for the planned action so I can fully commit to it. Even though I already believe in something, I still may need to ask questions to solidify my commitment."

"That's exactly right. I keep telling you how good you are, Paul. So now, tell me this: is there a difference between a *why* question asked at these two levels . . .," I said pointing to the CLOSED and OPEN rungs on the Ladder, " . . . versus a *why* question asked at the BELIEF level?" I asked, pointing to that rung on my Ladder diagram. "Keep in mind, if the parties involved are still at the CLOSED or OPEN rungs on the Ladder, they haven't gone through TRUST, RESPECT and CONFIDENCE yet. And, to make it even easier for you, I'll give you another hint. This is a test to see if you remember one of the two important psychological points I stressed about *why* questions."

"I remember you said for people who are important we explain the *why* until they get it," Paul said proudly. "You know, it's that 'tell them ten times using ten different methods' thing."

"Impressive!" I praised, amazed he remembered. "But it's the other psychological point I'm referring to."

"And the second point was . . . ?" Paul said racking his brain.

"When you ask a *why* question, it's an honest inquiry for information," I reminded, "but when someone else asks *why* of you, for some reason, their *why* questions sound like whining, criticism or a personal attack. This causes people to close down instead of open up."

"Oh, yeah."

"So, now answer my question. Is there a difference between *why* questions asked at the CLOSED or OPEN rungs versus when someone asks why after they've reached the BELIEF level on the Ladder?"

It took Paul only a second to think about his answer. "I would assume *why* questions at the lower rungs always sound suspicious as to whether they are honest inquires for information. At the lower levels the person being asked might wonder whether there is a hidden agenda or a possible challenge behind the *why* question. He may wonder why the person is asking, which may cause him to become defensive.

"However, when you are at the BELIEF level with someone, you know the person's questions are sincere. You know they don't have a hidden agenda or any ill-will in their questions; they are only asking why so they can understand what is being proposed."

"You are very good, Paul! You should trust your intuition because it serves you well," I commended. "So now let's go back to your question: When you are at BELIEF, do you accept things without question?"

"No. I may still ask questions for clarification and understanding," he answered.

"The good part is, when you are at the point in your relationship where you believe a person, you can accept direction with a lot fewer questions. You don't need the masses of information you might require at the lower levels on the Ladder before you support an idea. In fact, once you've reached the BELIEF level, it's actually possible to commit to something with little or

Stepping Forward Together

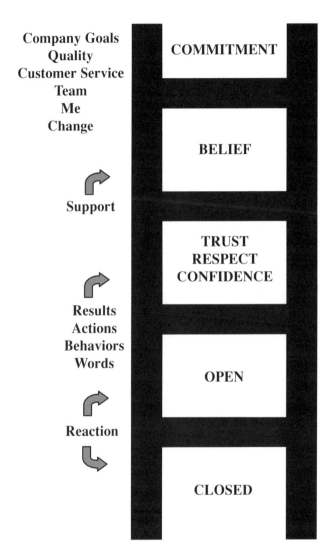

Company Goals
Quality
Customer Service
Team
Me
Change

COMMITMENT

BELIEF

Support

**TRUST
RESPECT
CONFIDENCE**

Results
Actions
Behaviors
Words

Information - Why
Goals / Direction
Roles
Expectations
Boundaries
Authority
Feedback

OPEN

Reaction

CLOSED

no information because of the strength of your belief. There comes a point, for example, where people will say to you: 'You're the general manager of the plant. You obviously know more about the production line than I do. You're the one who lives with the situation every day. If that's what you think we ought to do, I believe you. Do it!"

"Boy, that would be nice if I ever got to that point," Paul sighed.

"Oh, but you will. Remember, it takes time to climb this Ladder. The more people hear how you think, reason and come to conclusions, the more they will trust, respect and have confidence in what you say and do. Give it some time. There will come a day when people will believe you and they will commit to what you want. This is even true of your children. It may not be during the teenage years, but if your reasoning, thinking and conclusions are sound, there will come a day when your children will believe and accept your counsel," I promised.

"I guess there's always hope, isn't there?" he said with a sigh.

"When that day comes it's just a short jump from BELIEF to COMMITMENT. It's fairly easy to commit to someone when you believe them," I said, pointing to the top of the Ladder. "Even though people usually move past BELIEF to COMMITMENT rather quickly, there is a significant difference between these two levels on the Ladder. As always, I'll explain the difference by asking a question. Is there a difference between someone who *believes* in his religion versus someone who is *committed* to his religion?"

"Yes."

"What's the difference?"

"People who are committed to their religion *live* it," Paul offered.

"When do they live their religion? Do they live it just on a specific day of the week, at a certain hour of the day, or only when they go to church?" I pressed.

"No. They live it all the time."

"That's what commitment is, Paul. When people reach the COMMITMENT level on the Ladder they *live* their beliefs, values, principles and philosophies all of the time, no matter where they are or who they are with. A committed Christian, Muslim or Jew, for example, acts a certain way not because it is her religion, but because her faith defines her. It is who she *is*.

Stepping Forward Together

Consequently, she always behaves in certain ways and she maintains her personal integrity, never compromising her values or beliefs regardless of the situation. Her words, behaviors, actions and results are predictable because what she says and does is always in harmony with her defined character.

"You see, Paul, that's the kind of person I will commit to," I declared. "I will commit to people who are committed themselves. I will commit to people who are anchored firmly to their beliefs, values, principles and philosophies. I will commit to people whose personality and character is solid and predictable. I will commit to people who know who and what they are and who are fully committed to their beliefs and values no matter what.

"On the other hand, I find it difficult to commit to people who change their position, alter their beliefs, or discard their principles in order to fit in, achieve some advantage, or avoid a negative consequence. It is hard to have trust, respect, confidence or belief in someone who is wishy-washy, moody or unstable. Commitment in a relationship requires consistency in words, behaviors, actions and results."

Paul had gone inside himself so I paused to give him a moment to reflect.

"What you just said is true, Mac," Paul affirmed. "As you were saying that, I quickly thought of the people I'm the most committed to at work, and it's those people who are consistent in their performance. They're the ones who are the good, solid, stable workers. I'm committed to people who are consistent in the way they think and act."

"And that's how people will commit to you, too, Paul," I explained. "Over time, if your managers and employees haven't already witnessed it, they have to see you are consistent in your management philosophies and practices in order to commit to you. They have to hear consistent themes in your thinking, reasoning and conclusions. The more solid you are in your core values, management philosophies, and operating principles, the more your staff will believe you. The more congruent you are in every element of your life, the easier it is for people to commit to you."

"I'm sure that's true at home, too," Paul offered, making the connection himself. "I know my wife and children expect me to practice what I preach."

"You're right," I agreed. "The difference between the BELIEF and COMMITMENT rungs on the Ladder is that we seldom have to worry about people when they have reached COMMITMENT. We don't have to worry about our spouse because we know he or she is solidly committed to the marriage. We don't have to worry about our children because our kids have so firmly internalized our values, no amount of peer pressure can get them to falter. We know our employees will continue to work at the same high level, even when the manager is not around, because they are fully committed to the task.

"Committed workers don't just provide good service because they *believe* it's the right thing to do; they deliver exceptional customer service because serving people is a part of who they *are*. They don't just do quality work because it is a requirement of the job; they produce defect-free power tools because doing a less-than-quality job would violate their personal integrity. They don't work as a team because they're forced to; they step forward together because helping others makes them feel better about themselves. Committed people internalize these core values so completely there is no difference between how they act and who they are. And it's the conviction of their commitment that allows others to easily commit to them."

I wanted to make sure Paul was tracking what I was saying, so I gave him an example. I asked him if there is a difference between someone who is a "true"chef versus someone who, although he graduated from culinary school, is merely a chef by profession.

Paul was very quick with his response. He knew immediately where I was headed.

"Yes," he said. "A title-only chef cooks for a living; a 'true' chef lives to cook."

"Oooh! I like that. I couldn't have said it any better," I praised. "The difference between someone who is committed to her job and someone who isn't, is the committed person *IS* her profession. She thinks about her job all the time. She doesn't cook for a living; she lives to cook. She thinks about cooking while she's at work, while driving to and from work, while at home, and even when she is asleep. She gets great pleasure from reading cook books and searching for recipes. She scrutinizes cooking magazines for new ideas.

She thinks of ways to create new and exciting dishes. Even after she's toiled in a hot kitchen all day at work, she goes home and enjoys cooking for her family or friends during her time off.

"Don't you get it, Paul? If someone *IS* her profession, you never have to worry about her," I suggested. "The restaurant manager never has to worry about whether a 'true' chef will do her job. She will prepare a quality meal and do everything right because her food products represent *her*. She knows she will disappoint *herself* if the food is not presented well. The manager never has to force a 'true' chef to make changes to the menu or try new things because she is creating new dishes and testing new recipes all of the time. A committed chef will constantly be improving the efficiency and effectiveness of her kitchen because she wants to ensure the hot food gets out hot and the cold food gets out cold. Because the chef is committed, the restaurant manager can spend far less time managing her because she manages herself."

"*Managerless management*," Paul interjected.

"Exactly! That's what I want at Innovative Management Group," I continued. "As the owner of a training and consulting company, I don't want to hire people who just want a job doing training or consulting; I want to hire people who have training and consulting in their soul. I want to hire people who love to teach. I want to hire people who love to help others attain a higher level of excellence in their lives. I want to hire people who have a high need to solve problems. I want people working for me who cannot stand the thought of an organization failing. I want people who are so committed to helping others they refuse to remain on the sidelines when there are problems to be solved or people to be helped.

"Paul, if you work for me and I know training and consulting is in your heart, your head, and your intuitive senses," I said, motioning, with my hand, a complete immersion of him, "I don't have to worry about you. I don't have to worry about whether you will get on a plane to go see your clients. You would never think of letting a client down. I don't have to tell you what to read, or counsel you to stay abreast of what is going on in your assigned industries, because you are reading business journals and magazines in your spare time. The thought of not knowing something or using obsolete methods would drive you crazy. I don't have to encourage you to go to professional conferences to expand your knowledge and expertise because you want to stay at the top of your game. Committed people are always improving, always doing more. Committed people always do what is right; I just have to get out of their way and let them do it. In other words, I don't just *believe* they will do things well, I *know* it because they are that committed."

"That sounds great. And I'm sure it works that way in 'professional' positions. But what about in blue collar jobs," Paul challenged. "I seriously doubt assembly line workers dream about their jobs. I just can't see one of my workers pouring over the trade magazines that I read and getting jazzed about some new manufacturing process."

"I'm not saying all of your workers will be committed. But, if I were you, I'd do everything in my power to increase the odds that you'll have fully committed workers."

"How do I do that?" he asked.

"I'd start by hiring people who love working with tools," I suggested. "I'd find out in the job interview whether a candidate uses tools at home. I'd hire people who do carpentry, plumbing, auto mechanics and other handy work at home. These are the people who appreciate the value of a quality tool. Consequently, I believe they would be more quality-conscious on your assembly line because they wouldn't want someone buying a lesser quality tool than they would not use themselves.

"Since they will be making tools, I would hire people who like working with their hands. I would look for craftsmen who take pride in something they have made with their own hands. I would look for people who know how to turn raw materials into a final product, such as someone who builds furniture, welds wrought-iron sculptures, or sews their own clothes.

"Finally, since these people obviously know how to plan, design, and create a finished product of their own, I would regularly solicit their input on the entire manufacturing process to see if they know how to do it better, cheaper and faster. I would be totally OPEN with them. Rather than telling them about the *seven things that matter most*, I might even go so far as to let them define the business imperative, goals, roles, expectations, boundaries and authority for their position. I would solicit their thinking, reasoning and conclusions so I could develop mutual and reciprocal trust, respect and confidence.

"I'm not sure exactly what I'd do, Paul, but those are some of the ideas that come into my head regarding how to get blue collar workers up the Ladder to COMMITMENT."

"That was pretty good," he responded. "I wish we had more time because I'd like to get some more ideas from you."

"Paul, for once I'm sorry this long flight is quickly coming to an end because I've really enjoyed our conversation," I replied. "I just have a few more things to say about commitment before I wrap this thing up.

"I want to work and live with people who have gone beyond BELIEF to COMMITMENT. People who are committed to a personal relationship think about the relationship all the time. They are constantly striving to strengthen and enlarge the bond. They give of themselves freely. They sacrifice their personal wants and needs, if necessary, to maintain the relationship. They step forward together in unity. They dedicate their heart, mind, and soul to the relationship.

"I believe this is also true in professional relations," I added. "People who are committed to the team do what is best for the team. They are proud to be a part of the whole and are united behind their teammates. They play their position with enthusiasm and resolve. They are reliable and dependable. They step up to the plate and help others without having to be asked. They go the extra mile and willingly work extra hours if necessary to get the job done. Committed people suck it up and play when injured. They stay in the game and do whatever is necessary to make sure the team wins.

"That's why I want to get my employees all the way up this Ladder to COMMITMENT. I know I'll never have to worry about them," I emphasized. "Committed people never call in sick when they're not. They never abuse FMLA, hide behind a policy or union rule, or slack off when the boss is gone. Committed people want to stay in the game. They want to do what's right. They always step toward the action, rather than away from it."

I pointed to each rung on my diagram and showed Paul how people climb the Ladder of Commitment.

Beyond Belief to Commitment

"Committed people are the ones for whom you can be totally OPEN because you TRUST them, RESPECT them, have CONFIDENCE in them. You eventually reach a point in your relationship where your BELIEF in them is so strong, you make a full and unwavering COMMITMENT to them."

SEVENTEEN

Using the Ladder of Commitment

Our plane was on final approach. The flight attendants were busy picking up trash and getting the passengers to raise their seatbacks and tray tables to their locked position. I knew I had just a few minutes left with Paul so I pulled out the two printed 3x5 cards I'd placed in my shirt pocket when we began our discussion. I handed one card to Paul and held the other card in front of us so I could show him how to use the Ladder of Commitment to accelerate the commitment process.

"One of the reasons so many companies fail to get COMMITMENT from their employees," I said, pointing to the top of the Ladder and working my way down each rung, "is because they never get to the point where the employees believe management and management believes the employees. And the reason why they don't get to BELIEF is because managers and employees don't develop mutual and reciprocal TRUST, RESPECT and CONFIDENCE to the point where they will support one another. And that never happens because they don't step toward each other in the OPEN area to talk about the seven *things that matter most.* In other words, the reason so many companies fail to create enthusiastic and committed employees is because they are CLOSED organizations. There is no helpful or effective dialogue or communication going on between management and the employees. People come into work at those companies and do their jobs individually, but they don't step forward together as a team."

Paul said nothing, but I knew he heard and accepted what I said.

"So, can a company be successful if they are a CLOSED company?"

"No, not really," Paul replied.

"Of course they *can*," I countered. "Remember how earlier you felt only 10 percent of companies were OPEN. If that's the case, then the other 90 percent must be CLOSED. Does that mean the other 90 percent are not productive or profitable? Does that mean they are failing?"

"I guess not."

"No, of course not. Most of those companies are highly profitable. So, if that's the case, what difference does it make whether a company is OPEN or CLOSED if the company can be successful either way?" I inquired.

"It makes a whole lot of difference to the employees," Paul offered. "It's a lot more enjoyable to work at an OPEN company than a CLOSED one."

"Maybe so, but can't people have successful careers in a CLOSED company? Isn't it possible to live and work in a CLOSED environment?" I pressed.

"Sure, people can live and work in a place that is CLOSED. But it's not a lot of fun," he said. "And I doubt the employees become fully COMMITTED. They may comply with the company rules and do whatever they're told, but I doubt the employees will give their all in a CLOSED company. They'll probably just put in their time and try to make it through the days and years of their careers. More than likely, though, I think 'there will come a day' when they won't be able to put up with it anymore."

"Put up with what, Paul?"

"The lack of TRUST, RESPECT and CONFIDENCE at the CLOSED company."

"Wow. That was a great summation of the Ladder of Commitment. I think you've got it, Paul!"

"It just makes sense. It's all so logical."

"That's true," I agreed. "In fact, I don't think I told you anything tonight you didn't already know – at least subconsciously. All I did was make the subconscious conscious by putting everything into an easy-to-understand model called the Ladder of Commitment. Prior to learning about the Ladder, you may have had difficulty articulating the things you knew subconsciously. But now you have a method for interpreting how you think, reason and come to conclusions. Now that you know the key to *conscious management* you can help other people see what you see, hear what you hear, feel what you feel, think what you think, and intuit what you intuit. You now know your commitment is a result of your having a clear understanding of the *information, goals, roles, expectations, boundaries* and *authority* within your company. You also have *feedback* that tells you whether you are winning at work. Consequently, all you have to do is go into the OPEN and share these things with your employees and they, too, can win."

"I can't wait to get back into my office on Monday and start using what I've learned," Paul said enthusiastically. "I think the Ladder of Commitment is great."

"Can you hear the enthusiasm in your voice, Paul? Don't you get it? That was the very question you had that started our entire discussion tonight. You wanted to know whether it was possible to create enthusiastic and committed employees at work. At the beginning of our discussion your tone and attitude seemed to be one of despair. It seemed like you didn't think it was possible. But now you're all revved up and ready to get back to work and try it. I think you just proved the point"

"You're right, Mac. You've given me a lot of hope," said Paul.

"So let me reiterate a couple of things about the Ladder so we can turn your *hope* into TRUST, raise that trust to BELIEF, and convert your belief into COMMITMENT," I proposed.

"First of all, you now know you have to step *toward* the people with whom you want to have a committed relationship rather than going in the opposite direction. You have to take a risk and go into the OPEN with them.

"Second, you have to talk about the things that really matter in your relationship. You need to discuss and agree upon the seven *things that matter most*. This includes sharing *information*, particularly the business and personal imperatives and the reasons why things are the way they are. You need to agree upon common *goals* and make sure you're going in the same direction. In order not to step on each other's toes, you need to clarify *roles*, *expectations*, *boundaries* and *authority* to keep from having ambiguity and conflict in the future. And, of course, you must be willing and able to both give and receive *feedback* since that is what will keep your relationship strong and vibrant.

Stepping Forward Together

"Finally, you should use the Ladder of Commitment whenever there is conflict or difficulty in a relationship," I counseled. "Unfortunately, disagreements or arguments between two people (or two departments) have a high tendency to sound like criticism or personal attacks, particularly when *why* questions are being asked. You now know *why* questions are perceived as resistance, whining or complaints, instead of being accepted as an honest inquiry for information. This causes the parties to go to CLOSED. When people feel they are being attacked, the logical reaction is to defend one's position. But defensiveness is not helpful. The truth is the issue is seldom personal, it just seems that way. A key to healthy and productive relationships is to not take things personally, but instead to focus on the *things that matter most.*

"Every conflict and disagreement is caused by one of these seven things," I explained pointing to the *things that matter most* down the right side of the OPEN area of the Ladder. "The conflicting parties may lack *information*, have misinformation or have contradictory information that is causing the argument. They may have disparate or conflicting *goals* or be going in different *directions* that make them feel they are at cross purposes. They may feel the other person violated or failed to fulfill his or her *role*. Perhaps someone performed below *expectations* or felt what was being expected was unrealistic. Possibly someone overstepped his *boundaries* and *authority* and is playing in someone else's sandbox. Or she may have received *feedback* that left debris and put a crimp in the relationship.

"Paul, as I just said, the key to resolving conflict in a relationship is to go into the OPEN and discuss the real issues rather than take it personally," I declared. "The problem with a lot of people is, when they get in conflict with someone, they react poorly to the situation and 'lose their brain'. Instead of calmly explaining her position until the other person gets it – saying it 10 times using 10 *different* methods if necessary – she says the same thing over and over, gets louder and enunciates her words. That's how you can tell when someone has 'lost their brain' – she always gets louder and enunciates her words rather than changing the way she communicates. Have you ever 'lost your brain', Paul?"

"Yes, I have."

Using the Ladder of Commitment

"That's why I printed the Ladder of Commitment on this card so you can keep your brain in your pocket," I said placing my copy of the Ladder card in my shirt pocket. "That way, whenever you get into an argument and you start raising your voice and enunciating your words, you'll become conscious of it and realize you've lost your brains. You can then reach into your pocket, pull your brains out, and use the Ladder card to communicate effectively."

I pretended Paul and I were in an argument where we both had been speaking loudly and enunciating our words. Realizing I have lost my brain, I pull the card out of my pocket, hold it close to my face, and read the seven *things that matter most* printed to the side of the OPEN rung.

"Let's see," I quietly said to myself, "this argument is either being caused by a difference in or lack of *information* between us, conflicting *goals* and *direction*, failure to understand or a misunderstanding of our *roles* and *expectations*, overstepping of someone's *boundaries* and *authority*, or failure to give or receive *feedback* without becoming defensive. This is *not* personal between us, so don't take it personally. Stay focused on the things that matter and talk to Paul about those things instead of making it sound personal between him and me."

"That's neat!" Paul said, nodding his head up and down.

"And what's even better is, if both people know the Ladder of Commitment and both people have their brains in their pockets, it doubles the odds that someone will get a brain during an argument. Either party can reach into his or her pocket and discuss the *real* cause of the problem.

"That's why you need to teach the Ladder of Commitment to every-one you know," I suggested. "Teach it to your wife and children. Teach it to your managers. Teach it to your employees. Teach it to everyone in every organization. I'm going to give you a stack of cards when we get off the plane so you can teach it to others. That way you can help people stop taking things personally and start focusing on the *things that matter most* in a relation-ship."

"I'll do it, Mac. It's hard not to take things personally, isn't it?" Paul proposed.

"That's why so many relationships are damaged unnecessarily because people take offense when no offense was intended," I replied. "It's difficult to stay in the OPEN because people react to each other's subtle and not-so-subtle verbal and non-verbal reactions as they converse with one another. Far too often they interpret those reactions as negative and go to CLOSED. I believe that's why 80 percent of couples who attend marriage counseling end up getting a divorce. They get a divorce because sometimes the process of the counseling is structured to pretty much *guarantee* failure."

"What do you mean?" Paul asked.

"When we know a couple's marriage is failing, we tell them they need to work their problems out. We tell them to go to marriage counseling to try to save their marriage. And that sounds like great advice. The problem is the couple is hesitant to go to counseling because their intuitive senses tell them *not* to step toward each other. Their intuition tells them it is safer to *not* talk to each other. They're afraid of the *reaction* they will get if they try to work things out. And you know what? Their intuitive senses are extremely astute because the odds are high they *will* get a bad reaction if they move toward each other. And here's why.

"If a married couple is having problems and they sit down to address their issues, how long do you think it will take before one or the other person's face starts to contort in anger or frustration? How long before the vein on a person's forehead starts to bulge out, his face turns red, or her muscles tighten up because each is irritated with the other."

"Not long," Paul thought.

"When the couple is having problems and they start talking about those problems, how long before someone's tone changes, they get louder, they enunciate their words, or they use language that is forceful and direct?"

"Probably right away."

"And, when one person sees the other person is angry, each will become angry. When one is defensive, the other becomes defensive. When one raises his shields or arms his photon torpedoes, the other has to do the same to protect herself. In other words, where do they go on the Ladder?" I asked.

"To CLOSED," Paul knew.

"And we already know it is impossible to fix a relationship in CLOSED. That's why marriage counseling fails in so many instances: the couple feels they are being attacked during the session, and they close down," I proposed. "That's why I never had the couple face each other during marriage counseling because, when one could see the other person's non-verbal reactions to what was being said, it was too easy for one to take offense and become defensive. I also didn't allow them to talk to *each other* in the counseling session."

"That sounds weird," Paul said with a startled look. "So what did you do, Mac? Did you have them sit back to back or were they in different rooms? I'm not sure I understand how that works."

"I had them sit right next to each other, both facing forward, so they were *not* looking at each other. I gave them a Ladder of Commitment card and I had them talk to the Ladder, rather than to each other. That way they could talk about the *Ladder* instead of each other. This removed the couple from the line of fire when comments were made, and it kept them from feeling personally attacked. Subconsciously, the Ladder became the target instead of the marriage partner. I know it sounds strange, but it worked really well. They could hear each other perfectly, but they were really talking to the Ladder instead of each other," I explained.

"You're going to have to show me how that works because I'm not sure I understand the concept," Paul proposed.

"OK, let's assume my marriage is faltering and I'm sitting down with my wife in a marriage counseling session. The counselor has taught me how to use the Ladder to talk about our marriage without causing defensiveness. I'll show you what I would say, but this role play may seem a little weird because I'm going to have to pretend you are my wife. Here goes."

"I love you, Mac," Paul joked in a falsetto voice.

"I doubt it, since we're here for marriage counseling," I rebutted.

I held the Ladder card in front of us, pointed to the top of the Ladder, and started the role play by talking to Paul (my wife).

"*Thirty-three years ago when we stood at the altar and put rings on each other's fingers I believed, then, that we both thought we were making a COMMITMENT to each other. In fact, we both made vows to that effect. However, since then I feel I have become CLOSED toward you as exhibited by my words, actions, and behaviors. Do you agree that I have been acting CLOSED toward you?'"*

Paul said he (my wife in the role play) agreed with my assessment.

"'And I feel you also have become CLOSED toward me. Is that also true?'"

Paul said it was.

"'If that's the case, we are both at the bottom of this Ladder instead of at the top where we felt we wanted to be when we began our relationship." I continued. *"But I don't want to be at the bottom of the Ladder with you. I still want to be committed to you, and I hope you want to be committed to me. I want our marriage to work out and I will do everything I can to make that happen. But I first need to know if you still want to be committed to me?'"*

"I think so," Paul answered, assuming that is what my wife might say.

I told Paul he gave the answer I typically heard when I was counseling couples. In a troubled marriage, one or the other partner may not easily be able to say yes. She may not have the trust, respect and confidence that the marriage can be saved. Therefore, she can only answer with a tentative *hope* rather than a real commitment.

"What if, instead, my wife had said no, Paul? What if she said she *didn't* want to work it out?"

"I guess it's time to get a divorce," Paul said in a futile tone.

"There's no guessing about it. If one person doesn't want to be married to the other person, the marriage is over. They can go to counseling, they can talk to their pastor, or they can sit down and talk to each other. But unless the one who doesn't want to work it out has a change of heart, there is no hope the marriage will survive. If either party is unwilling to do everything they can to save the marriage, it is just a matter of time before they get a divorce.

"If someone doesn't want to continue the marriage, there's no need to share information, agree upon goals, clarify roles and expectations, define boundaries or authority, or give each other feedback. The marriage is over. The only thing to discuss is how to get out of the marriage without hurting anyone."

"I agree," Paul affirmed.

"Fortunately, that *isn't* what you said in the role play. You said you

Using the Ladder of Commitment

'think' you still want to be committed to me, and that's enough to have hope we can fix our marriage. So let's talk about what it will take to get my wife and me back up the Ladder to COMMITMENT.

"You see, Paul, we don't have to talk about the *past*. All we have to do is talk about what we will do in the *future* to build mutual and reciprocal trust, respect and confidence so we can support one another, believe each other, and fully recommit to being married to each other. We don't have to talk about who did what to whom. We don't have to bring up past issues of what one person said or did to violate the other's trust, respect, or confidence. All of that is in the past. It's done. It's over. The issue is not what one person has done to hurt or offend the other, but what we *WILL* do from this day forward to never hurt or offend each other again in the future.

"I *NEVER* let people talk about the past in marriage counseling. It was not helpful and could only open old wounds. I forced them to stay focused on the future. I got them to share information and discuss their *future* goals and direction together as a unified couple. We talked about *future* roles and expectations. We agreed upon the boundaries and authority each would abide by from that day forward. And we defined how they would give each other feedback in the future should things not go as planned.

"I got the couple to talk to each other about what they *would* do as a *couple*, not what they *did* to each other *separately*. It wasn't an issue of their trying to work through differences or make changes individually. It was an issue of whether they would step forward together and do everything in their power to re-establish trust, respect, confidence and support in their marriage. I knew, if they got stuck in the past, they would never fix their marriage. But if they would stay focused on the future and not take things personally, there was a strong possibility their marriage would survive."

"Wow, wow, wow!!!" Paul said shaking his head. "I'll say it again. I think this Ladder of Commitment is fantastic. Everything you've said is right on target."

"I believe the reason why 80 percent of couples who go through marriage counseling end up getting a divorce is because they spent the entire time focusing on the *past* instead of the *future*. They talked about what *caused* the problems instead of what they would do to *fix* them. They talked about *him* or *her* instead of *us*. The only way to save a marriage is to stay focused on the future and talk about the things that really matter. It does not matter who did what to whom. It only matters what *THEY* will do differently in the future to save their marriage."

"Maybe if my first wife and I had done that when we went to counseling we could have saved our marriage," Paul sighed.

"Now, just in case you thought I was talking about marriage – which I never was because this conversation always has been about business – let me give you an example of how I would counsel an employee who is performing poorly at work," I suggested.

I held the Ladder card out in front of us and told Paul when I first hired him I thought I was making a COMMITMENT to him and he was making a COMMITMENT to me and the company. I thought he wanted to do the job I wanted him to do. But as our work relationship has progressed, I've started to feel CLOSED toward him as I saw him do things that violated my TRUST, RESPECT and CONFIDENCE. I also suggest Paul has become CLOSED toward me and the company. Our relationship has become strained. Finally, since he and I both understand the Ladder of Commitment, I remind him our relationship will never work out if either of us remains CLOSED.

"*'I still want you to work here, Paul,'*" I said in a role play of how I would counsel him. "*'I still think you can be successful and we can recommit to each other if you want to. Do you still want to work here?'*"

"Well, I need the job," he replied.

"*'Is that a yes or a no?'*"

"Yes."

"*'Great. That means there is still hope,'*" I replied.

I explained if an employee says he or she doesn't want to work for a company or manager, the manager should immediately accept the employee's resignation. If the employee doesn't want to do the job, it's time to get a divorce. The reality is the employee may already have separated from the company anyway; he just hasn't left yet. In other words, the employee *IS* going to leave the company; it's only a matter of when and who files first.

I returned to the role play.

Using the Ladder of Commitment

"'*I'm glad you want to work here, Paul, because that's what I want, too. So let's talk about how we can make that happen. You see, I'm not interested in the past; I'm only interested in the future. I want to know what you will do differently from this day forward to build my trust, respect and confidence so I can support you, believe you, and fully recommit to you as an employee in my department. Let's talk about what information you need, what goals and direction you must work toward, and what role you will play in the future in order to keep your job. Let me explain what I will expect from you. Let me redefine your boundaries and authority so there is no confusion or ambiguity from this day forward. And let me reiterate that you must be receptive to my feedback from now on if you want me to believe you are sincere in your desire to fix the problem.*

"'*Paul, I love you. I would never do anything to purposefully harm you. I want you to have a happy, successful, independent and self-sustaining career. Everything I do is designed toward that end. So don't fight against my feedback and counsel; I'm on your side. Now, do you understand that these are the conditions for your future employment and do you accept them?*'"

"What if the employee says he doesn't accept the conditions?" Paul wondered.

"Then you accept his resignation," I proclaimed. "If he doesn't want to fix the relationship after you, the boss, have declared what is required, he's already decided he no longer wants to be employed by you. He either accepts your feedback and steps forward with you, or he steps away from you toward CLOSED. And that will eventually end the relationship. There is no middle ground. People are either moving up the Ladder or they are moving down. There is no lingering on the Ladder except at the top or bottom where people either reach COMMITMENT or stay CLOSED."

"Man, I really love this Ladder," Paul exclaimed. "It makes counseling people so much easier."

"I told you at the beginning I consider the Ladder of Commitment to be the Holy Grail," I reminded. "It is the key to everything because everything is a trust, respect, confidence and support issue. That's why you need to keep the Ladder card in your pocket at all times. Or glue it to your forehead if you have to. Use it in everything you do as a manager, as a husband, as a father, and in every other role where you interact with other human beings. The Ladder of Commitment is the key to getting people to step forward together." I looked out the window and could see we were just about to land in Las Vegas. There was only time for me to teach Paul one last point, even though I had so much more I wanted to share with him about the Ladder of Commitment.

"Dang it! This is the first time I've wanted a flight to last longer," I said starting to speak a mile a minute.

"Me, too, Mac. This has been a very helpful and enjoyable discussion. I can't tell you how much this has meant to me to learn about the Ladder of Commitment. I'm definitely going to use this at work and at home."

"I'm glad I could help. So let me give you one more tool before we part ways," I proposed. "If someone violates your trust, respect, or confidence after they've earned it, *should* you go down on the Ladder?"

"I think people *do* go down on the Ladder, but I don't think they necessarily should," he said.

"I disagree. I actually think they *should* go down on the Ladder if their trust has been violated," I corrected. "I think if they *don't* go down on the Ladder – if they continue to trust people who are not trustworthy – they may eventually get hurt or have someone take advantage of them. So they *should* go down on the Ladder. The problem is where do people generally go on the Ladder when their trust is violated?"

"They go to CLOSED," he said.

"And where should they go?" I pressed.

"They should go to OPEN and talk about what the person did to violate them," he rightly suggested.

"Paul, have you ever violated someone and you didn't realize it until someone told you later?"

"Yes. Unfortunately I've done that a lot."

"If that person goes to CLOSED instead of staying OPEN, you can't fix the problem, can you?"

"No."

Using the Ladder of Commitment

"I think it should be unacceptable at work or at home for people to go to CLOSED and stay there because doing so doesn't allow the other person to fix the problem. Therefore, it should be mandatory that a person must say something when they go to CLOSED. The problem is, people don't want to be OPEN when they've been violated. They've already had at least one bad reaction and don't want another one if they were to OPEN up. Therefore, to make it safe for both parties, I've established a groundrule at my company and in my home that whenever a person goes to CLOSED, their mouth must open. And here are the words they must say," I said, while turning to Paul for one final example.

"Paul, I just went to CLOSED." I paused to see if he would respond to my comment. "If I tell you 'I just went to CLOSED,' where am I on the Ladder?

Paul thought for only a moment before declaring enthusiastically: "You're OPEN!"

"Cool, huh? If I *tell* you I'm CLOSED, I'm really OPEN. But the ball is now in your court. What are you going to do with it?"

"I'm not going to take it personally. I'm going to reach into my pocket, pull out my brains, and use the Ladder of Commitment card to discuss what I did to close you down, knowing it probably had something to do with one of the seven *things that matter most*," he said proudly.

"Paul, I am so impressed with how much you have internalized from our discussion tonight. I believe you are now committed to using the Ladder of Commitment in both your professional and personal lives. And if I can get you to the top of this Ladder in just the few hours we've been together, then you, too, can get other people to the top of the Ladder by explaining it to them. Teach them the Ladder so they can see what you've seen, hear what you've heard, feel what you've felt, sense what you've sensed, and think what you've thought during our discussion tonight.

"Use the Ladder of Commitment at work and at home to talk about the seven *things that matter most.* Remember, everything is a trust, respect, confidence and support issue. Help people go inside themselves so they can make the changes necessary to build committed relationships where everyone involved will want to step forward together. This is the key to *conscious management* and *managerless management.* It is the key to creating enthusiastic and committed employees. More important, I believe the Ladder of Commitment is the key to a happy and successful life!"

More Thoughts About the Ladder

The long discussion I had with Paul on the flight home from Philadelphia that night got me thinking even more about the Ladder of Commitment. Even though we talked for almost five hours, I was disappointed there wasn't enough time for me to share more of what I know about the commitment process. When I went into my office the next day I decided to jot down some additional key points about each rung on the Ladder. I wanted to offer quick advice, words of wisdom, pithy statements or axioms that would further explain how to climb the Ladder from CLOSED to COMMITMENT.

KEY POINTS REGARDING THE **CLOSED** RUNG ON THE LADDER

- At the beginning of a new relationship or situation, most people are hesitant or uneasy to commit themselves fully. They start out CLOSED and have to climb to COMMITMENT.

- Even new employees and newlywed couples are CLOSED at the beginning of the relationship. Although, logically, one might assume a new employee would be committed to a job she applied for, that usually is not the case. A new employee *hopes* she has made the right job choice and she *hopes* her new company will be a good place to work. But she won't know that until she gets further into the relationship. Similarly, newlywed couples are not necessarily committed to each other. They *hope* they married the right person and they *hope* their marriage will work out. Hope, however, is not COMMITMENT. Hope is merely wishing some day there will be mutual commitment in the relationship.

Stepping Forward Together

- Most people respond CLOSED to proposed changes or new ideas. Although there are a lot of reasons why people respond CLOSED, there are two primary reasons why people resist change. Every change makes people *uncomfortable* as it disrupts their routines and takes them out of their comfort zones. The disruption to the routines also causes people to become *incompetent* as they now have to learn new routines. Since people don't like feeling uncomfortable or incompetent, they tend to resist whatever will make them feel that way.

- Some of the most common reasons why people react CLOSED to a proposed change are:

  ▶ Fear of the unknown
  ▶ Fear the change will negatively impact them
  ▶ Fear they may lose their job
  ▶ Fear they may not be able to perform successfully after the change
  ▶ Fear the change will fail or they will fail because of the change
  ▶ Fear of loss of status, power, authority, territory, etc.
  ▶ Failure to accept or understand the need for the change
  ▶ Not believing the change will actually make a positive difference
  ▶ Constant or too frequent changes, making them not want to commit to *this* change since there may be further changes down the road
  ▶ Unsuccessful changes in the past making them skeptical to commit to something that might fail or go away
  ▶ Lack of follow-through or commitment by management to past changes
  ▶ Accepting the change means what they have been doing was wrong
  ▶ Already like what they are doing
  ▶ Lack of involvement of employees in the change
  ▶ Hoping "this too shall pass"
  ▶ "Been there, done that"
  ▶ "Here we go again"

- Since being CLOSED is a natural first response to any change or new situation, don't fight or worry about it when people appear resistant. Accept the natural hesitancy and move on. Go into the OPEN and share information until people get it.

More Thoughts About the Ladder

- Twenty percent of people in an organization will resist change every time. Don't waste time and energy trying to convince them. Focus on the 80 percent and get them up the Ladder. The 20 percent will figure out they either need to get on board or leave.

- People go to CLOSED whenever they *wonder*. For example: they wonder whether they are loved, they wonder whether they are appreciated, they wonder whether management cares about them, or they wonder whether working hard or sharing their ideas will actually make a difference. When people wonder, they usually remain CLOSED until what they are wondering about has been addressed. You can get a person out of CLOSED much faster by going into the OPEN and sharing the information that will explain whatever they are wondering about.

- When someone doesn't answer questions truthfully – such as "How are you?", "How was your meal?", or "How do I look?" – it doesn't mean the person is CLOSED. It could mean they don't want to bore you, impose on your time, or hurt your feelings by going into detail. Being OPEN doesn't mean a person must be totally honest. Even in our closest relationships, most people are wise enough and kind enough to *not* be totally honest. Sometimes the worst thing a person could do in a relationship is to be totally honest. Total honesty tends to close people down.

- People often seem to go in the opposite direction from that which is right. Instead of being OPEN and moving toward a person with whom they have a problem, they move away from that person. They become defensive when they should be listening. They spend less time with people they don't like instead of taking time to get to know the person better. Abraham Lincoln once said to a companion when he saw another man walking toward them: "I don't like that man. I need to get to know him better." Lincoln knew he needed to step toward the person he didn't like, rather than away from him.

- If you go to CLOSED and stay there, you have already decided not to fix the situation. Refusing to fix the problem should never be an option in the workplace or at home. Therefore, when someone goes to CLOSED, her mouth must open and she must say these words: "I just when to CLOSED." If she *tells* people she is CLOSED, she is actually OPEN.

Stepping Forward Together

KEY POINTS REGARDING THE OPEN RUNG ON THE LADDER

- If you want to move people up the Ladder to COMMITMENT, you must get them to be OPEN and receptive to doing so.

- Managers must open up to employees *first*. Employees wait for a signal from management that it is OK to be open.

- The primary thing that determines whether a person will OPEN up is the *reaction* he gets when he does. If the reaction is good, a person tends to open up more. If the reaction is bad, the person tends to close down.

- Bad reactions don't have to be dramatic to close people down. The bad reaction could be as simple as a perceived negative look, tone, posture, pause, or any other unenthusiastic or off-putting comment or gesture.

- A bad reaction does not have to be directed at the person to close him down. Just witnessing a bad reaction can close people down. The bad reaction also doesn't have to happen at the company where the person works. Bad reactions at previous employers can close someone down at his current company. And, in some cases, the bad reaction doesn't have to happen at all to close the person down. Just the mere hint a bad reaction might happen can cause someone to close down.

- Unfortunately, most people tend to close down after a single bad reaction. Many wonderful ideas have been squelched because the person could not handle one negative response to her idea. If you react poorly to the bad ideas, you may never get the good ones.

- Most of what a manager does is manage reactions. You need to manage your own reactions to keep your employees from closing down. You also need to manage the reactions of your employees, customers, other managers, bosses and anyone else with whom you come in contact.

- People need to gain confidence in how you react. It is difficult to step toward someone who could fly off the handle at any moment. If you are in control of yourself, more than likely people around you will be in control of themselves.

More Thoughts About the Ladder

- Instead of *reacting*, you should *respond*. Reactions are impulsive. Responses are thought out. Pause to think before you respond.

- The amount of openness a person exhibits is inversely proportionate to the amount of punishment he receives for opening up.

- Contrary to what some people may assume, you don't have to have trust, respect or confidence in someone to OPEN up to that person. Nor do you need to *know* the person. All you have to do is be willing to take a chance and risk being open. However, most people will only risk being open one time. The reaction they receive determines whether they will open up again.

- People cannot get committed to something if they don't know what it is. One of the main reasons why management fails to gain the enthusiasm and commitment of employees is because they fail to provide employees with the information needed to become enthusiastic or committed.

- There are seven important things that need to be shared in the OPEN area to get people to move up to the next rung. These seven elements are the *things that matter most* in gaining the commitment of employees. Employees need significant background *information* about a proposed action before they will commit to it. (This background information must include the business and/or personal imperatives for taking the action. The imperative tells employees why the action is necessary.) Once the background information is known, the employees are in a better position to understand the *goals* and *direction* they must undertake. In addition to the goals and direction, employees need to understand their *roles, expectations, boundaries*, and *authority*. Finally, employees need on-going *feedback* to let them know whether they are winning or losing.

- In order to understand the *goals* of a company, the employees need a lot of background *information* first. They need to know why the goals are important and there must be a viable business imperative for the proposed action. They need to know how the goals were set, whether the goals are realistic, how the new goals compare to past goals, and what the plan is for achieving the goals. Most important, employees need to know what is in it for them when they reach the goals.

Stepping Forward Together

- While many managers spend a great deal of time helping employees understand what they are supposed to do and how to do it, sometimes they overlook the key issue of *why* a job must be done and *how* it fits into the company's overall goals. Both elements are key for helping employees feel personally invested in their jobs. Therefore, you need to:
  - ▶ Make a specific connection between the employee's job responsibilities and the company goals. This entails explaining the *why* behind the job responsibilities.
  - ▶ Educate all employees about other work units so they understand *how* their job fits into the business operation as a whole.
  - ▶ Discuss the purpose of projects before explaining the mechanics.

- The meaning of your communication is the *response* you get. If you get the wrong response, change the way *you* communicate.

- How well you communicate is determined not by how well you say things but by how well you are understood. If you can't explain it so other people can understand it, you may not understand it yourself.

- It is useless to argue with someone who is philosophically grounded. Once he has defined his vision, values, principles, beliefs or philosophies, it is futile to try to argue against what he believes to be core to who he is.

- You can accelerate the process of moving people up to COMMITMENT and show how much you value and respect them by listening to their input regarding decisions that affect them.

- Employees don't feel the same commitment as the executives because they are too distant from the information and decisions. Management needs to lessen the distance between them and the front-line employees.

- Most communication problems can be solved by proximity. The more time you spend with your staff the more they will open up to you. Get out on the shop floor and mange by wandering around. You will find it much easier to resolve employee issues when you are visible and accessible to the workers.

- With many more options available for how to communicate with each other, as well as increased geographic dispersion of people who need to collaborate, people have become increasingly reliant on technical means of communication rather than face-to-face interaction. But when it comes to developing trust, there is no substitute for face-to-face engagement, particularly at the beginning of a task or relationship. Since conflicts often arise at work, and conflict resolution by phone or on-line can lead to misunderstanding, periodic meetings for check-in and team maintenance are an absolute necessity.

- Openness in many businesses tends to diminish the higher one is on the company hierarchy. Contrary to what one might think, executives are often less likely to be OPEN because they have more at stake. By the time an executive has moved up to her position in the company, she has invested a great deal in her career. She may be very hesitant to jeopardize a position she has worked hard to attain. A $6-per-hour front-line employee can more easily get another job if she is fired for her openness than can a $600,000 per year executive.

- It is easier to get other people to open up when you are open. One way to get other people to be honest about their weaknesses and faults is for you to be honest about yours. By exposing your vulnerability, you reveal your humanity and approachability.

- Silencing discussion and squelching dissent signals you are infallible. When you communicate you are perfect, there is no need for anyone to help you with anything. Therefore, what you really are saying is you need no one's SUPPORT.

THE IMPORTANCE OF EXPLAINING WHY

- The number one question anyone has whenever you make a change is "why?" Since you know in advance people will wonder why, you can better build rapport and gain people's support by explaining the *why* before anyone asks.

- Always state the *why* first, then the *what*.

- As stated earlier, for people who are important, we explain *why* until they get it. Everything can be communicated clearly and simply. We just need to find different ways to communicate in terms others can understand.

- The meaning of your communication is the *response* you get. If you get the wrong response, change the way *you* communicate.

- When a person cannot find a different way to communicate, he tends to press his point harder by speaking louder and enunciating his words. Loud language and enunciated words should be a significant signal that the person has lost his brain because people with a brain find a different way to communicate.

KEY POINTS REGARDING THE
TRUST, RESPECT AND CONFIDENCE RUNG ON THE LADDER

- Contrary to what some people may think, it is impossible to build trust by attending a trust-building seminar and playing trust-building games. There are only two ways to build trust. First, we trust people when we hear how they, think, reason and come to conclusions. Second, we trust people who earn our trust by their words, actions, behaviors and results.

- *Everything* is a trust, respect and confidence issue. Every word we say, act we take, behavior we exhibit and result we achieve either builds trust, respect and confidence or it diminishes them.

- Every single person can tell you exactly how to earn his trust, respect and confidence. Ask your boss, employees, spouse or children and they will tell you what pleases and displeases them. They can tell you what makes them happy and what would anger them. They know how you can move up the Ladder in your relationships with them.

- The tangible indicator of trust, respect and confidence is SUPPORT. Support is what every husband wants from his wife and wife wants from her husband. It is what every parent wants from children and children want from parents. It is what every manager wants from employees and employees want from management. Support is what the union wants from company executives and the executives want from the union. People want to feel supported in everything they do.

- People have a tendency to go to CLOSED when someone violates their trust, respect or confidence after having earned it. When that happens, don't go CLOSED, go into the OPEN and discuss what the person did to violate you.

More Thoughts About the Ladder

- If you violate someone's trust, never try to defend your actions. Just apologize quickly, atone for your actions, and turn away from your offending behavior. Apologize with the same amount of energy you used to offend the person.

- The Ladder has two legs. One leg represents the personal elements of life and the other represents the professional elements. One leg also symbolizes one's management abilities (planning, organizing, assigning tasks, focusing on *content*, etc.), and one leg symbolizes one's leadership capabilities (inspiring, motivating, mentoring, focusing on *process*, etc.). The people we admire the most are those in whom we trust, respect and have confidence in both personally and professionally. We most admire bosses who are both good managers and good leaders.

- Yelling, screaming, threats, intimidation, belittling, harassment, a condescending tone or an autocratic style never build trust, respect and confidence. Fear is the opposite of trust. It never moves people in the right direction; it just moves them away from the threat. We trust and respect those who treat us well and shun those who treat us poorly.

- You cannot talk negatively, disrespectfully or critically about someone and expect to build trust, respect and confidence. You cannot complain to others about a person without damaging the relationship you have with the person you are complaining to. Talking behind someone's back never develops trust, respect and confidence – it destroys it. Either the third party will agree with you and lose trust, respect and confidence in the person you are complaining about, or they will disagree with your assessment of the person and lose trust, respect and confidence in you.

- Trust is the willingness to believe that others will behave in reliable, predictable, non-harmful ways. It is one of the most important conditions for healthy and productive relationships. It contributes to a sense of safety that allows us to let ourselves be known to others and to try new things. Without trust, we are more guarded in our interactions with others, less willing to share information or other resources, and reluctant to work collaboratively with others.

Stepping Forward Together

- People come to work with different assumptions about trust and how it is built. These beliefs are typically formed and reinforced in early life experiences, including cultural differences. The beliefs take three forms that I call "flat line," "above the line" and "below the line."

  "Flat line" people approach relationships neither trusting nor distrusting others. They wait to see whether the other person can be trusted and either move up or down the Ladder accordingly.

  "Above the line" people approach relationships based on the belief that others are fundamentally trustworthy. They start from a position of trust, maintaining this assumption until the other person does something that is perceived as untrustworthy.

  "Below the line" people start from the position that it is better not to trust others until the others have demonstrated they are worthy of that trust. They have a wait-and-see approach.

  The potential for conflict between these three points of view is high and can, ironically, contribute to a difficult beginning for everyone, increasing the likelihood of misunderstanding. As part of the team formation and start-up process, it's a good idea to find out where each of the members is starting from and to discuss what will help them develop a foundation of trust.

- When people come together for the first time, they usually don't trust each other. Trust, respect and confidence have to be earned. Conscious managers find out whether the people they are interacting with are above the line, flat line, or below the line people so they know how hard they will have to work to gain the trust, respect and confidence of others.

- Trust is slow to develop and quick to lose. Trust is built over time, through shared experiences in which members show themselves trustworthy by communicating openly, following through with commitments, and acting effectively with and for the team.

- Knowing it takes a long time to build trust, respect and confidence (and only seconds to destroy it), should cause you to take great care to ensure you do all you can to protect the trust between you and others. Sometimes all it takes is one bad reaction to destroy what has taken years to build.

More Thoughts About the Ladder

- If someone violates your trust, respect or confidence after having earned it, you *should* go down the Ladder, but not to CLOSED. You should be OPEN and discuss the violation. Many violations of trust, respect and confidence are done unintentionally or by mistake. The way to re-establish trust when it has been damaged is to openly discuss the infraction that violated the trust. If you are the one who has violated someone else's trust, you can regain their trust by apologizing and admitting your mistakes quickly. If trust is violated and you confront it successfully, the relationship usually becomes stronger because of having worked through the violation.

- If you have a problem, concern or issue with someone, go directly to that person. Do not go to a third party. Going to a third party often violates trust, respect and confidence. If you feel you need input or advice from a third party before going to the person with whom you have a problem, make sure your motivation is only to get their input and not to solicit the third party's support, intervention, or any other action that would violate trust, respect or confidence.

- We trust and respect people who roll up their sleeves, help out and work along side us.

- We have greater trust, respect and confidence in those who admit their mistakes.

- You cannot build trust, respect and confidence by presenting problems without also offering solutions.

- You cannot violate confidentiality *and* build trust. You cannot gossip or talk behind someone's back and expect to earn their respect.

- She who mistrusts the most should be trusted the least. She who is disrespectful of others will not be respected by others.

- He whom we trust, we take under our wings and give our full confidence and support.

- Employees join unions because of trust, respect and confidence. Since the workers don't *trust* management to take care of them, they turn to the union for support. Since they don't feel *respected* by management, they unite with the union whose promotional campaign promises they can "get respect by joining the union." Since they don't have *confidence* management will treat them fairly, they turn to the union to represent them in fighting for their perceived rights.

- Proper delegation is a trust, respect and confidence issue. It is difficult to delegate to employees in whom you do not have trust, respect or confidence.

- Every time you share information with your employees or invest in improving their knowledge, skills and abilities, you send a significant message that you trust, respect and have confidence in them.

- Survey after survey shows the number one thing employees want from management is *respect.*

- Advice or constructive criticism is more readily accepted when people are convinced of your unconditional trust, respect and confidence in them.

- It is difficult to trust, respect and have confidence in people who are inconsistent, moody or wishy-washy in their values, beliefs, philosophies, principles, words, actions, behaviors or results.

- Honesty and integrity are essential for building and maintaining trust, respect and confidence. You cannot lie, exaggerate, cover up or distort the truth and build trust, respect and confidence.

- There can never be true mutual and reciprocal trust, respect and confidence when one person *feels* superior or inferior to another.

HOW TO GAIN SOMEONE'S SUPPORT

- The tangible indicator of trust, respect and confidence is SUPPORT.

- The reason why you are not supported is because you either do not have the trust, respect and confidence of the other person; that person can sense you do not trust, respect or have confidence in yourself; or that person only has trust, respect and confidence in his own way of thinking and no one else's.

More Thoughts About the Ladder

- "There will come a day" when people will want your support and you will want the support of others. The phrase "there will come a day" is a great motivator in getting people to do what you want them to do.

- The best approach is to gain the support of the people you need *before* you need it. Talk openly with your employees, boss, the Human Resources Department, the Union, your spouse, children and anyone else who is important to you to build their trust, respect and confidence in advance of the day when you will need their support.

- Listed below is what I call: The ABCs of SUPPORT. It clearly defines what level of support can be given.
  - ▶ Approval
    - ✓ Authority to approve/disapprove
    - ✓ Authority to kill/not kill
    - ✓ Authority to grant/not grant time, resources, staff, etc.
  - ▶ Buy-In
    - ✓ Believe it is the right thing to do
    - ✓ Agree with or trust enough to proceed
    - ✓ Are willing to step forward as a team
    - ✓ Agree to not veto, thwart or hinder in any way
    - ✓ Are willing to provide tools, resources, staff, money, etc.
    - ✓ Will champion the cause
  - ▶ Consensus
    - ✓ Can live with it, although you may not agree
    - ✓ Will actively support
    - ✓ Understand it enough to proceed

- People want more that just your verbal support. They also want the support of your time, talents, resources, money, and other indicators you truly are behind them.

- Both customer loyalty and employee loyalty are tangible indicators of trust, respect and confidence. When customers trust and have confidence they will have a consistent experience with your products and services, they show their support by patronizing your business. The same is true of employees. When employees trust, respect and have confidence in their leaders, they show their support of those leaders by faithfully following them.

- Getting productive performance from people is not so much a matter of having quality employees as it is one of having supportive management. Employees will flood you with ideas if you listen to them.

How to Know When a Relationship Is Over

- In some relationships, there eventually comes a day when you have to say, "We are done!"

- You should always do everything you can to salvage a relationship before you decide to end it.

- People go in the opposite direction from that which is right. In estranged relationships people tend to move away from, rather than toward, their perceived antagonist. The only way you can fix a relationship is to OPEN up to the person and discuss the *things that matter most.*

- You cannot fix a relationship if you are CLOSED. If you go to CLOSED and stay there, you've already decided not to fix the situation. If you stay CLOSED it is just a matter of time before the relationship ends.

- A relationship, such as a marriage, is over when either party has decided not do everything in his or her power to develop trust, respect and confidence in the relationship. Although people can live, work, or interact with someone in whom they do not trust, respect or have confidence, they cannot do it forever. "There will come a day" when the lack of trust, the disrespect, and the overwhelming doubt will totally destroy the relationship.

- If a relationship is over, end it. Don't drag it out. Managers often delay the inevitable in a false belief they are being kind. The kindest thing you can do is let people go before the relationship becomes so damaged it is impossible to support the employee with a painless termination and a kind job reference.

- If you don't improve or terminate bad employees, your good employees will lose trust, respect and confidence in your leadership.

- If you end a relationship properly, it should never be perceived as firing someone or getting a divorce. Rather it merely is "setting them free" to pursue other opportunities. When you have to let someone go, you set them free because they will never be successful at your company or under your leadership. You are setting them free to go somewhere else where they *can* be successful. The same is true in a divorce. If the marriage will never be successful or happy, the couple needs to set each other free so they can find someone with whom they *can* have a happy and successful relationship.

KEY POINTS REGARDING THE **BELIEF** RUNG ON THE LADDER

- BELIEF always follows TRUST, RESPECT and CONFIDENCE; it never precedes it. In order to believe someone, you have to trust what she says, respect her opinion, and have confidence she knows what she is talking about.

- You can tell whether someone truly believes something or whether he is just giving lip service.

- For people to step forward together as a team, they have to believe it is in their own best interest to do so.

- When you truly believe someone, it is possible to do what she says without question. People at a high level of trust, respect, and confidence don't need to know the reason before they commit to something. "Because I said so," the famous answer of parents and some managers, can be an acceptable reason for people who have reached BELIEF.

- Employees need to believe the company executives are in agreement with, unified around, and committed to the goals and direction of the company before they will commit to it. The same is true of parents. Children are more apt to accept parental guidance when the parents are unified in their values, philosophies, principles and beliefs.

- What convinces people most is your conviction. People will believe you when you believe in yourself. Convince yourself that your thoughts, ideas and experience are valuable, and others will believe it, too.

KEY POINTS REGARDING THE
COMMITMENT RUNG ON THE LADDER

- One great difference between BELIEF and COMMITMENT: belief is a feeling, commitment is an action. Commitment transforms a belief into reality.

- People who commit make a fundamental shift from passive to active orientation in their roles and responsibilities. They willingly invest themselves in their work.

- Committed people keep their commitments even at great sacrifice. They come into work when they are sick, they play when they are injured, and they do what is necessary even when they don't feel like it.

- Commitment means seeing things through to the end, not doing something half way or half-heartedly.

- Until commitment is made, there are only promises, hopes, wishes and dreams.

- If you truly believe in someone's ideas, you will prove your belief by committing the time, energy, money and resources necessary to successfully implement the idea.

- People commit to causes and other people, not to organizations.

- Employees can tell you exactly what it would take for them to feel totally committed at work. The same is true of managers. They can tell employees what the employees must do to receive the managers' unwavering support and commitment. So ask them; and then do it!

- Committed employees are loyal employees. Committed employees are more likely to be productive and go the extra mile for the company. Committed employees invest themselves fully and act like partners instead of employees.

More Thoughts About the Ladder

- Commitment to an organization involves commitment to its values, purposes and people. Its intent is not personal gain, but rather commitment to those beliefs, practices, and relationships that benefit all involved. You build commitment by consistently exemplifying and communicating the high values and right purposes of the company.

- In order to get commitment *from* employees, management must be committed *to* the employees.

- Commitment cannot be bought with higher pay. Commitment is a result of how employees feel about their manager, their colleagues and the company.

- Employees must have the desire and willingness to commit to their work. Managers can provide a wonderful work environment, but the employees still have to *make* the commitment to be productive.

- If you are committed to your spouse or partner, accept that he or she is the *only* one for you and stop looking. Stop looking elsewhere for someone who might be better than your companion. Stop negatively comparing your spouse to others. Stop coveting what you don't have and appreciate what you do. Most important, stop looking lustfully at members of the opposite sex and focus on your spouse.

- If you are committed to your job, accept it as the *best* job for you and stop looking elsewhere. Stop looking through the help wanted ads for another job. Stop comparing your job, your company, your boss or your income to what others may have. Stop coveting what you don't have and appreciate what you do. Most important, stop longing for another position and focus on the one you have.

- Commitment often requires the sacrifice of one's own opinion or plan and the acceptance that one may be wrong.

- People who are committed do things the right way, not their own way.

- At the level of COMMITMENT you get to a point where it no longer matters who is giving and who is receiving. Both parties are content with either scenario. Likewise, when there is pain and suffering for one, the other also experiences the grief.

- People in a committed relationship stay in the relationship no matter how tough the situation may be. Committed married couples, for example, stay together through thick and thin, health and sickness, and good times and bad. Stated another way: When the grenades are flying, the committed person doesn't go AWOL.

- You can tell when employees are committed to the company mission because the company mission becomes *their* mission.

- It is impossible to receive commitment from someone you are not committed to.

- For someone to fully commit, he must get "it" intellectually, emotionally and intuitively. It must appeal to his head, heart, and gut.

- Too many employees are focused on WIIFM instead of WIN. They're concerned about "what's in it for me" instead of "what is needed," "what is noteworthy," or "what is noble."

USING THE LADDER OF COMMITMENT

- When you know how to use the steps on the Ladder of Commitment, you can accelerate the process of getting people to COMMITMENT by going into the OPEN and discussing the seven *things that matter most.*

- In the fast-paced markets of the global economy, there is precious little time to get people up to speed. The sooner you go into the OPEN area and talk about the seven *things that matter most* the sooner you will gain your employees' COMMITMENT.

- Just as people cannot *not* communicate, they also cannot *not* impact trust, respect and confidence. People are either moving up the Ladder or they are moving down. There is no lingering on the Ladder.

- The whole purpose of the Ladder of Commitment is to get people to the point where they trust, respect, have confidence in, support, believe and are committed to one another. The Ladder is a tool to get people to step forward together as a team where everyone holds each other in high regard and values each other's contribution regardless of title, office, or job responsibilities.

More Thoughts About the Ladder

- You cannot push or pull people up the Ladder. They must be willing to climb to COMMITMENT themselves.

- One only gets to the top rung on the Ladder by consciously climbing one rung at a time. Then, suddenly, all sorts of powers and capabilities, which you never thought possible, are opened up to you.

- The Ladder of Commitment allows you to both establish a company culture and a company language.

- Work relationships, like marriages, rarely stay the same. They may erode over time or strengthen and grow deeper. Relationship maintenance is the conscious effort to nurture bonds with key people.

- Some of the traits important to relationship maintenance are:
  - ▶ An honest desire for productive solutions, regardless of blame
  - ▶ An awareness of the role of emotions – our own and those of our adversaries – particularly feelings of being threatened or of losing control
  - ▶ Proving trustworthy, and staying trustworthy
  - ▶ Maintaining clear agreements and expectations
  - ▶ Dealing with people and problems directly
  - ▶ Being open and honest about motives and avoiding hidden agendas
  - ▶ Sharing information freely
  - ▶ Soliciting feedback and responding well when feedback is given
  - ▶ Giving credit and exposure

INNOVATIVE MANAGEMENT GROUP

To take advantage of the experience of Mac McIntire and the associates at Innovative Management Group, call, check the website, or write:

702-258-8334

www.imglv.com

840 Trotter Circle
Las Vegas, Nevada 89107

Innovative Management Group:

- works in collaboration with your management team to match your strategic objectives at every level of your company

- helps you assess and modify your organization's systems, structure, processes and people to ensure alignment with your vision, mission, philosophy and values

- conducts quality improvement workshops that teach work groups how to:
  - solve complex problems,
  - make collective decisions,
  - release greater creativy, and
  - increase ownership and comitment to your company's strategic goals

- provides custom-designed training programs that dramatically improve the leadership skills of your executives and managers by taking the "real work" issues of your company and weaving them into the skill development materials presented in the training

- helps you define your service strategies, integrate customer service values at every level of your day-to-day operations, and develop committed service employees